Please renew/return this item by the last date shown.

So that your telephone call is charged at local rate, please call the numbers as set out below:

	From Area codes 01923 or 0208:	From the rest of Herts:
Renewals:	01923 471373	01438 737373
Enquiries:	01923 471333	01438 737333
Minicom:	01923 471599	01438 737599

L32b

29 JUL 1974
20. FEB. 1974
30. APR. 1974

22. JUN. 1972
25. APR. 1975

-6. JUL. 1972

28. MAY 1975

27. MAR. 1973

11. JUL. 1973
-1. AUG 1975

19. FEB. 1976

A HISTORY OF SCENT

By the same author

THE SCENTED WILD FLOWERS OF BRITAIN

THE ROSE—A COMPLETE HANDBOOK

THE COTTAGE GARDEN

A HISTORY OF SCENT

ROY GENDERS

HAMISH HAMILTON

LONDON

First published in Great Britain, 1972
by Hamish Hamilton Ltd
90 Great Russell Street, London WC1
Copyright © 1972 by Roy Genders
SBN 241 01906 0

Printed in Great Britain by
Ebenezer Baylis and Son Limited
The Trinity Press, Worcester, and London

TO MAUREEN

ACKNOWLEDGEMENTS

THE author acknowledges with gratitude the interesting information so freely provided by the world-famous perfume houses of Messrs. Lancôme, Lanvin and Coty of Paris and London and by Yardley and Elizabeth Arden of London and New York. I am grateful to Messrs. Floris, perfumers of London; the Minnesota Mining and Manufacturing Co. of the U.S.A. for information concerning Microfragrance, and Messrs. Wilsons of Sharrow Mills, Sheffield, for information on their snuffs and modern snuff-taking.

My thanks are also due to The Antique Porcelain Co. Ltd. of New Bond Street; to Messrs. Sotheby and Co. and Messrs. Christies; also to Taylor of London; Messrs. Jeremy Ltd.; The Old School House Antiques; and Messrs. Bracher and Sydenham Ltd. of Reading for so kindly allowing me to make use of a number of photographs of snuff boxes, scent bottles, pomanders and vases. I have also had much interesting correspondence with Mr. F. Terry Newman of the P.P.R. Survey on the Psychological Reactions of Perfumes and am indebted to him for his kindness in replying to my letters.

Finally my thanks are due to Mr. Christopher Sinclair-Stevenson for his kind help in revising my manuscript and for his many valuable suggestions.

The line drawings throughout this book are by my son, Mr. W. A. Genders, whilst the manuscript was prepared by Doris Gatling.

CONTENTS

LIST OF ILLUSTRATIONS

To smell those odours that do rise
From out the wealthy spiceries:
So smells the flower of blooming clove;
Or roses smother'd in the stove:
So smells the air of spiced wine;
Or essences of Jessamine!
So smells the breath above the hives,
When well the work of honey thrives;
And all the busy Factors come
Laden with wax and honey home;
So smell those neat and woven bowers,
All over-arched with oringe flowers;
And Almond blossoms, that do mix
To make rich these aromaticks:
So smell those bracelets, and those bands
Of Amber chaft between the hands,
When thus enkindled they transpire
A noble perfume from the fire . . .
When as the meanest part of her,
Smells like the maiden pomander,
Thus sweet she smells, or what can be
More lik'd by her, or lov'd by mee.

TO THE MOST FAIR AND LOVELY
MISTRESS ANNE SOANE

ROBERT HERRICK

CHAPTER ONE

THE MYSTICAL QUALITY OF SCENT

Smell the most neglected of our senses – Emotional response – Stimulation of scent – The olfactory senses – Odours of the saints – The mystery of scent.

OF the five primary senses—touch, taste, smell, sight and sound— smell is unique in that there is no word in the English vocabulary to define it. We may say that a certain odour has a violet- or vanilla-like scent or it may be likened to one of the fruits, recalling the perfume of the raspberry or peach; but there is no word to describe a particular odour as there is 'bitter' or 'sweet' as applied to taste, or 'sharp' or 'soft' as applied to sound.

Scent is the most neglected of the senses yet according to the Kenya-born anthropologist, Dr. Louis Leakey, early man survived for twenty million years because of his distinctive body odour which turned the stomachs of predatory animals. Because of this, they left him alone, until he had learnt to protect himself by the use of weapons. It was only then that the unpleasant smell of his body began to disappear. Dr. Leakey arrived at this conclusion by his observations in the wild of baboons and chimpanzees, both of which sleep in trees. Baboons frequently lose their young to predatory animals but only rarely does the chimpanzee which resembles man in many ways, not least in its body odour, suffer in the same way.

Macrosomatic animals, like the dog, which go about on four legs with their noses close to the ground, have their smelling organs developed to a greater extent than man who relies on his sight rather than his sense of smell for survival; though in primitive man, smell is more acutely developed than in more civilized society. This may account for the ability of the Indians of Peru to track down an enemy over considerable distances, working entirely by scent, in the same way that a hound will take up the 'scent' of a fox. In dogs (and rabbits) the degree of pigmentation of the olfactory mucous membrane covers a larger area than in man. It is also more darkly coloured and is therefore more sensitive. For this reason the sense of smell is more acutely developed in people with dark skins.

Unlike the warrior Indians of Peru who by necessity must rely on their sense of smell to protect themselves and their families and to hunt down game for food so as to ensure their survival, the sense of smell in modern man is now almost entirely used as a means of enjoyment, whether partaking of food or drink, or in the use of perfume to assuage body odours, or for sexual attraction. In his *Bulwarks of Defense* (1562), William Bullein said: 'Man only doth smell and take delight in the odours of flowers and sweet things.'

Smell is the most subtle of our senses and that most difficult to regulate or define. It is possible to close the eyes or block the ears to protect oneself from seeing or hearing something unpleasant, but one cannot stop breathing for more than a few seconds and so it is not possible to exclude the sensation of scent or smell for a greater length of time. It is possible to breathe through the mouth though the sensations of taste differ from the olfactory sensations which are more delicately defined.

Rousseau expressed the opinion that the sense of smell is the sense of imagination, with the property of refreshing the memory and vividly recalling our past life; and Walter Savage Landor said: 'Sweet scents are the swift vehicles of still sweeter thoughts.' But though a particular odour is readily recognized wherever it is experienced, its play upon the imagination is determined by its associations. The resinous smell of sawdust in the timber yard immediately recalls days spent in the felling of timber in pine woods, whilst the musk-like smell of honey swiftly brings back warm August days by the sea, for this was the time of year when the Buddleia produced its graceful honey-scented racemes and always it grew near the sea and bloomed when summer holidays were in full swing.

In a programme about the old steam railways on BBC Television which took place on Boxing Day, 1970, the interviewer asked each of those who had spent a lifetime as a steam engine driver, to describe his most outstanding memories of days spent with the old engines. Almost without exception the men replied that it was some special smell they remembered with most affection. The smell of the old engine shed on a winter's morning with coal burning in the fire box, and the smell of oily rags were amongst the things they remembered best. But most made mention of the smell of apple blossom as they came down into Worcestershire soon after leaving the grime of Birmingham's New Street station and the industrial Midlands. 'Ah,' said one of them in his broad Yorkshire dialect, 'it were like 'eaven, you drove with thi' 'ead out of cabin window, takin' it into thi' lungs. A'll ne'er forget it, it were wonderful. In the modern closed-in cabins you can't smell a thing and it's the one thing I miss most of all.'

When on active service during the First World War, Rupert Brooke's most impressive memories were of the vicarage garden at Grantchester and the old-fashioned scented flowers which grew there:

> Just now the lilac is in bloom,
> All before my little room;
> And in my flower beds, I think,
> Smell the carnation and the pink . . .

'Of all the senses,' wrote Dr. McKenzie in his *Study of Smells* 'none surely is so mysterious as that of smell . . . the nature of the emanations that stir it to activity is still unknown . . . its effects upon the psyche are both wide and deep, at once obvious and subtle.'

Scents and smells and even their descriptions, act at once upon the delicate nerve centre that lies beneath the mucous membrane of the nose and so play upon the imagination as to bring about an emotional reaction which may be either pleasant or unpleasant as the case may be. The olfactory nerve is only one of twelve cranial nerves that directly lead to the cerebrum.

The subject of emotional floral response is so great that at least seventy-four aspects have been covered extensively and from earliest times formed the basis of folk medicine, herbalism and homoeopathic flower healing. To many women, cigar smoke acts as an aphrodisiac whilst clove and lavender scents have a powerful attraction for the male who equates them with cleanliness. It is on record that the world-famous portrait painter, Pietro Annigoni, becomes exhilarated by the scent of old leather-bound books and by the aroma of burning wood and will have perfume in his studio

to create atmosphere between himself and his sitter. Yehudi
Menuhin, the celebrated violinist, has said that he considers scent
to be more elusive than music, stirring in one subconscious thoughts
and emotions. He has told of Indian musicians who, when playing
far from their native land, will light sticks of incense before taking
up their instruments. This they do to bring back memories of their
homeland and to create an atmosphere around them which will
enable them to perform most favourably. Thomas Moore, in
Lalla Rookh or *Night of the Harem*, tells of 'the young Arab, haunted
by the smell of her own mountain flowers as by a spell, the
Sweet Elcaya, and that courteous tree, which bows to all who seek
its canopy'.

But odours and exhalations go further than this. They can coerce
and compel and inspire compulsive actions quite out of character.
The scent of the white jasmine can transform a woman into a
nymphomaniac after the slightest inhalation and the tuberose has a
similar effect on some women.

There are those who are unable to work creatively without
emotional stimulation and, before taking up his pen, Guy de
Maupassant would invariably place on his desk a bowl containing a
mixture of ether and strawberries when in season, though what he
used at other times for inspiration, we do not know. Strawberries
and ether give off a scent resembling the leaves of wild strawberries
when dying, a scent which Lord Chancellor Bacon said was one of
the most delicious of all: 'Next to the scent [of the double white
violet] is the musk rose; then strawberry leaves dying, with a most
excellent cordial smell.'

Through the centuries, scent has always excited the strongest
emotions in man, usually acting as a stimulant as it did to
Maupassant. It was John Kay, physician to Queen Mary Tudor, who
in 1552 wrote imploring his fellow beings 'to smell unto an old
sweete apple for there is nothing more comforting to the spirits'.
In the *Song of Solomon* it is written: 'Comfort me with apples for
I am sick of love.'

Goethe has told how Schiller found similar comfort in the smell
of ripe apples but which to Goethe acted like a poison. He recorded
the story of his calling on Schiller one day. Not finding him at home,
he seated himself at Schiller's desk to take notes of various matters.
Soon, he began to feel most uncomfortable, 'but I did not know to

what I should ascribe this wretched and unusual state until I discovered that a dreadful odour issued from a drawer which I opened and found to my astonishment that it was full of rotten apples. I immediately went to the window and inhaled the fresh air, by which I was instantly revived'. Meanwhile Schiller's wife came in, and informed Goethe that the drawer was always kept filled with well ripened apples because their aroma was so beneficial to her husband and he was unable to work without it.

It was in 1877 that C. T. Kingzett, when walking in a Surrey pine wood, became so refreshed and exhilarated by the scent of ozone formed by the volatile of the leaves producing oxide of hydrogen and camphoric acid, that he decided to manufacture these reagents artificially by the decomposition of turpentine. He was to form the Sanitas Co. of Bethnal Green to market his product, from which he duly made his fortune, for its qualities quickly became appreciated throughout the civilized world.

Not all scents refresh and stimulate, however, and Dr. Hampton has told of a friend, a girl in her teens, who would become excited and agitated when approaching a bean field in bloom. Her heartbeats would increase rapidly, her breathing would quicken and after a few minutes she would become exhausted. But as soon as the field had been passed, the girl would quickly return to her normal self. Because of their power to stimulate the emotions, the Romans used bean flowers as love charms and considered the plant to be sacred.

Montaigne believed that physicians might draw more use from odours than they do: 'For myself, I have often perceived that according to their strength and qualitie, they change and alter and move my spirits, and work strange effects on me.'

There are those who are so stimulated by scents that they break into hilarious laughter, whilst in others, scented flowers and leaves will often bring about a feeling of intense cheerfulness. Writing in 1597, John Gerard was scientifically correct when he said of the Sweet Basil that 'it maketh men merry and glad'; and William Langham in *The Garden of Health* (1579) said that to carry about one the powdered leaves of Rosemary would 'make thee glad, merry, gracious, and well beloved of all men'. For a similar reason, during mediaeval times, scented leaves were placed beneath door mats and cushions, and they would release their fragrance when anyone entered the home or sat down. Many Arabs have a comparable practice. In the entrances to their homes, they place a charcoal brazier on which they throw incense, fragrant woods and aromatic gums. When guests enter, they wrap their cloaks around the brazier for a few moments, so that they may become impregnated with a lasting perfume.

The peoples of the East were in fact the first to use perfumes to stimulate sexual emotion. Attraction between one person and another, however, may depend upon a natural scent of the body rather than one applied to it, for there are sweetly scented odours given off by the body at certain times which are so delicate as to be imperceptible to all but the person attracted by them.

Experiments carried out at the Primate Research Centre at Beckenham, Kent, revealed that the sexual desires of male monkeys depend upon hormones given to the females. When these were given oestrogen hormones (which naturally reach their maximum concentration in the body at the time of ovulation), the males quickly responded with vigorous love-making.

It has been suggested that the male monkeys were attracted by the hormone smell and that the same experience may take place between human beings. In a similar manner, butterflies attract their mates by secreting perfume on to their wings during courtship. With the butterfly, however, it is the male that is scented, the fragrance differing amongst the various species. Longstaffe, in his *Butterfly Hunting in many Lands*, describes the scents of more than a hundred species, but it was Dr. Carpenter who told of the function of scent in butterflies after watching the mating habits of certain African species. He observed the male hovering over the female, first protruding and then withdrawing its scent brush and scattering over his mate a delicately perfumed dust, like talcum powder.

The scent is due to an essential oil secreted at the base of a tuft of scales or hairs which are coated with a wax-like substance. This fixes the scent. These scented hairs lie in a groove at the extremity of the wings and are brought into use only when mating so as to concourse the scent. In some species, the hairs are present on the abdomen, from which the scent scales on the wings are inoculated with the perfume by means of a stroking action. It was the German botanist, Fritz Muller, who in 1877 first described the scents of butterflies and moths, recognizing it as a sexual characteristic. With the silkworm, on the other hand, it is the female that is scented and it has been observed that the male can detect her smell from a distance of more than six miles.

Scientists claim that the odours given off by humans can be used to determine not only their sex but their attire. They may also be used to detect crime and disease. To illustrate this, in 1965 the Illinois Institute of Technology carried out the experiment of 'bottling' people, so that the odour given off by their bodies could be accurately recorded. Volunteers were placed in large 'bottles' of purified air, the out-going air being trapped in containers and analysed. Each person was then placed in certain categories as determined by the results of the experiment, and upon physical examination of the person the information was seen to have been accurately recorded. A red-haired woman, for instance, emits a most pleasing smell from her body which has a special attraction for the opposite sex.

So sensitive is the nervous system to changes of temperament that the natural smell of a person can alter with the mood he or she is in, and perfume worn on the skin of a woman will change its scent entirely during emotional stress. For the same reason, a dog or any other animal may attack where it is able to detect, not by sight but by the smell of fear given off by the body, when one is afraid.

The human nose, however, is from ten to a hundred times more sensitive than the most accurate laboratory test in detecting odours, as Dr. Roland Harper made known to the British Association at Cambridge in 1965. Whilst the gas chromatograph can detect a thousandth of a millionth of a gram of certain substances, the human nose is able to take that from a tenth to a hundredth part further. Musk is one of the most powerful and penetrating of all scents, being detected with the nose in concentrations a million times smaller than is necessary for other substances. The human nose is indeed so sensitized that Dr. Harper has told of the nurse in a mental institution who could identify the freshly laundered clothes of each patient in her ward merely by holding them to her nose for a few seconds.

Olfaction is usually considered to be the lowest, the most animal, of our senses. It is certainly the most primitive and, in man, no evolutionary change has occurred since the beginning of time, for olfactory development is linked with the habits of the different species. Thus upright man relies almost entirely on his vision for survival, so neglecting his sense of smell. It may with truth be said that the sense of smell in modern man has been maintained more by the mouth than through the nose for we have come to appreciate the sensation of flavour in food and drink more than in those objects which merely have a pleasant perfume. What we recognize as flavour in food is really its odour which is appreciated by our sense of smell, being transmitted from the sensory cells present in the lining of the nasal cavity. Those who no longer take comfort from the use of tobacco have come to enjoy their food all the more and, perhaps for the first time, have found pleasure in fragrant plants and perfumes, as the sensory cells are no longer blocked with nicotine.

Though smell and taste are so closely related, they differ widely in their capacities: taste is able to appreciate only four sensations whilst those of the olfactory organ are virtually without end. Those who have lost the powers of smell are also unable to taste.

The apparatus which allows us to distinguish between scents and smells is contained in the epithelium linings situated at the top of the nose. They resemble tiny rods from which protoplasmic filaments known as the olfactory 'hairs' project into the mucous membrane, the watery substance which covers the inside of the nose. The end of the olfactory cell tapers into a nerve-fibre which comes into direct contact with the central nervous system. The olfactory cells which are present in all forms of animal life, from the lowly sea-anemone to human beings, have the function of passing the scent from the nose to the nervous system, thus acting immediately on the emotions.

The olfactory 'hairs' are present in the upper region of the nose, being situated just to one side of the mainstream of air which enters through the nostrils. The same thing happens when we eat or drink for then the mouth opens, the aroma is taken up through the nose, whereupon the molecules of the odorous substance come into contact with the olfactory cells, stimulating them by molecular vibration. These cells are in direct contact with the nervous system and determine our powers of differentiation as to whether or not we are able to appreciate a particular food or drink.

Compared with sight and hearing, scent is the most delicate of the senses, at times being scarcely perceptible; yet Fischer and Penzoldt found that they could detect, by smell, one milligram of chlor-phenol evaporated in a room of 230 cubic metres, the equivalent of 1/230,000,000th of a milligram to every cubic centimetre of air.

The remarkable sensitivity of the olfactory senses would lead one to suppose that the degree of response was equally sensitive, but this is not so, for whereas the reactionary time for auditory sensation is about 0.15 of a second, that for smell is 0.5 of a second. Only one sensation registers more slowly and that is pain which takes 0.9 of a second to react on the nervous system.

The nerve endings of the olfactory cells may become oppressed by a scent of excessive strength as when used in too concentrated a form or when experienced at too close range. Should this occur, the nerves may be quite incapable of appreciating the scent. One example is musk when used in concentration; another is the narcissus and Madonna Lily when indoors in a warm room. Indol is present in both flowers, as it is in lilac, privet and the tuberose (Polianthes tuberosa). These are flowers which, on account of their scent, have always been used in quantity to decorate salons and apartments on special occasions when they would, if inhaled for too long a time, cause headaches and distress to those susceptible. When fresh and inhaled from a distance, the flowers smell sweet and pleasing but when inhaled near to or when the flowers begin to fade, they take on animal-like overtones. This is due to the indol, an alcohol closely related to methyl indol (scatol) which is the active principle of civet and when inhaled in excess may also cause nausea and depression. It was the poet Cowper who said that he was unable to enter into conversation 'where there was civet in a room'. Indol occurs amongst the products of putrefaction, hence the likeness of the dying lilies to the smell of a dead rat.

Gerard the herbalist, who in the sixteenth century looked after the gardens at Theobalds for Elizabeth's Chancellor, Lord Burghley, and later had his own garden in Holborn, described the lilac's scent as being oppressively sweet, 'troubling the head in a strange manner and exciting the sexual instincts'. As the flower begins to fade, the sweet-scented compounds become broken down into simpler substances which have the same evil smell. The first products of decomposition are mostly sweet-smelling, as they are in the human body, and this may account for the sweet smell observed by those attending many of the saintly figures of history at the time of their deaths.

St. Thomas à Kempis is credited with the statement that the chamber of the blessed Leduine was so deliciously fragrant that people would press their faces as near to her as possible, and when St. Mark's tomb was opened at Alexandria in 827 for the conveying of his body to Venice, 'so sweet an odour spread through the city, that all the spiceries of Alexandria could not have caused the like'.

When the grave of St. Alban was opened, in obedience to a sign from heaven, people were amazed at the fragrance of his remains; and the same has been told of St. Thomas à Becket, when his remains were removed from his shrine at Canterbury and destroyed at the command of Henry VIII. And when St. Aldhelm's tomb was opened at Malmesbury Abbey 350 years after his death, a fragrant emanation was wafted from the open tomb into the faces of those who stood by.

The sweet odour of the saints may be akin to that indefinable scent which Havelock Ellis said is so often perceptible when people are gathered together on solemn religious occasions. It is something which seems to emanate from the soul rather than from the body. On the other hand, Burton, in his *Anatomy of Melancholy*, tells of Louis XI of France who lived a life so corrupt that 'all the odoriferous perfumes his courtiers could get would not ease him and still he smelled a filthy stink'. St. Joseph of Copertino was apparently able to recognize the sins of the flesh by their odours, and St. Paconi could even 'smell out' heretics.

The sense of smell quickly becomes tired by some scents, that of the violet being the most widely quoted example. At first, the scent is sweet and pleasing, but the olfactory nerves are rapidly fatigued and the longer the flower is inhaled, the more completely does the scent fade, leaving only the faint smell of cucumber or damp moss.

The violet scent is caused by a ketone of the ionane type which makes it one of the most difficult of all flowers to use for the extraction of its perfume. Shakespeare had observed this quality and wrote that the scent was

> Sweet, not lasting
> The perfume and suppliance of a minute.

Towards the end of the nineteenth century, de Parville, the French scientist, stated that the perfume of the violet had an injurious effect on the voice, and there is a record of the experience of the celebrated singer, Madame Marie Sass, who, when once a guest in the home of Baron Anthony de Rothschild, could take no part in a concert after smelling a bunch of Parma violets presented to her on the occasion; the scent acted upon the nerves and brought about the tumefaction of the vocal chords. For this reason, teachers of singing forbid the use of perfume made from those flowers which, like mimosa, also have a violet-like perfume.

Professor Zwaordemaker has shown that when the olfactory nerve endings have become fatigued by a certain smell, they are also insensitive to other scents which may resemble it though differing in chemical composition. This would seem to indicate that the nerve endings are equipped with separate receptors which have different responses to different smells.

Not all perfumes smell the same to any one person. Dr. Harper has demonstrated the effect of the substance methyl salicylate on several people in the United States and Great Britain. He found that whereas Americans described it as being sweetly scented, people in Great Britain thought it had the unmistakable smell of carbolic. But even to those whom he questioned in Wales and Scotland the smell differed greatly from that experienced by Englishmen. And for some, it had no smell at all, simply because the olfactory mucous membrane is covered with pigment which differentiates the degree of perfume. We know that a dark-haired person has a keener sense of smell than one who is fairhaired whilst albinos have no sense of smell at all—hence the difficulty in making a classification of scent.

Anosmia, the absence of smell, is occasionally met with in negroes who have lost pigment, as well as in albinos; and in albino animals which are unable to recognize the foetid smell given off by poisonous plants and may die in consequence. In parts of Virginia where Lachtanthus tinctoria with its poisonous roots is prevalent, farmers will keep only black pigs who are able to smell out the plant and so leave it well alone.

Darkness of pigment may act in the same way as black soil or black polythene sheeting which more readily absorbs the sun's heat than does light-coloured material. Substituting scent for heat, the scent of a flower, imperceptible to someone with a lighter skin, may be detected at a distance by a dark person, who is better able to absorb odours. And, because of the build-up of nasal pigmentation, an old person has a keener sense of smell than a young one.

Professor Ogle has shown that there is pigment in the ear and eye as well as in the nose. In the eye it is in contact with the rods of the retina and he supposed that the pigment must be associated with the reception of the sensory impressions. This may account for the inability of an experienced wine taster to carry out his task when unable to see the wine. If the eyes are closed during the 'tasting', the aroma from the wine vanishes completely.

Odours in solid form are better able to retain their perfume than they are in liquid form. This is because, when solid, the odorous molecules within the solid evaporate slowly—hence the high regard in which scented woods and roots were held in ancient times by people in the East, since their fragrance was retained for many years.

It might also be thought that liquids would be more odorous than non-volatile substances, but this is not so. A piece of sandalwood of some thickness is just as fragrant as perfume extracted from the wood, which readily loses its scent upon evaporation.

CHAPTER TWO

PERFUMES OF ANCIENT EGYPT

The Garden of Eden – The early spice traders – The Incense Road – Solomon
and the Queen of Sheba – Temples of the Nile – Aromatics for embalming –
Egyptian women and their love of perfumes.

SINCE man first appeared on earth, perfumes have been a part of
his existence. The first Book of Moses called Genesis, written some
4,000 years before the birth of Christ, at about the time of the
building of the Temple of the Sphinx and the great pyramid of
Cheops, tells that 'the Lord God planted a garden eastward in Eden
and out of the ground made the Lord God grow every tree that is
pleasant to the sight and good for food . . . and a river went out of
Eden to water the garden'. We do not know whether or not the
trees were fragrant nor is there any mention of flowers in Genesis,
for trees and ferns were the first plants to cover the earth's surface,
providing shade from the heat of the sun, and food and the mystical
quality of scent.

The river which watered the Garden of Eden 'became four heads',
one of which, named Pison, irrigated the land called Havilah where
gold was to be found and bdellium and onyx. There have been
various translations of 'bdellium', one being 'crystal', but the Greek
word of the same spelling was the name given to the Balsamodendron
from which an aromatic gum is obtained and which the scriptures
call myrrh. If such a derivation is correct, then this is the first
mention of a scented plant in the Bible.

Myrrh was from earliest times recognized as the most valued
possession of civilized man, for the use of alcohol in which to dissolve
the essential oils of flowers was then unknown, and myrrh was the
only substance which could provide a powerful and lasting scent. It
is a yellow gum-resin secreted by the prickly shrub Balsamodendron
myrrha, to be found in Arabia and in that part irrigated by the
Tigris and Euphrates; a region known as Babylonia at the time of

Moses. Here, at the junction of the two mighty rivers, was supposedly situated the earthly paradise, the Garden of Eden.

Sir William Willcocks, who surveyed the entire region at the beginning of this century, concluded that the Babylonian Tablets of the Creation were correct in naming this vast low-lying land Eden, which in the language of those who inhabited the area signifies 'a plain'. It was, in the time of Moses, approximately at the centre of the civilized world which extended from the Nile in the west to India in the east and from the southernmost tip of Arabia to the Black and Caspian Seas in the north. It is an area of intense heat and aridity and from earliest times was the centre of the perfume trade. Here were to be found the most potent of the scented woods and leaves from which the resinous gums were obtained.

Early man must surely have been aware of the preservative properties of spices and gums as well as their value for flavouring food and drink. The cooling properties of trees and shrubs with scented foliage were another important advantage for those who inhabited the warmer parts. Not only did they provide shade for early man and for domestic animals but, just as Professor Tyndall has shown that a spray of perfume when diffused through a warm room is able to reduce the temperature by preventing the passage of heat rays, so too do those plants with fragrant foliage bring about a reduction of air temperature around them. They were also appreciated for their powers of refreshment and recuperation from the production of ozone formed by the oxidization of the volatile oils. Newton in the *Herbal of the Bible* (1597) said that it was the custom for the peoples of Palestine at that time to stick branches of fresh green leaves over and about their beds because of their cooling properties; and for the same reason they would bedeck their living-rooms with fragrant foliage.

The ancient Egyptians were the first people to show an appreciation of perfume, using them for religious rites and funeral honours, and also for their toilet, massaging their bodies with fragrant oils to give elasticity to their sun-baked skin.

They first began to import aromatics about 2000 B.C. and Genesis tells us that they were carried to Egypt by Ishmaelite traders who went 'from Gilead, with their camels, bearing spices and balm and myrrh' (Joseph was sold to Potiphar by these merchants). Ancient Ishmaelia was then the hub of the important caravan routes which traded spices and aromatics and was situated in the most southerly part of Palestine. It later became the kingdoms of Edom and Moab, territory now under Jordanian sovereignty.

The 'balm' mentioned in Genesis was not, however, the celebrated Balm of Gilead which later came to be cultivated around Jericho in the mountainous country of Gilead, situated between the Sea of Galilee and the Dead Sea. This plant, Commiphora opobalsam, grew only in the southernmost part of Arabia, called Felix Arabia, until introduced into Palestine during the time of Solomon. It formed one of the gifts of 'spices' brought to Solomon by the Queen of Sheba whose country occupied that part of Arabia now known as the Yemen.

The 'balm' carried by the traders was most likely the exudation of Pistacia lentiscus, a fragrant terebinthine obtained by making incisions in the stem and which appears as pale yellow transparent drops. It is known in commerce as 'Mastick' and was used by the Egyptians for burning as incense and by the children of Palestine to chew, for it was believed to strengthen the teeth and gums. At a later date the Greeks flavoured a liquor made from grapes together with the gum, which they called 'Masticke'.

In Joseph's time, Jericho was the principal trading post for aromatics and spices, many of which arrived by camel and donkey train from Babylon on the Euphrates. One of the most highly prized aromatics brought by the traders was spikenard, whose scented roots were obtained from the valleys of the Himalayas. From Babylon, the caravans would set out for Jericho, following the Euphrates in a northerly direction and stopping first at the royal city of Mari, birthplace of the patriarch Abraham, the most important city in the East until it was overrun by the Babylonians in 1700 B.C.

From Mari, the caravan would turn in a westerly direction, crossing the inhospitable Syrian Desert by way of the oasis at Palmyra, still a watering stop for tribesmen, then southwards to Damascus. From here, the traders would follow the green valley of the Jordan as far south as Jericho on the northerly shores of the Dead Sea and there unload their precious cargo for the Ishmaelite traders to collect.

Canaan, the strip of land extending from Hamath to Gaza, along the Mediterranean coastline, was the next destination to traders after leaving Jericho. It was here that Jacob and his family lived and here that his son Joseph was sold to be taken with the Ishmaelites 'down into Egypt'. Canaan was also the central market for the purple dye, famed throughout Egypt and used by the royal household for colouring their robes. This dye was obtained from the shellfish Murex which took on its deep purple colouring only when out of the water and directly exposed to the heat of the sun. It was so precious a commodity that Canaan was known as the 'Land of Purple' and no caravan train would make the journey into Egypt without taking with it at least a small amount. From this time, purple became the symbolic colour of royalty throughout the world for it was so costly that no other people could afford to use it. In the Greek language, the dye was called Phoenicia and those who collected it were the Phoenicians, a people who occupied that part of Canaan to the north of the Sea of Galilee extending to the Mediterranean. Here too grew the dense cedar forests of Mount Lebanon, indigenous only to that area. The cedar is one of nature's most handsome creations, growing to a great height and spreading out its branches horizontally for a considerable distance, the evergreen leaves appearing in small tufts like those of the larch. Oliver Goldsmith hailed the beauty of Lebanon's cedars and of the 'balm' that grew in Gilead:

> Ye hills of Lebanon, with cedars crowned,
> Ye Giliad groves, that fling perfumes around.

The Egyptians believed that the wood of the cedar was imperishable and that it had the property of preserving for ever anyone it enclosed. It was therefore much in demand by the Pharaohs for the building of ships and for making the doors of their temples. It was also used for coffins, whilst the fragrant wood was burnt as incense as an offering to the gods. Cedarwood oil was used to rub over the body after bathing and was included in the most expensive cosmetics and unguents.

In the museum at Palermo one can see a tablet, dating from about 2700 B.C., which tells how the King of Egypt imported large numbers of cedars, the forty ships he sent to the port of Tyre to take on the load returning laden with the massive trunks. The tree was so important that, in 2350 B.C., Cheops I had reason to send an expeditionary force to Canaan, to prevent a Bedouin attack on the country which was to be made simultaneously from Arabia in the south and Syria in the north. His campaign was completely successful, the Egyptians destroying much of the land occupied by the 'desert people' and returning with large numbers of prisoners.

By 1950 B.C. Sesostris I, in order to safeguard the forests of the Lebanon and to ensure supplies, had brought Canaan under full control, setting up a consular office at Tyre which was then the most flourishing port of the ancient world. It was at about this time that Abraham and his wife Sara entered Canaan from the kingdom of Mari and followed much the same route as the caravans which brought spikenard and aromatic gums from Babylon to Jericho.

Ishmaelia was also the terminus of another important spice route taken by the caravans bringing frankincense and myrrh from the Yemen, and known as the Incense Road. Frankincense exudes from the smooth-barked tree or shrub, Boswellia serrata, all parts of which are fragrant. After myrrh, its fragrant gum was the most prized substance of the East and was the one most widely used as incense. Like myrrh it was found only at the southernmost tip of Arabia and on the coast of Somaliland where it grows on rocky hillsides and in desert ravines, and its collection and transportation presented the utmost difficulty. Here 'in fortunate Arabia', wrote Dionysius, 'you can always smell the sweet perfume of marvellous spices, whether it be incense or myrrh', for both grew plentifully in the spice kingdoms of Minaea and Sheba. Here, gardens of unprecedented beauty were washed by a great natural dam which collected the waters of the river Adhanat. The lush vegetation resembled that of Eden when it was watered by the Tigris and Euphrates, and the kings and queens of southern Arabia were well able to exploit the favourable situation to the advantage of their country.

Almost daily, the spice caravans consisting of large numbers of the finest camels travelled along the tortuous coastal road of the Red Sea, fanned by fresh breezes which made their journey tolerable. Before reaching Ishmaelia, they had to cover twelve hundred miles and frequently came under attack from marauding tribesmen. It was a journey of extreme difficulty but the cargo was valuable, for the spices that they carried were much in demand by the Egyptians.

For two thousand years, this distant corner of Arabia continued to supply the civilized world with Frankincense. Then in about 1000 B.C. the empire of Solomon, which extended from Jerusalem to

Damascus and as far south as the flourishing port of Ezion-Geber on the gulf of Aqabah, caused serious difficulties for those using the Incense Road. For the first time, it was necessary to pass through Israeli territory before continuing the journey into Egypt, and Israel, now a prosperous empire, showed no friendliness at all towards its neighbours in the south.

At this time, however, Sheba was ruled by a queen who, besides her fabulous beauty which few had ever gazed upon, was an astute business woman and a superlative diplomat. Realizing that a hostile Israel could terminate her lucrative trade with Egypt, she lost no time in despatching her agent to Jerusalem to arrange an immediate interview with Solomon since her country's economy relied on an uninterrupted flow of incense to Egypt.

II Chronicles tells that 'when the queen of Sheba heard of the fame of Solomon, she came to prove Solomon with hard questions at Jerusalem, with a great company, and with camels that bare spices, and gold in abundance, and precious stones'. It was no easy task for a woman to undertake a journey of more than two thousand miles across some of the most desolate country in the world, and it proves Sheba's queen to have been a woman of considerable courage and daring. Brought up in a life of luxury, probably never before having left her native land, she did not spare herself from making the hazardous journey when the trading future of her country was at stake. Nor did she entrust the urgent business to a delegate, but went herself, laden with all manner of gifts for Solomon. He must have been greatly impressed by the courage and business acumen of his guest; 'and when she was come to Solomon she communed with him of all that was in her heart.' She also brought seeds of the precious myrrh.

On the walls of the magnificent temple at Der-el-Bahari in Upper Egypt, built in 1500 B.C. by Queen Hatshepsut who ruled as co-regent with Thutmos III, there is a relief painted in the most brilliant colours which depicts the traffic in the precious resins and gums. It describes in great detail the expedition which set out from Ezion-Geber on the queen's behalf to far-away Punt, a legendary place in Somaliland, situated at the easternmost tip of Africa. Five barges left the chief port of the Red Sea under the captaincy of Nehsi, laden with copper and turquoise to be exchanged for thirty-one incense trees, together with a cargo of ebony, sandalwood, ivory and apes. The relief shows how the incense trees were brought back, with their roots in deep boxes and probably covered with soil to prevent them from drying out, as modern nursery growers sell trees and shrubs in containers with the soil ball intact, so that there will be as little root disturbance as possible. The natives who came back with the trees supervised their unloading and, before returning home, may also have planted them in the queen's garden to ensure that this was done in a satisfactory manner. According to Pliny these trees were so sacred that, when removing the gum for use in the temples, the men were to be kept free from pollution.

There are numerous reliefs which tell of the extensive use of incense and perfumes in ancient Egypt. At the base of the Sphinx at Giza is to be seen a granite tablet of King Thutmos (1425–1408 B.C.) offering incense and libations of oil to the god created by Chephren in his own likeness but with the body of the sacred lion. It records that one day, when resting at the base of the Sphinx, he heard it say that it was far from happy with its body covered by sand, whereupon the king had the sand removed and recorded this act for posterity.

Fragrant woods were first used as offerings to the gods and burnt on altars in temples throughout Egypt, the daily ritual being performed by the priests who lived in compounds attached to the temple. They were provided with food and wine and with linen for their clothes whilst large quantities of incense were stored in rooms specially set aside for the purpose.

The word perfume, from the Latin per, 'through', and fumum, 'smoke', shows that the origin of the word lay in the burning of incense, both to 'offer up' the gratitude of the people to the gods for favours received, and to ask for their blessing in time of trouble. The Egyptians believed that their prayers would reach the gods more quickly, wafted by the blue smoke which slowly ascended to heaven, and the belief has persisted: 'Of your well perfumed prayers,' wrote John Crashaw in 1646. Since the heavy intoxicating smoke also brought on religious ecstasies, the burning of incense was employed in all forms of primitive worship.

Every temple at Luxor and at Memphis smoked with the fragrant woods of Arabia during the more important festive occasions, whilst offerings were made in the streets and in the homes of the people. Karnak, situated on the left bank of the Nile, near Thebes, was the largest and greatest Egyptian temple. Here an inscription and a relief show the commanding figure of Ramses III, exhorting Amun to bring him victory in battle and reminding him that he has already sacrificed thirty thousand oxen to him and 'sweet smelling herbs and the finest perfumes', which would have been used to cover the bodies of the oxen to counteract the oppressive stench whilst burning.

At Heliopolis, city of the sun where the fiery orb was worshipped under the name of Re, incense was burnt thrice daily. Resinous gums were offered with the rising of the deity; myrrh when in the meridian; and a concoction of sixteen fragrant herbs and resins at the setting. This was the most expensive offering made and was known as Kyphi or Khepri. It was described by Plutarch and Dioscorides, and was adopted by the Greeks and Romans at a later date. The French chemist, Loret, has stated that its chief constituents were Acorus calamus, Andropogon, Schoenanthus, Cassia, Cinnannomum, Peppermint, Pistacia and Convolvulus scoparius, which were dried and powdered and then mixed together. Equal quantities of Juniper, Acacia, Henna and Cyperus longus were macerated in wine and added to honey, resin, myrrh and raisins steeped in wine. The whole concoction was beaten up, made into a paste and allowed to solidify. It was then ready to be placed in the burner as an offering to Re who reigned supreme at Heliopolis until the founding of the royal house at Thebes and the inauguration of the new god Amun. From the days of Chephren, builder of the Sphinx, the kings took the title, Son of Re, and this they retained until the time of Cleopatra.

Plutarch said that the aromatic substances included in the perfume Kyphi 'lulled one to sleep, allayed anxieties and brightened dreams' and he concludes with the observation that the perfume is 'made of those things that delight most in the night', from which it would appear that the incense was burnt at night in the homes of those who could afford to buy it as well as for an offering to Re.

Democrates said that spikenard, crocus (saffron) and bdellium were also included in the recipe, and this is confirmed by Plutarch. Myrrh was also mixed into the perfume Mendesium, the other ingredients being oil of ben and cinnamon which was found in Nepal and Sikkim and is the 'Kayu-gadis' of Malaya. The fragrant bark may have found its way into Persia and Babylonia from the valleys of the Himalayas, together with the hairy roots of Valeriana jatamansi, the Spikenard of the Scriptures. They were the most prized of aromatics for, although obtained under extremely difficult conditions, they never deteriorated during transportation, their fragrance actually increasing the dryer they became.

Cinnamon was also used in the perfume known as Metopium, which contained honey, wine, resinous gums (including myrrh) and almonds. It was rubbed on the feet and legs and, like most of the concoctions made in the temples which contained only wine and honey and natural herbs, was also taken internally to sweeten the breath.

At the opening of the tomb of Tutankhamen in 1922 a large number of exquisitely made vases were discovered, some of them containing unguents which, when opened, released a faint but quite distinctive perfume. The vases which were of calcite had been sealed by the crystallization of salts in the unguent, and the contents, though solidified, released the smell of spikenard when melted by the warmth of the hand.

Egyptian flask, 1380 B.C.

At a meeting of the British Association held at Oxford in 1926, Chapman and Plenderleith described the detailed analysis they had made of the substance, concluding that about ninety per cent of it consisted of animal fat, and that its scent was due mostly to the presence of olibanum or gum-resins of local origin, together with some matter resembling Indian spikenard. The substance was described by those who made the discovery as being somewhat sticky, 'consisting of yellow nodules, together with a chocolate coloured body'. Dating from 1350 B.C. it had retained its scent for more than three thousand years and confirmed the opinions of

Herodotus and Democrates who, on visiting Egypt during the Hellenistic Period, declared that the people were masters of the art of perfumery.

It was during this period in her history, that the Egyptians became familiar with the art of floral extraction as depicted on the walls of the temple of Edfu. This relief shows perfume being distilled from the flowers of the white Madonna lily, Lilium candidum, one of the oldest plants still to be found in cottage gardens everywhere. A floral perfume, green in colour, was also obtained from the flowers of the Henna, every part of which plant is fragrant. This perfume was known as Cyprinum and, as would be imagined from blossom so powerfully scented, the perfume was heavy and lasting. It is believed that this was used to drench the sails of the royal barges during the Hellenistic period.

At all important feasts fragrant gums were offered to the gods, one of the most lavish offerings being that made to Isis, wife of Osiris, god of the earth's fertility and ruler of the after life. Osiris was the best loved of all the gods for he was the most easily understood, and Isis was the most revered of all goddesses. Her feast day was a great occasion when an ox filled with myrrh and frankincense was made the sacrificial offering while fragrant oils were poured over it to counteract the smell of burning flesh. So great was their love for Isis that the Egyptians erected an exquisite temple at Philae in her honour and as late as A.D. 500 pilgrims came from all parts of the East to place scented flowers on her altars.

But it was in their important religious processions that the Egyptians made their most lavish display of perfumes. On one occasion during the Ptolemaic dynasty, a hundred children, each carrying a golden chalice filled with incense and myrrh, marched in procession and they were followed by camels laden with three hundred pounds of cinnamon, saffron and orris.

The crowning of Egyptian kings was accompanied by a ceremony of the utmost splendour when incense was offered to the deity on behalf of the people, to give thanks for past favours and to ask for a happy and successful reign. Warrior kings, returning from a victorious campaign, would be greeted by the chief priests dressed in their robes of office who would walk before them carrying censers filled with burning incense and chanting prayers to the deity.

Their belief in the transmigration of souls led the Egyptians to devote much time to the embalming of dead bodies since they believed that, when the soul departed, it entered successively into the bodies of animals of the land, of the water, and of the air, before returning to the human form. It was therefore essential to preserve the body in the likeness of the living person so that the soul upon its return would recognize the body it had left. It has also been suggested that embalming developed from the wish of wealthy Egyptians to preserve the bodies of their ancestors in as near perfect a condition as possible so that future generations could contemplate the features of their predecessors.

On special occasions, the mummified bodies were brought from the tomb to be displayed before friends and relations and a priest was invited to offer incense and libations and to pour fragrant oil over them. They were then wiped with a towel before being replaced in the tomb.

The Egyptians believed that as soon as the soul returned to the body, the dead person could go on living exactly as before, spending an eternity in the tomb but leading the life to which he had been accustomed. Consequently, jars were filled with food and drink and with precious ointments to apply to the body and were placed in the tombs to be renewed by the gods whenever the occasion arose. To help preserve the strength of the departed, small statues were also left in the tomb to carry out the more unpleasant tasks which might have to be performed there during the period of re-incarnation and so that the recipient of the new life would have more leisure for his favourite pastimes of hunting and fishing.

In the Museum of Fine Arts at Boston there is a sarcophagus dating from the XIIth Dynasty (c. 2000 B.C.) and made of cedar wood. It still retains the unmistakable scent for which the wood is famous and on the side is painted a likeness of the mummified person, surrounded by jars of ointments and of food for his survival in the after-world. He is shown sitting in an upright position and in front of him stands a priest with a censer, fumigating his body with incense and offering libations.

This was the first act in the burial rites of a person of high rank. Afterwards would begin the embalming of the body, to enable it to arrive at the end of the long journey in a state of preservation. For this, aromatics were required in considerable quantities by those whose families were prepared to pay for them, and for this purpose alone, large amounts of fragrant gums and oils were imported from all parts of the East, especially Arabia.

After first removing the brains, then the intestines by means of an incision made in the side of the body with a sharp stone, oil of cedarwood was injected, and the stomach was filled with myrrh and cassia before being sewn up. The body was then placed in natron in which it was kept for seventy days so that the flesh could dehydrate. Natron is a sesquicarbonate of soda, found at the oasis of Wadi Natrun, one of several areas of hollow ground into which the Nile at one time overflowed.

At the end of seventy days, the body was removed from the natron and was then ready for wrapping in linen bandages which had first been smeared with scented ointments. Almost a mile of bandaging was used to entwine the body of a person of wealth and in the folds were placed amulets, small charms made of gold, stone or coloured glass to watch over the body of the mummified person through eternal life.

The wrapping completed, the body was then placed in a cedarwood coffin, made to the size and shape of the body. Only cedarwood was used, for it was both durable and fragrant, and it had to be brought from the Lebanon, almost a thousand miles away. Indeed, it was so highly prized for coffin making and ship building, that a later dynasty was forced to safeguard the supply by extending the kingdom to bring the Lebanon into its orbit.

The most expensive method of embalming cost a talent, about £500 in today's money, but this excessive use of aromatics was reserved only for kings and the very rich. Embalmers were regularly appointed for the purpose and were considered to be at the lower end of the social scale. In Thebes alone, one quarter of the town was employed in the manufacture of coffins and of tools for the embalmer's trade. Coptic jars, consecrated to Am-Set, were made to hold the intestines. Another vase held the smaller viscera and was dedicated to Ha-Pi. Into a third were placed the heart and lungs and a fourth, decorated with the head of a hawk, held the liver and gall bladder. The jars were then filled with fragrant oils and sealed down before being placed in the tomb. Favourite animals, such as cats and dogs, were also preserved by embalming and were often placed in the tombs with mummies.

After the embalmed body had been placed in the coffin, it was laid on a bier and the cortège made its way to the necropolis, the priest dispensing incense about the bier during the journey, the family mourners and friends following in slow procession (such a scene is depicted on a wall painting in the tomb of Amenemonef at Thebes). Upon arrival at the tomb, the rites were performed and incense was burnt before the body was lowered into the ground and sealed. In the Louvre is a drawing on papyrus, dating from the XVIIIth Dynasty, which shows the entrance to a tomb and a shaft by which the soul, in the form of a bird, is flying to be reunited with the body in the depths of the burial chamber, surrounded by jars of ointment and food vessels.

The coffin or sacophagus was usually painted in brilliant colours with an eye on the side, through which the dead person could 'see', and a doorway, by which he could leave and enter when-ever he desired, during his long stay in the tomb. Decorations with text, taken from the Book of the Dead, which gave instructions as to one's behaviour in the after-world, were also made on the coffin.

It was during the New Kingdom period extending from 1500 to 1000 B.C. and especially during the Ramses dynasty, that the most ornate cedar coffins, lined with silver or gold, were made. Ramses the Great, for instance, is said to have built himself a vessel of cedarwood of 280 cubits, covered inside and out with a layer of pure gold. By conquest, Ramses extended his dominion to Arabia and Persia, encircling the whole of the Middle East. Before he died at the age of almost a hundred, he had built up a flourishing trade in spices and aromatics, increased the welfare of his state, and founded large towns like Tanis and Quantir in the delta of the Nile. At his death in 1235 B.C. the power of Egypt was supreme, the country rich and prosperous. But the pinnacle of Egyptian civilization had been reached and soon the rot set in. By 1000 B.C. most of the country lay in ruins, the tombs pillaged and the temples desecrated. But the Near East was still the only region in the known world where the most potent of the scented woods and leaves would grow. The Egyptians, with their refined tastes and habits, were the first to use perfumes for personal adornment; and this practice, and their system of bathing, were later adopted by both the Greeks and Romans.

The Egyptians used pastilles to sweeten the breath and the
2*

Egyptian unguent flask,
1300 B.C.

women would cleanse their bodies with scented toilet waters. In addition, besides their use of perfumes, the women of Thebes, who were considered to be the most beautiful in the East, applied paints and powders to the face and a black powder known as Kohl to the pupils of the eyes to increase their size and brilliance. This was made from antimony and was applied with an ivory bodkin; it is still use as a basic ingredient for mascara. The attractive green shading on the eyelids was made from powdered lapis-lazuli, and necklaces and bangles of beads made from fragrant gums and scented woods were worn on the neck and arms.

Perfumes and unguents, in daily use for anointing the body, were manufactured in the laboratories of the temples. One such room can be identified in the great temple at Edfu, begun by Ptolemy III in 237 B.C., and dedicated to the god of the sky, the falcon god Horus, son of Isis and Osiris. It is situated on the left bank of the Nile, sixty miles south of Luxor, and on the walls of the perfume labora-tory, a room in almost complete darkness, are numerous inscriptions which clearly reveal the manner in which unguents and perfumes and ritual oils were made, the most subtle scents taking as long as six months to concoct and mature.

The priests alone were in charge of perfumery and in the temples was stored the greater part of all the aromatics brought into the country. They were kept in pots and vases made of onyx, alabaster and glass and in beautifully carved boxes of wood or ivory. Only the wealthy could afford such luxuries, the poor rubbing their bodies with palm oil which was produced in quantity for the purpose.

Both men and women of high rank considered perfume an essential accessory. Though the men only used them for festive occasions, the women, during the Late Period, improved their appearance with all manner of cosmetics. Indeed, the women of Thebes had their toilet boxes and dressing cases filled with bottles and jars containing everything imaginable for beautifying the body including Henna (Lawsonia inermis) leaves to rub on the cheeks and hands, for creating a rosy tint, Kohl to accentuate the beauty of the eyes, and scented oils to pour over the body.

In the beautiful temple of Hatshepsut at Thebes, carved out of the mountain face, there is a painting in the most brilliant colours which shows a lady of the court going through the daily routine of her toilet. She is attended by four maidens, two of whom pour fragrant oil over her body whilst a third massages her shoulder with one hand and, with the other, holds up a lotus flower for her to smell. The fourth maiden holds a polished copper mirror before her, that metal having been introduced into Egypt by Ammenemes III in about 1800 B.C. Later, when the copper mines of Sinai became exhausted, mirrors and embalming tools were made of bronze. Censers and wine bottles were also made of copper or bronze, though a material known to the Egyptians as 'brilliant' soon became fashionable. This was a type of quartz which was given an enamel-like finish after being dyed with the brilliant blue and green compounds of copper. But alabaster was most commonly used to store unguents on account of its density and coolness which prevented rapid evaporation.

With each dynasty the use of perfumes increased and with the advent of the Macedonian princess Cleopatra, who governed Egypt from the city founded by her countryman Alexander the Great in 336 B.C., they were used in abundance. Cleopatra, who ruled from 40 to 30 B.C. when the kingdoms conquered by Alexander had already fallen to the Romans, seduced Mark Antony by her lavish use of perfume in the hope of recovering her lost territories. Both Plutarch and Shakespeare have described her first meeting with the Roman when the purple sails of her barge were so saturated with perfume that

> The winds were love sick . . .
>   From the barge
> A strange invisible perfume hits the sense
> Of the adjacent wharfs.

Nile barges of the Egyptian kings and queens, dyed with the symbolic purple of royalty, were washed with scented waters for all state occasions whilst perfume bottles, made of glass or terra cotta, were prominent amongst the gifts presented to important visitors. In the British Museum there is a scent bottle of Egyptian design, made of richly coloured glass and dating from the fifth century B.C. It was discovered on the island of Rhodes and dates from the time of the domination of the country by Alexander the Great. It was probably given to a person of high rank when on a visit to Egypt at the time.

Rhodes scent bottle, 640 B.C.

Herodotus, the Greek historian who visited Egypt on several occasions during the Hellenistic period, has described in his *Enquiries* the country, its people and customs with the eye of the experienced traveller. He tells of seeing priests with shaven heads for the first time on his travels, and of Egyptian scholars who wrote from right to left. At festive banquets he saw slaves anointing the heads of the guests whose wigs of human hair gave protection from the heat of the sun and improved their appearance if they were bald or turning grey. Each guest was also crowned with a chaplet of scented flowers, white madonna lilies, the saffron crocus and that sacred and most fragrant of all flowers, the lotus, cradle of the sun. Wreaths of fragrant leaves hung from the walls to cool the atmosphere, incense burners on which aromatic woods were thrown were placed at intervals about the room and blind musicians played sweet music on eight-stringed harps.

The lotus was the most noticeable of the flowers of ancient Egypt and, in its forms of white and blue, grew wherever the water was still. The Egyptians believed that the creator had sprung from a lotus flower so that from an early date it became a symbol of re-incarnation. It still grows everywhere, in pools and marshlands, taking root in the mud and spreading wide its leaves, like large circular discs. The flowers open at daybreak and close at eventide in accordance with the rising and setting of the sun, and this caused the Egyptians to believe that the sun itself had ascended to its heavenly position from a flower of the lotus. In the Berlin Museum there is a statue of the infant sun god arising from a partly opened lotus flower to spread his light around the world and then to retreat into the flower as it closes in the evening.

The Blue-flowered Lotus or Water-lily, Nymphaea coerulea, was held to be sacred on account of its soft delicate perfume. It is shown in its colour of soft sky blue in a painting on the walls of the tomb of Menkheper at Thebes, dating from about 1500 B.C. The painting depicts four men seated at a funeral banquet and each is holding and smelling a lotus flower; another painting in Thebes depicts both living and dead inhaling the delicious scent, here shown as a symbol of immortality. The Blue Lotus was also the flower of the handsome young Memphis god, Nefertum, who, in the Book of the Dead discovered in the tomb of king Tutankhamen in the Valley of the Kings, is shown arising in all his beauty from a Blue Lotus bud, its long thin elegant petals pointing heavenwards.

Egyptian women copied the lotus lily for the arrangement of their hair in one of the more popular styles during the New Kingdom period. The hair was worn long, worked into many small plaits or curls, and the wealthy employed a private hairdresser to attend to the daily ritual. A stone carving on a sarcophagus at Deir-el-Bahari shows one such lady attended by her coiffeuse. She is holding in one hand a circular copper mirror with its decorated ivory handle and in the other holds a bowl of perfumed oil which the attendant massages into her scalp and uses to set her hair into the latest style. Wigs were arranged in similar style with the long curls flowing almost down to the waist.

In the Brooklyn Museum, New York, one can see a statue of a lady dating from about 1300 B.C., carved in ebony, her long plaits completely covering the back of her head and shoulders with a peculiar-looking cone-shaped object resembling a hat perched on top. It is, in fact, a cone made of metal or wood and containing fragrant pomade. This melted in the heat of the sun and covered the head and shoulders with a perfumed grease which seeped into the skin. When the lady retired for the night, this was massaged into the skin, improving a neckline whose beauty of form the Egyptian

Egyptian unguent vase,
1000 B.C.

women enjoyed as their birthright. At all religious festivals, wealthy women would cover their heads with ornate head-dresses made of beaten gold and inlaid with precious stones or coloured glass which protected the hair-style and accentuated their beauty.

The death of Cleopatra brought to an end the grandeur of Egypt with its then unparalleled appreciation of beauty and good living. For more than four thousand years perfumes had been used on a gigantic scale and almost all had been obtained from abroad, from Palestine, Persia, India and Arabia in ever-increasing quantities. The Jews were to continue this practice begun by the Egyptians both in their religious rites and for their personal enjoyment.

CHAPTER THREE

PERFUMES OF THE JEWISH PEOPLE

The Children of Israel – Exodus – The holy anointing oil – Frankincense –
Perfumes of the Promised Land – Myrrh and Spikenard, most precious of
substances – Sweet-smelling henna.

THE Exodus of the Hebrew people from the land of Goshen began
about 1240 B.C. and lasted forty years. Goshen was then a province
of Egypt which covered the eastern part of the Nile Delta, and
formed a large area of low-lying swampland infested by crocodiles.
The higher ground, however, which at certain times of the year was
irrigated by the fertile waters and alluvial deposits of the Nile, was
suited to corn growing, whilst the Israelites grazed their sheep over
the rich pasturelands further to the east. For several centuries, the
peace-loving Children of Israel, who were of farming stock and
knew no other trade, tended their flocks and grew their corn. Their
hosts were the Hyksos, people of Asiatic origin who had settled
there centuries before and were also of farming stock, so that a
bond grew up between the two peoples which lasted for nearly four
hundred years.

The last of the Hyksos kings of Egypt was Amenophis IV, a
mystic whose sole occupation was the adoration of the sun god Aton,
and who took little or no part in either the everyday life of the
people or in the affairs of state. In his strange cult he was supported
by his wife, the beautiful Nefertiti, who assisted him in the building
of Akhet-Aton on the east bank of the Nile. There they lived in
almost complete seclusion but imposing upon the country a religious
doctrine which was completely alien to that practised during the
two thousand years of Hyksos rule. As he had no son, Amenophis
chose as his successor Tutankhamen, who continued to rule from
Akhet-Aton for a short time until his death in 1345 B.C. when the
people rejected the cult of Aton and returned to the older religious
beliefs. Though reigning for less than ten years and dying before he

was twenty, the young king had assisted in repudiating the cult of Amenophis IV (Akhnaton) and the way was now open for a new dynasty to restore the country to its former greatness. Ramses was one of the generals who had destroyed the new religion inaugurated by Amenophis IV but when he ascended the throne as Ramses I he was already an old man and left the affairs of the country in the hands of his son Seti. Upon his death two years later, Seti's son accepted authority and was to rule as Ramses II for sixty-seven years, during which time Egypt resumed much of her former glory. The second Ramses was an extraordinary character. He had six wives in his lifetime and produced more than a hundred children; he brought under cultivation large areas of the kingdom which had hitherto produced nothing and, to store the grain, he built large 'treasure cities' at Pithom and Ramses in Israelite territory, using forced labour to make bricks and silos; 'And the Egyptians made the children of Israel to serve with rigour and they made their lives bitter with hard bondage in mortar and in bricks.'

Under the new king, the Israelites' position changed completely. No longer could they live the lives of nomadic farmers to which they were accustomed, tending their flocks untroubled by their rulers. They were now forced to work in gangs, supervised by Egyptian overseers, who can still be seen depicted on tablets, sitting on boulders with a cane in their hands, ready to strike any man who would not remain at his task. Quite unused to this type of work, the Children of Israel must have found it hard and exhausting, for there was little time to be lost if the granaries were to be ready for the harvest, and large areas of the land of Goshen, where previously sheep had grazed, had now been sown with corn: 'And it came to pass in those days, when Moses was grown up, that he went out unto his brethren and looked on their burdens: and he spied an Egyptian smiting an Hebrew, one of his brethren. And he looked this way and that way and, when he saw there was no man, he slew the Egyptian and hid him in the sand. And when Pharaoh heard this thing, he sought to slay Moses.'

Though Moses had been born in Egypt, he was of Hebrew stock and to save his life had no alternative but to flee the country. We can imagine the consternation amongst the Hebrew people after the killing of the overseer. Here was someone who had the courage to stand up for the rights of his people, and almost overnight he became their respected leader. Moses lost no time in leaving, seeking refuge in the mountainous country beyond the Gulf of Aqabah, a land occupied by the Midianites, descendants of Abraham's second wife, Ketura. It was shortly afterwards that Moses married Zipporah, daughter of the high priest. But Moses was greatly disturbed for in his heart he knew that his people were being exploited and he decided to return, to do whatever he could to relieve their sufferings.

The death of Ramses at this time must have seemed to the Israelites a most opportune moment to throw off the yoke of oppression; but to return to their homeland, they would first need permission from the new king. Moses, as their spokesman, lost no time in seeking an audience with him but his pleas made little impression for no country would wish to release so valuable a pool of cheap labour. Only the ensuing series of plagues finally brought about a change of heart in the king who agreed to release the people of Goshen hoping that the infections would go with them. Canaan, the homeland of the Hebrew people, was, however, under Egyptian occupation—Egypt's jurisdiction extended over the whole land, from Gaza in the south to the port of Tyre in the north—and Moses believed that if they took the coastal road by which they had originally entered Egypt during the time of famine, they would be sure to meet with a hostile reception, at every stage of the journey.

It was therefore decided that they should leave in a southerly direction, crossing the Gulf of Suez and taking the route used by the Egyptian labourers as they worked their shifts in the copper mines of Sinai. From the new towns of Ramses and Pithom the exodus began, about ten thousand Israelites having collected their belongings, their oxen and sheep to follow Moses, their chosen leader, to the land of their fathers. But it was to take them forty years of the most appalling hardships before they had sight of the Promised Land.

Near the fort of Migdol, which guarded the incense road to southern Arabia, they encamped for their first night. Moses knew this part of the country well, both the terrain and the tides. At the time, the narrow isthmus at the most northerly part of the Gulf was thick with reeds over which the tidal waves of the Red Sea ebbed and flowed incessantly.

When the tide was at its lowest, it was possible to cross the isthmus by walking over the reeds, in the same way as the pilgrims of old carried the body of St. Cuthbert from Lindisfarne to the Northumbrian coast and to the safety of the abbey at Chester-le-Street when the monks feared an attack by the Vikings on their Holy Island priory. Only in the Old Testament is this stretch of water known as the Reed Sea—this being the correct translation—for the Red Sea is entirely free from reeds, whilst its depth would prevent a crossing on foot anywhere.

After negotiating the isthmus, the Israelites continued their journey south under the most appalling conditions which must have made them long to return to the moist pasture-lands of the Nile Delta with its ample supplies of food and water, in spite of the laborious tasks they had to perform for the kings of the new dynasty. But there was to be no turning back and they continued their journey as far south as the oasis of Rephidem. Here they caught large numbers of quails for it was springtime and the birds had begun their migration to Europe from the east coast of Africa. Here, too, they had their first sight of Manna, 'the bread which the Lord had given them to eat'. To the Children of Israel, manna was like hoar frost which covered the ground after a cold night, but Moses knew it was edible and highly nutritious. From earliest times it had been gathered by wandering tribesmen for food and to sell to tradesmen who passed through the Sinai Peninsula. It is an exudation of the pink Tamarisk, a tree or shrub which grows in dry coastal districts, T. mannifera being indigenous to Sinai. The sticky exudations are caused by a minute insect which enters the plant's tissues by piercing a hole in the bark, thus causing the sap to flow out in tiny white beads which quickly solidify before dropping to the ground. The bushes and the ground around them do indeed appear from a distance to be covered with hoar frost.

Father Breitenbach, Dean of Mainz, when on a visit to Sinai in the fifteenth century, was fascinated by this substance, the Bread of Heaven of the Bible, and wrote that it 'falls about daybreak, like hoar frost and hangs like beads on grass, stones and twigs'. He described it as being sweet to the taste, like solidified honey, and of having a sweet, honey-like smell. To this day it is collected, always in the early hours of the morning, by Bedouins as an important part of their diet and to export to the many tourist centres of the Near East, for in the warm climate it will keep for many years: 'And Moses said unto Aaron: Take a pot and put an omer full of manna therein and lay it up before the Lord, to be kept for your generations.' Exodus tells that the Israelites ate manna throughout the entire forty years of their journey, 'until they came to the borders of the land of Canaan', for it grows in all parts of Palestine and Arabia and the exudations continue throughout the year. The Bedouins still press it into cakes and consume it with dates and on this mixture they can subsist for the whole day.

Turning north, the Israelites stayed for a long time at Rephidem (now Feiran) and it was here that one of the most momentous happenings in the history of the world took place.

Rephidem was the most important oasis in the south of Sinai and here Joshua won his decisive battle, beating off an attack by the Amalekite tribesmen who were indignant at having a host of unfamiliar people making use of their sole supply of water. At Rephidem, during the early days of the Christian Church, a chapel was built which gradually attained the stature of a monastic foundation. It was later to be known as St. Catherine's Monastery and became a centre of pilgrimage for Christians everywhere. Here, in 1859, the German von Tischendorf made one of the most stupendous theological discoveries of all time. He found in the chapel a fourth-century manuscript which was later purchased by the British Government and is now in the British Museum. It is known as the Codex Sinaiticus and in it is contained the whole of the New Testament and much of the Old.

Shortly after leaving Rephidem, Moses decided to pitch camp at the foot of Mount Sinai and, going up into the mountain, he spoke the wonderful words of the Ten Commandments, declaring for all the world to understand, a new faith in one omnipotent God. It was on Mount Sinai that Moses gave to his people a moral code which has since been the foundation of man's faith: 'I am the Lord thy God, thou shalt have no other gods but me.' Since this time, the Ten Commandments have remained the pillar of Christian code and conduct; they were the basis of Christ's teaching. The glory of God shone upon Mount Sinai for six days, covering it in a cloud of great brilliance. Then, as an offering, the children of Israel were commanded to bring gold and silver and fine linen; rams' skins dyed red; and oil for the lamp, together with spices for the anointing oil and sweet incense to burn.

As an Egyptian, Moses would have been familiar with the use of
fragrant oils and the burning of incense, and would know of the
trees and shrubs which grew in Sinai and Arabia and provided gums
and fragrant woods for offerings. The Israelites were to take this
knowledge with them to the Promised Land.

During the remainder of their sojourn in the wilderness, they
were to make use of large quantities of incense in the ceremonies
of sacrifice and in consecrating the priests. Aaron and his sons, the
chosen priests, were to make daily offerings of bullocks and rams;
and so that 'there would be a sweet savour before the Lord', incense
was used to cover the bodies. There was also an altar on which
Aaron was instructed to burn 'sweet incense every morning: and
when Aaron lighteth the lamps at even, he shall burn incense upon
it; a perpetual incense before the Lord throughout your generation'.
This burning of incense Moses had seen performed in a similar
fashion in the temples of Egypt, since when it has been a significant
part of all religious ceremonies throughout the world.

In Exodus there are explicit directions given to Moses for making
the holy anointing oil: 'Take thou also unto thee principal spices, of
pure myrrh five hundred shekels; and of sweet cinnamon half so
much, even two hundred and fifty shekels; and of sweet calamus
two hundred and fifty shekels; and of cassia five hundred shekels;
and of olive oil, an hin [about a gallon]. And thou shalt make it an
oil of holy anointment': and it was to be used only on sacred occasions.
In Exodus it clearly states that 'whosoever shall make like unto that
to smell thereto, shall be cut from his people'. The penalties decreed
by Moses against the private use of incense and anointing oils would
seem to be proof that the Jews, like the Egyptians, were now
beginning to use perfumes for their own vainglory, chiefly as a
means of seduction, a method used by Judith when she sought out
Holofernes and asked him for the liberation of her people.

It was decreed that only pure frankincense could be used for
making the holy incense, which meant that supplies would have to be
obtained from tribesmen coming up from southern Arabia on their
way into Egypt laden with this expensive commodity. They would
meet the Israelites going in the opposite direction, and would
possibly exchange the frankincense for other aromatics the Israelites
had collected during their days in the wilderness.

Since earliest times, frankincense has been valued on a par with gold and there is a manuscript dating from the time of Henry III which tells that, after the rebuilding of Westminster Abbey, Edward the Confessor so wished to make the Abbey unique in its attractions, that he endowed it with a relic beyond price—part of the frankincense offered to the infant Jesus by the three Eastern kings, Kaspar, Melchior and Balthazar who went to recognize his Divinity, taking with them what were then considered to be the three most precious things known to man: gold, frankincense and myrrh.

Together with gold and myrrh, frankincense used to be offered in three silken bags on the Twelfth Day after Christmas, in the Chapel Royal in the Palace of St. James, at one time by the Sovereign in person. The *Daily Post* of January 7, 1742, recorded one such scene: 'Yesterday being the 12th day, his Majesty also the Duke and Princesses, went in state to the Royal Chapel . . . and, according to the ancient custom of the Kings of England, presented three purses filled with gold, frankincense and myrrh, in commemoration of the presents offered by the Magi.' George III was the last monarch to perform the ancient ceremony in person. Now, the monarch is represented by the Lord Chamberlain, attended by the Yeomen of the Guard. He places on the alms dish three purses, each of which contains £10 for distrubution to the needy and which replace the ancient offerings.

The purification of Hebrew women, as ordained by law, also increased the consumption of frankincense and of other aromatics. The purifying took place throughout the year, oil of myrrh being used during the first six months, and different aromatics yielding sweet odours for the remainder of the time. Esther had to undergo this ritual before she was presented to Ahasuerus who chose her to be his wife.

Frankincense is the gummy discharge of Boswellia carterii or B. serrata, both being closely related to the terebinth tree which is large in stature with compound leaves divided into numerous serrate leaflets and with greeny-white flowers opening star-like and tipped with pink.

The gum exudes from the bark in brittle, round drops which are white or pale yellow, and glisten in the sunlight. Though bitter to the taste, the gum gives off a balsamic odour when warmed by the heat of the hand or when burnt. Frankincense is mentioned on twenty-two occasions in the Bible, sixteen times in relation to its use in religious worship and three times as growing in the royal gardens of Solomon.

Frankincense, Boswellia serrata

Ecclesiasticus speaks of 'a pleasant odour like the best myrrh, as galbanum and onycha'. It has been suggested that Galbanum was obtained from the plant Galbanum officinale which grew on Mount Amonus in Syria, though Dr. Hower of Kew, an authority on the plants of the Bible, has said that the true Galbanum is rare in the Holy Land. The exudation referred to in Ecclesiasticus may have been obtained from Ferula galbaniflua, a turnip-rooted perennial native to Persia and Syria with stems five feet in height. If the stems are broken, a milky juice wells out, solidifying in the air and emitting a pleasant balsamic odour, unless it is burnt when it smells most unpleasant.

Of the other ingredients used to compound the holy incense, stacte (which in the Hebrew language means 'droppings') could be a reference to the exudations of myrrh or of any other gum-discharging plant of the Near East. Dioscorides believed it to be an unguent made from myrrh and origanum, which grows abundantly in Palestine.

Onycha has defied description, and though numerous theories

have been put forward as to its meaning, the generally accepted version is that it was the small mollusc Strombus lentiginosus, found on the shores of the Red Sea and from which a fragrant essence was obtained. It was finely ground into powder to mix with other ingredients, to act as a binding agent in the making of incense.

From Rephidem, the Israelites were to take many more days before reaching the oasis at Hazeroth from where they crossed the awesome Wilderness of Loneliness, a journey of several hundred miles, before arriving at Ezion-Geber, an oasis at the extreme northerly tip of the Gulf of Aqabah. It was here that the caravans arrived at the end of their twelve-hundred-mile journey from Felix Arabia and here they would come upon the Israelites. Within two centuries it was to become a part of the homeland of the Jewish people, being the most southerly outpost of King Solomon's empire, a place of great commercial and strategic importance. Here, the spice traders stopped to water their camels before beginning the journey into Egypt. Ezion-Geber was also the terminus of the famous King's Highway which ran northwards, through the kingdoms of Edom and Moab, along the eastern bank of the Dead Sea and past Mount Nebo from which Moses had sighted the Promised Land. This was the caravan route which took the Arabian traders and Sheba's queen to Jericho and Jerusalem and northwards to Damascus where they exchanged their precious spices for those brought from Babylon and the valley of the Euphrates. Altogether, it was a journey of some two thousand miles from southern Arabia through some of the most desolate and inhospitable country on earth.

However, because they could not obtain permission to cross through Edom, the Israelites took neither the King's Highway nor the valley road which leads straight to the oasis of Oboth, situated near the southern end of the Dead Sea about four hundred miles away. Instead, they chose to go by the sun-baked plateau known as the Wilderness of Sin, to Kadesh in the Land of the South, the territory of the Negeb. A few miles north of the oasis of Kadesh is the Wadi Qudeirat which had the largest supply of fresh water in the Negeb and where the children of Israel first saw their future home-land. From the country around Hebron, Moses sent out twelve scouts to survey the land of Canaan which lay to their left and had been under Egyptian occupation since 1500 B.C. They returned with the news that Canaan was indeed the 'land of milk and honey', where grapes and figs grew in profusion but where every city was heavily fortified and garrisoned by the Egyptians. Many of the towns were walled and most of the inhabitants well armed. It was a terrifying sight for the Israelites who were totally unskilled in the art of warfare.

After leaving Mount Nebo, they crossed the Jordan, which may be forded at several points in summer, and pitched camp in Gilgal. Only Jericho which guarded the road to the fertile plains of Canaan now stood in their way: 'And when the people heard the sound of the trumpet and the people shouted with a great shout, and the wall of the city fell down flat, and they took the city.' (Recent excavations in Jericho reveal that the city caught fire in about 1200 B.C. and authorities believe this to have been the result of an earthquake so severe as to leave not a single stone standing.) The Israelites were now in control of both sides of the Jordan and of the fertile valley through which the river enters the Dead Sea. They had arrived in the Promised Land. However, almost two centuries were to elapse before Israel under David finally subjugated the Philistines and the country was free to enjoy a long and prosperous peace. For forty years, David, poet and soldier was to rule over Israel, for the most part from Jerusalem, extending his kingdom from the Orontes to Ezion-Geber near the shores of the Red Sea, 'unto the borders of Egypt'. David inaugurated a Civil Service to administer the country and, after taking over the kingdom of Edom, brought under his control the most important iron and copper deposits in Palestine. He also had an outlet to the Red Sea so that his ships could begin trading with Africa and Arabia, obtaining aromatics in return for iron and fruit. When Solomon his son became king, Israel was already an Empire with a navy of ships bringing gold and silver, ivory and apes, and he built forty thousand stalls for his horses and chariots. Solomon was the first of the great industrialists, a fore-runner of the steel 'kings' of America, for not only did he have large quantities of iron and copper at his command but he had the most accurate scientific knowledge of how to extract and refine it; and, from Ezion-Geber, the centre of the mining industry, Solomon's cedarwood ships carried it to all parts of the known world. His fleet rivalled the bulk carriers of modern times which transport iron ore from the Australian deposits to Japan and America for the smelters of Nagasaki and Philadelphia to refine.

The Bible tells us that all came to hear the wisdom of Solomon, 'all kings of the earth', but mostly they would come to discuss trading agreements, the queen of Sheba being one of the first to make the journey, wishing not only to ensure that her caravans would be permitted to pass through his territory into Egypt but also to enquire as to what opportunities there would be for supplying Solomon with incense and other aromatics from southern Arabia. The queen must have made a deep impression on Solomon: 'Thy wisdom and prosperity exceed the fame which I heard,' she told him, and Solomon duly responded to her flattery for 'he gave her all she desired, whatever she asked and she turned and went back to her own country'.

It is possible that the queen made the journey to see Solomon on behalf of all the kingdoms of southern Arabia who were exporters of spices in some form or another, for shortly after her visit it is recorded that Israel obtained the 'traffic of the spice-merchants of all Arabia', together with large quantities of ivory, silver and gold which his merchant fleet brought from the east African coast. These he used with great extravagance to decorate the temple he had built entirely of cedarwood according to the pattern given him by his father David and stripping the forests of the Lebanon for the purpose. From the felling of timber, first by the Egyptians, then by Solomon, the forest never recovered, and today only a few ancient trunks show where the vast plantations had once been. Probably the last of the cedars were removed for building the temple of Diana at Ephesus, one of the wonders of the ancient world which was ravished by fire on the night Alexander the Great was born. Like Solomon's temple, it had been built of cedar as the peoples of the ancient world believed the wood to be imperishable. Horace alludes to the smearing of books with cedarwood oil to preserve them, and to give them fragrance they were kept in cedarwood chests. This gave rise to the ancient proverb when praising any work of importance, that it was 'worthy of being cased in cedar'.

In the Song of Solomon, all the fragrant spices and flowers known to the Hebrew people or which grew in Israel in 1000 B.C. are mentioned.

While the king sitteth at his table, my spikenard sendeth forth the smell thereof.

A bundle of myrrh is my wellbeloved unto me; he shall lie all night betwixt my breasts.

My beloved is unto me as a cluster of camphire in the vine-yards of Engedi.

Who is this that cometh out of the wilderness like pillars of smoke, perfumed with myrrh and frankincense, with all powders of the merchant?

Thy lips, O my spouse, drop as the honeycomb; and the smell of thy garments is like the smell of Lebanon.

Thy plants are an orchard of pomegranates, with pleasant fruits; camphire, with spikenard, spikenard and saffron; calamus and cinnamon; with all trees of frankincense; myrrh and aloes, with all the chief spices.

I rose up to open to my beloved; and my hands dripped with myrrh, and my fingers with sweet smelling myrrh, upon the handles of the lock.

His cheeks are as a bed of spices, as sweet flowers; his lips like lilies, dropping sweet smelling myrrh.

His countenance is as Lebanon, excellent as the cedars.

Myrrh was the most widely found of all the aromatics of the East and has continued to be used by the medical profession and in perfumery right up to the present time. For the Israelites it had a special importance. As bathing was not always practical in a land where water was rarely to be found away from the Jordan valley, it was the custom of the women to carry, beneath their clothes, a small linen bag containing myrrh and other fragrant substances. This was usually suspended from a cord around the neck and lay in the hollow between the breasts. Here, the solidified myrrh would release its fragrance from the warmth of the body and this would be enjoyed both by the wearer and by those in close contact. Today, women often wear their perfume in the same place and though it may be more exotic, it is not so lasting, as the small bags of myrrh released their scent for several months before needing to be replaced.

Myrrh is most common in southern Arabia and grows there with frankincense. It is collected by the Arab people to this day exactly as it was in Solomon's time, from the beards of goats which nibble at the shrub. The sticky exudation is made into cakes and sold in the markets of the East. Distilled with alcohol, it is used in the manufacture of quality soaps and shampoos and also as a fixative for perfumes.

Like labdanum, it has a narcotic effect when immersed in wine or spirits and was given to those on their way to crucifixion by compassionate Jewish women, during the occupation of Palestine by the Romans. Inhaled, it quickly numbed the senses and St. Mark's Gospel says that they gave Christ 'wine mingled with myrrh: but He received it not'. Myrrh was also used at the burial of our Lord. St. John's Gospel tells that Nicodemus had come to Jesus by night and brought a mixture of myrrh and aloes, 'about an hundred pound weight. Then [after the Crucifixion] took they the body of Jesus and wound it in linen clothes with the spices, as the manner of the Jews is to bury their dead'.

Balsamodendron myrrha and Boswellia serrata, the Frankincense tree, are of the same family Burseraceae, most of them plants of subtropical America. Closely related to the orange, they have small white flowers and privet-like leaves which are covered with minute glandular dots. These are oil cells and, when pressed, release an invigorating resinous smell. The wood also releases a pungent orange-like scent when burnt. The same smell is present in Rue, a herb which has been grown in English gardens since Roman times and which gives its name to the larger order, Rutales. With their small leaves and heath-like habit, most members of the order are especially suited to withstand hot arid conditions, for transpiration is reduced to a minimum. Indeed, the plants will grow almost anywhere, on barren hillsides and in ravines, which is where they are usually to be found.

Of the same family is Dictamnus fraxinella, a shrub so liberally endowed with resinous oil glands that, in the warm climate of southern Europe and the Near East, it is perpetually surrounded with a transparent film of resinous vapour which when lit burns with a brilliant glow; it may have been the 'burning bush' which Moses encountered in Sinai, at the very place over which St. Catherine's Monastery was built. A pleasing scent is given off by the vapour which burns without harming the foliage of the plant.

'Aloes' was the fragrant wood of the shrub-like tree, Aloescylum agallochum, which has been used in the East for burning as incense since the earliest times. It was usually accompanied by myrrh and the smoke or paste used to fumigate clothes and bedding. The aloe is

closely related to the yucca, both being of the Lily family. Belonging
to the same genus is the Dracaena, the Dragon tree of Tenerife, but
only aloe wood is fragrant. They are plants with aerial stems and
thick leathery leaves, arranged in two rows in rosette fashion. The
leaves grow upright and terminate in a point; they are water-storing,
to enable the plant to survive long periods without rain. As the
cactus is to the New World, so is the aloe to the Old World, being
present in most parts of Africa and the Near East. The wood of the
species A. agallochum is scented like cedarwood whilst the bark may
be removed and rolled after the manner of cinnamon. It burns
slowly on a charcoal fire, releasing a delicious balsamic perfume.

The cinnamon known to the peoples of Palestine and the Near
East would be the species Cinnamomum glanduliferum which is
present in the more remote valleys of Nepal and Bhutan. It is an
evergreen tree of considerable stature, the leaves being broad and
leathery, pale green above, white on the underside and entirely
covered in pellucid dots. When crushed, they release a pleasant
aromatic scent. But it was the bark that was in most demand. Known
in perfumery as Nepal Sassafras, it is brown and readily peeled from
the tree without causing it to die. The strength of its odour varies
with the age of the tree, being less pronounced as the tree becomes
older. The pieces were rolled, one inside another, to make for easier
transportation and, in the dry warmth of the East, the bark dried
rapidly. This enabled it to be finely ground before it was placed on
burners with myrrh and frankincense. The bark was also used to
flavour food and wines whilst its essential oil is a powerful bac-
tericide. The ancients were scientifically correct when they believed
that those substances possessing a pungent smell would give
protection against plague and they carried cinnamon about with
them for the purpose, in the same way that, in Hogarth's day,
London doctors carried pieces of camphor in small boxes or in the
end of a walking stick, to inhale discreetly whenever attending those
suffering from contagious diseases. It is believed that, for the
same reason, the Hebrew people imported from southern India the
wood of the 'camphor' cinnamon which, when cut into pieces and
boiled, yielded a white crystalline camphor after it had cooled. This
is the finest of all forms of camphor and is widely used to inhale for
a head cold. The wood was also burnt during epidemics.

In 1885, Messrs. Schimmel and Company of Leipzig discovered

that safrol was present in the oil of Cinnamomum camphora and that it could be separated in a state of absolute purity. It is safrol that gives the pleasant smell to cinnamon bark, resembling that of the clove but with undertones of orange and bergamot. Proverbs gives advice against the lures of the adulteress who has covered her bed with the tapestries of Egypt and perfumed it with myrrh, aloes and cinnamon.

It was usual for the wealthy to fumigate bedclothes by placing them over a brazier full of burning aromatics and, as there was no way to clean clothes except by washing them and in the desert water was scarce, wearing apparel was also fumigated in this way. Supplies of aromatics were constantly needed, and the Psalms tell that myrrh, aloes and cassia were mostly used for this purpose and gave to the wearer a sense of cleanliness and well-being. In the Odyssey, Homer alludes to the custom, which was also followed in the East, of placing small bags of aromatics between bedding and garments, in the same way that the country housewife places muslin bags of dried rosemary and lavender in drawers and linen cupboard.

The 'cassia' of the Scriptures was obtained from the shrub Cinnamomum cassia, all parts of which are fragrant. The bark was peeled into sections whilst the young twiggy branches also release a pleasing scent when burnt. The plant is found from Afghanistan to central China and yields the cassia oil of commerce. The most fragrant oil is that obtained from the young bud-stalks but the leaves also yield a brightly coloured distillate with the smell and taste of cinnamon.

The oil was obtained by a most primitive method. The plants were first stripped of their bark whilst the young twigs and leaves were removed and tied together in bundles for transporting to the distillation centre. They were then boiled in large vessels and, from the aromatic juice, oil of cassia was obtained by distillation. Today, most of the oil comes from China and Malaya, the principal centres of production in China being the provinces of Kwang-Si and Kwang-Tung. The oil is of amber colouring and is powerfully scented. In Palestine, cassia oil was mixed with the more readily obtainable olive oil, the olive tree being common to all parts of the Holy Land. The oil was used to rub on the feet, and also to massage into the scalp as it kept the hair dark and greasy and prevented baldness. The dried leaves and bark of cassia were mixed with other aromatics for burning so as to fumigate the house and to impart their sweet perfume to clothes.

Cassia fistula, a native of India and Burma, was cultivated in Egyptian gardens but it should not be confused with the 'cassie' of perfumery, which, with its golden-yellow flowers borne in drooping racemes and its thread-like stamens crowned with brown anthers, diffuses the sweet lemon-like perfume of its relations the laburnum and sweet pea. Sprays of cassie were used by Egyptian maidens to make chaplets and wreaths to decorate the hair.

The flowers of Cassia fistula are followed by pods as straight as a reed pipe and often as much as three feet in length. Each pod contains up to a hundred seeds covered in a sweet-smelling brown pulp which in the East is used to flavour snuff tobacco. From the flowers, a yellow volatile oil with the smell of honey is obtained by distillation. Often known as the Indian Laburnum, Cassia fistula has ash-grey bark and is one of the most handsome of eastern trees though it possesses only limited commercial value.

The rose of Sharon of Biblical times is believed to be the Rock Rose, known also as the Cretan Rose as it is present on the island of Crete and throughout Greece and Macedonia as well as in Syria and Palestine. Its botanical name is Cistus ladaniferus, but it is usually known as Labdanum and, like myrrh, was one of the bases for all ancient perfumes. Its highly resinous gum is in the form of a black exudation secreted from the stems and from the glandular hairs present on the underside of the leaves, and it is collected by shepherds who comb it from the fleeces of their sheep, exactly as they did in ancient times. Dioscorides, alive at the time of Christ, has described in detail the method by which the gum was also obtained, saying that it was collected from the beards and thighs of goats which feed upon the leaves. Pierre Belon, a French physician and traveller in the Near East in the sixteenth century, narrates the method of collecting labdanum on the island of Crete and his *Observations* of 1555 were confirmed by Tournefort a hundred and fifty years later. The descriptions of the two men substantiate the accuracy of writers who had described the method some two thousand years earlier.

In Crete, a special instrument called a Ladanisteron is used to remove the gum from the plants. This ensures that it is not in any way contaminated by perspiration from the hands. The instrument is made in the form of a double rake and has leather thongs three feet in length instead of teeth and is used like a whip. When charged with the resin, the thongs become cylindrical and rope-like. The resin is removed with a knife and is moulded into cakes which are placed in baskets before being packed into small wooden boxes. To prevent their adhesion during transportation, the cakes are placed between layers of bay leaves.

Labdanum is also collected on the island of Cyprus, in the Pylienia district on the north-west of the island, an area of hilly country stretching from Yallia to Leuka. Here, the resinous gum is gathered from the coats of browsing animals and is not as pure as that of the Rock Rose, for other resin-bearing plants such as Inula odora and Erigeron viscosum are also visited by sheep and goats. For this reason, Cyprian labdanum lacks the powerful scent of that collected solely from the Rock Rose and is usually fortified by mastic. When used as incense, Cretan labdanum is most pleasing for it does not contain animal hairs which give off a noticeable odour of ammonia when burning.

Pure labdanum is reddish-black in colour with a balsamic odour which may be compared to that of ambergris. It is highly inflammable and burns with a clear flame. Its price is fixed according to its purity which is determined by placing a small piece on the edge of a copper stove known as a 'mangol' which is filled with glowing charcoal. If the labdanum quickly melts into a transparent liquid and gives off a pleasing balsamic scent, it is graded as being of superior quality accordingly. Labdanum is also soluble in rectified spirit, when it forms a gold-coloured solution with a smell that is narcotic and stupefying, quite different from the odour given off when it is burning.

Cistus ladaniferus and its related species which are wide-spread across southern Europe, from Spain and Portugal to Greece and Bulgaria, are found throughout Palestine, and are also indigenous to all the major islands of the Mediterranean including Sicily and Rhodes. It grows amongst rocky outcrops, making a low-spreading bush with rough grey bark, the younger wood being covered with short white hairs. The leaves which are about an inch long are also covered on both sides with glandular hairs whilst the flowers are of pinkish purple, shaded with yellow at the base. Curtis' *Botanical*

Magazine observed that 'it is one of the most ornamental of hardy shrubs, being at once pleasing to the eye and grateful to the smell; the whole plant in warm weather exudes a sweet glutinous substance, which has a strong balsamic scent, so as to perfume the air to a great distance'. It blooms in June and July and though the flowers are fleeting, they appear in continuous succession for at least eight weeks provided the sun is shining. Most species secrete a resinous gum (though some do in greater quantities than others), and its collection from the living plants is unique amongst the economic products of the vegetable kingdom. It is during the mid-summer months that the exudations are most active and this is the time for harvesting it; but so tedious is the process, that the most efficient worker, skilled in the use of the ladanisteron, is able to collect no more than two pounds a day.

But by far the most precious and expensive of all the ancient aromatics was spikenard, around which an aura of mystery has persisted until recent times. Few knew where it came from, nor was it understood from what part of the plant the fragrant substance was obtained. It was not an exudation, neither was it wood nor bark. It was held in high esteem by the early Egyptians, and Solomon appreciated it for its sweet perfume, coupling it with the sweetly scented flowers of the camphire, Lawsonia inermis, which were used to bedeck those attending marriage ceremonies and important feasts.

Spikenard, Valeriana Jatamansi

Some idea of its costliness may be deduced from St. Mark's Gospel which tells that when Christ was at the house of Simon the leper in Bethany two days before the feast of the Passover, as he sat at supper, 'there came a woman having an alabaster box of ointment of spikenard, very precious; and she brake the box and poured it on his head'. The woman's name was Mary, Martha's sister, and she was making an act of supreme generosity, for of all her possessions, none would have been more precious to her than the box of spikenard oil.

In St. John's Gospel, Jesus is again in Bethany and he has raised Lazarus from the dead. Lazarus was the brother of Mary and Martha, both of whom, the Bible tells us, were much loved by Jesus. Whilst He ate His supper, with Lazarus sitting beside Him, Martha waited at table. It was then that Mary once again brought out her 'box' of spikenard, pouring it over the feet of Jesus and in all probability massaging it into his feet before wiping away the surplus oil with her hair. St. John says that the whole house was filled with the odour of the ointment—as, when the spikenard was used in such quantity, it certainly would be. Seeing this extravagant use of the oil, Judas Iscariot asked why the oil was not sold for its full value of three hundred pence and the money given to the poor. Judas, however, had entirely missed the meaning of Mary's action for she was revealing, by her complete unselfishness, a love for Jesus that few had shown him during his days in Galilee.

Our Lord quickly came to her aid, telling Judas to 'leave her alone' and explaining that she had performed this act of generosity as a symbolic preparation of his entombment, as was the custom of the time; when relatives and neighbours would wrap the body before burial in those aromatics which retained their perfume for a considerable time. Mary's spikenard would have been mixed first with olive oil for, by Jewish law, the sacred oil containing more than one aromatic was to be used only by the priests of the temple for anointing the tabernacle and to burn on the altar of incense.

The Mountain or Indian Nard of Dioscorides was to be found only in the more remote valleys of the Himalayas, from Kumaan to Sikkim, growing at a height of 15–17,000 feet, consequently it was extremely expensive, for only very small quantities ever reached the civilized world. Its botanical name is Nardostachys jatamansi,

3

'Nard' for short (this is a Persian word, as its transportation from
the valleys of the Himalayas was mostly in the hands of Persian
carriers). In the Tamil language, the word 'nar' denotes anything
possessing fragrance, whilst spikenard is a generic name used in
ancient times for any kind of powerfully scented plant. Jatamansi is a
Hindu word signifying a 'lock of hair' for the most fragrant part of
the plant is that portion of the stem just above the root which is
covered with fibres from the petioles of the withered leaves. These
hair-like filaments are formed so closely together that they have the
appearance of a lock of hair.

The true Spikenard or Mountain Nard was first recognized as
being of the valerian family by the French botanist, Candolle, who
described it in his *Plants of the Valerian Family*, and this was
confirmed by the orientalist, Sir William Jones, some years later.
In his *Memoir*, Candolle's illustration of the plant clearly shows the
long hairy stem. Beneath the hairy fibres, the central woody column
is formed of numerous sections, held together by joints which
resemble the vertebrae in a sable's tail. Its shape led the ancient
peoples to believe that spikenard was, in reality, the end of an
animal's tail and gave rise to much confusion as to its identity.

This hairy stem with its reddish-brown fibres is the only part
which is used in perfumery and is about as thick as the little finger.
The plant is perennial, extremely hardy and of such easy culture
that it is surprising it has always been such a scarce commodity.
Its scent is heavy and somewhat peculiar, like a mixture of Valerian
and Patchouli, though more pleasing than either. However there are
those who find it disagreeable and it is far less highly esteemed in
modern perfumery than it was in ancient times.

Dioscorides knew three kinds of Nard, the Mountain Nard which
is the true Spikenard; Celtic Nard or Valeriana celtica; and the
False Indian Nard, V. walchii, which is found only in hilly country in
parts of Northern India near the Ganges, and provides the Indian
perfume Tagar, also the drug Tagara, mentioned by Sanskrit
writers.

The so-called Celtic Nard is found in the Swiss and Tyrolean
Alps. The roots and lower part of the stem are black and highly
fragrant, resembling Patchouli, and with a particular attraction for
the inhabitants of Turkey and Persia who use it to add fragrance to
their bath water.

To eastern peoples, spikenard has always been a most precious commodity, not only for the heaviness of its perfume which has a greater appeal to those living in warmer climes, but because, like myrrh, it retains its scent for a considerable time. Even when freshly dug up and in the 'green' state, the hairy stems diffuse a heavy perfume but, as with orris root, this becomes more pronounced as the stem dries. The longer it is kept, the heavier does its scent become. It was as precious to the Egyptians as it was to the Hebrew and Roman peoples. Horace promised his fellow poet Virgil a cadus of wine (the equivalent of fifty bottles) in exchange for a small onyx box filled with spikenard. It was used as an oil and as an ointment, also, when finely ground, to mix with frankincense and cinnamon for burning as incense.

One of the most beautiful of all plants, indigenous to the Holy Land, is the Camphire of the Song of Solomon. From its leaves, henna is obtained to be used in the most sophisticated of modern salons for dying the hair dark red as in Biblical times. It is believed to have been planted in the Hanging Gardens of Babylon, to form hedges, for the scent of its flowers exceeded that of all others. It was one of Milton's 'odorous bushy shrubs' which grew in the Garden of Eden and Thomas More wrote of its 'odorous coral branches'. It was planted throughout Palestine to protect vineyards from prevailing winds.

The small white flowers are borne along the twiggy stems and were, like cassia, woven into chaplets by Egyptian maidens. In Cairo, until recent times, sprigs of blossom were sold in the streets during summer, with the cry of 'Oh odours of Paradise; Oh flowers of henna!' much as violets were once sold in London.

Mohammed held the scented flower of the henna in most esteem, declaring it to be 'the chief of the sweet-scented flowers of this world and the next', though he likened 'the excellence of the violet to the excellence of El-Islam above all other religions'.

Mohammed also used henna to dye his beard and Mohammedan women use it to colour their hair and their bodies. The dark brown paste is obtained from the dried and powdered leaves and, as it is a vegetable colouring agent, it coats the hair without penetration and is therefore harmless. The longer the preparation remains on the hair, the darker does the hair become. For its safety, it is preferred by many hairdressers for hair tinting, and it is also used to convey other preparations to the hair. The compound hennas were introduced in 1914 by the Parisian firms of L'Oréal and Broux, and for the first time it was possible to fix the shade required so that it remained after the client had left the salon.

CHAPTER FOUR

PERFUMES OF ASSYRIA AND PERSIA

The tower of Babel – The women of Assyria and their use of perfumes – Subjugation of Egypt – The Persian rose – Alexander the Great – The Lydians and their love of saffron.

I T was at Babylon on the Euphrates, near the site of the earthly Paradise the Garden of Eden, that King Nebuchadnezzar built the famous Hanging Gardens to please his homesick wife Amytes, daughter of the last King of Media, a country which lay to the immediate north. The Babylonians were ardent lovers of fragrant flowers and trees and made daily offerings to their gods of cedarwood, calamus, myrtle and of other fragrant herbs. In a recently discovered text of ancient Babylon, King Nabonidus is described as 'filling the temples with the odour of incense' and it is said that all flowers used in the terraced gardens of Nebuchadnezzar, his successor, were scented:

> . . . rich fruits o'erhang
> The sloping vales, and odorous shrubs entwined
> Their undulating branches.

After Solomon's death in 1000 B.C. when constant quarrelling between the tribes of Israel brought about an end to the house of David, there arose in its place two independent states, Israel in the north and Judah in the south; and within three hundred years of Solomon's death, both had fallen to the all-conquering Assyrians.

Setting their sights westwards in the hope of world conquest, the Assyrians under King Ashurnasirpal II set out from Ashur on the Tigris in 880 B.C. They left in the expectation of reaching the Mediterranean ports of Tyre and Sidon in the shortest possible time, which they accomplished by following the caravan route to Damascus. They slaughtered and plundered all before them, and left behind Assyrian settlers in the once flourishing but now vanquished cities.

Unlike the Jews, the Assyrians worshipped many deities, chief amongst them being the Sun god Baal, whose symbol was a bull's head, and Astarte, referred to in Judges as Ashtaroth and who, like Isis in Egypt, was synonymous with the moon. Herodotus has described at length the temple erected at Babylon in honour of Baal which consisted of seven towers, raised one upon another and believed to have been the notorious Tower of Babel.

The 'tower' was made up of seven equilateral squares the sides of the base being 290 feet in length. According to Herodotus, in the uppermost part was an ornate couch occupied by a woman, lavishly attired and redolent with perfumes, chosen by the god for his own enjoyment: 'the natives declare—but for my part I do not believe it, that the deity himself comes down and sleeps with her on the couch.' Inside was a statue of Baal in pure gold and valued at 800 talents, worth about five million pounds in today's currency values. In front of the statue was an enormous altar, also made of gold, on which each year a thousand talents' worth of pure frankincense were burned. The Assyrians also set up altars to their most revered rulers such as Nimrod and Semiramis, queen at the time of the country's greatest splendour. These were erected on high ground so that the incense could the sooner reach the deity in heaven, and by the side of each were carved tablets showing the priest of the temple, holding in front of him a small wicker basket; in this he carried the incense and aromatic gums to be used in the sacrifices. Herodotus maintains that, from Arabia alone, the Assyrians received each year as a tribute one thousand talents of frankincense for offering to Baal, and this is confirmed by Assyrian documents of the eighth century B.C. which tells of trade relations with Sheba and the neighbouring land of Minaea.

Herodotus also mentions the Assyrian women who would 'bruise with a stone, wood of the cypress, cedar and frankincense and upon it poured water until it became of a certain consistency. With this they anointed the body and face to impart a most agreeable odour'. When removed on the following day, it left the skin in a soft and beautiful condition and impregnated with a delicious scent. The historian, in his wanderings, visited most parts of the Near East during the fourth century B.C. and is said to have obtained much of his information at first hand. From his conversation with a priest in Egypt, he learnt of the remarkable destruction of Sennacherib's army in Judah, due to multitudes of rats which swarmed over the warriors by night, spreading plague with such remarkable speed that the army was unable to engage in combat.

He was greatly interested in the customs of the times and has told of Assyrian women who would perfume themselves with the most expensive scents and rubbed pumice over their bodies after bathing, to give the skin a delicate smoothness. To the corners of their eyes, to make them appear larger, they applied stibium, a preparation of antimony similar to the kohl used by the Egyptians; and they painted their lips and face with bright red paint. The men painted their faces with white lead and would plait their hair like the women. No one devoted more care than the Assyrians to the hair and beard. Their hair was a mass of curls falling over the shoulders and the men would spend hours plaiting their beards, using fragrant oils and pomades to help achieve the desired effect. The kings spent even more lavishly on improving their appearance. They had gold thread interwoven in their beards and wore on their heads tall conical turbans encrusted with pearls and studded with precious stones. At their banquets, fragrant cassolettes were kept constantly burning, to scatter their scents throughout the apartments and on the clothes of those in attendance. Fragrant waters were also sprinkled over the guests and upon the floor.

Assyrian perfumes were famed throughout the ancient East. Scent bottles made of glass or alabaster and which had once contained liquid essences were discovered during the excavations at Nineveh by Sir Henry Layard in 1845. The expedition was sent out by the British Government under the leadership of Thomas Rawlinson, and it was here that one of the most important discoveries in the history of archaeology was made when the library of King Ashurbanipal, greatest of the Assyrian kings, was uncovered and more than twenty thousand cuneiform tablets were sent back to the British Museum to be deciphered. Ten years later, Rawlinson and Hincks had translated the Assyrian script which gave a new meaning to much of the Old Testament which had hitherto remained unintelligible to Biblical scholars.

By the year 720 B.C. the Assyrians were in control of all Palestine, including the city of Samaria, then the capital of Israel's northern

Assyrian scent bottle, 600 B.C.

kingdom, though Judah to the south still remained intact. Twenty years later, King Sennacherib and his army set out from Mesopotamia and within weeks had occupied the whole of Judah except for its capital Jerusalem. But Jerusalem did not fall. For some reason unknown to us, the Assyrians turned south to march against Egypt but at Lachish were overcome by the plague, which wreaked such terrible destruction that those who survived immediately returned to Nineveh. Twenty years later, Sennacherib, like his father before him, fell to the assassin's hand and was succeeded by his grandson Ashurbanipal. Within a decade (664 B.C.), the Assyrians again set out on their conquest of Egypt. From Nineveh and Ashur they went, following the ancient spice route and passing the site of Abraham's birthplace at Mari, and so to Damascus. Jerusalem and all Judah were subjugated, the Assyrian armies continuing their slaughter as far as the Nile, conquering first Memphis, then Thebes, stripping the temples of their precious stones, vestments, and silver and gold, which they took back to Assyria. Even the temple gates were removed and according to Homer there were more than a hundred. The Assyrian Empire now stretched from the Nile to the Indus and was by far the most powerful ever known, held in fear throughout the East. Yet at the very moment when she reached her pinnacle of power, the peoples beyond her northern boundary were already plotting to attack her. These were the Medes, who occupied that part of Iran which bordered the southernmost shores of the Caspian Sea and whose king, Cyaxares, had been able to unite the peoples of western Asia under his command. In the south, Semitic tribes, known as the Chaldeans, assisted by the Babylonians, were pressing north, and the

Assyrians found themselves caught in a pincer-like movement. Ashur on the Tigris, then Nineveh, were the first to fall, and all that was left of the Assyrian army retreated in disorder to northern Mesopotamia. Hastening to their aid, the Egyptians reached Haran in Syria and laid siege to the town, but they were unable to take it and returned south again, back to their own country. This once great power was completely humiliated, and would never regain her former glory.

Ashurbanipal the conqueror died by his own hand in 636 B.C. By then he had adopted female dress and painted his face like a woman. He is also said to have had his hair styled like his wife's and he used scent just as lavishly. Following his defeat at the hands of the Medes, he built himself a pyre of fragrant woods and gums and, after lighting it, lay on the top with his personal treasures and died by asphyxiation in the sweet-scented smoke.

The power of Assyria was shattered for ever and the country was divided between the Medes who took the north and east, and the Babylonians and Chaldeans who took the south and west, including Judah, with Nebuchadnezzar as their king. In 497 B.C. he ordered an onslaught to be made on Jerusalem. The royal house of David was ended, and Judah, depopulated by mass deportations, became a province of Babylonia. But the might of Media was to last for only sixty years after the destruction wrought on Ashur and Nineveh for in 550 B.C. Cyrus, king of the Persians, defeated his grandfather Astyages at Ecbatana, and Media was annexed to the Persian kingdom, which by 500 B.C. was to dominate the entire western world. Under Cyrus 'the Liberator' the peoples of the Fertile Crescent were able to return to their homes and, in the reign of his successor Darius I, they were assisted in their rehabilitation, the temples being rebuilt and trading with other nations encouraged. Emissaries of Darius travelled abroad as far as Lydia in Asia Minor and Thrace in southern Europe, to the Mediterranean coast of north Africa and to the lower reaches of the Nile.

The Persians borrowed their taste for perfumes and cosmetics from the Medes whose king Astyages had adorned himself with a wig of flowing ringlets perfumed with the most expensive scents, and had coloured his eyes with mascara, his face with henna. The Persian kings wore crowns of myrrh and of sweet-smelling labyzus, and aromatics were constantly burnt in golden braziers to fumigate their apartments. Such indeed was their love of perfumes that Persians of high rank had gardens of exquisite beauty made for their pleasure. Xenophon has given us some idea of their use of fragrant flowers for he relates that the gardens were enclosed by hedges of red roses, and white jasmine and lilacs filled the flower beds which were edged with violets and with other scented plants.

The red rose would most surely be Rosa gallica or R. rubra, native of Persia, the Balkans and islands of the eastern Mediterranean. It is one of the oldest plants known to man and is still cultivated in modern gardens. It was used to adorn the shields of Persian warriors at the time of their supremacy and, according to Ibn Khaldun, the province of Farsistan provided an annual tribute of 30,000 bottles of rose water to the treasury at Baghdad. Athenaeus (c. A.D. 220) tells that red rose petals were used to cover the floors of the royal apartments to a depth of eighteen inches on the occasion of Cleopatra's first meeting with Mark Antony.

The red rose was in great demand throughout the East for not only did the flower possess valuable astringent properties but its perfume was known to increase as the petals dried. During his lifetime, Nero is said to have spent the equivalent of £50,000 on the importation of the dried flowers from Persia, to perfume his apartments. Following the Roman invasion of North Africa, the red rose was introduced into Italy and eventually reached France and England. Pliny the Elder, who perished in the destruction at Pompeii, described it as being of brilliant red with a rich perfume. With its ability to retain its fragrance when dried, and for several years afterwards, it earned for itself the name of the Apothecary's rose, and from the French town of Provins, near where it grew, the dried petals were sent to all parts of Europe. In June 1429, the town made a gift of red rose petals to Joan of Arc, on the occasion of her visit, shortly after raising the siege of Orleans.

During the nineteenth century, the red rose was grown at Mitcham in Surrey, 'for the druggists' to use. It was of bright red colouring 'with one range of petals'. It was the same flower which grew in the Temple Gardens during Shakespeare's lifetime and was taken as its symbol by the House of Lancaster in the Wars of the Roses. It may be recalled that Edmund, brother of Edward I, first Earl of Lancaster and second son of Henry III, was also Count of Champagne and his territory included the town of Provins.

The red rose was the emblem of his second wife Blanche, widow of Henry of Navarre, and upon his return to England in 1277, Edmund also adopted this rose as his emblem. He had no issue by his first wife, and it is likely that his descendants continued to use the rose as their heraldic device.

A hybrid of the red rose, possibly from a crossing with the ancient Damask rose, is depicted on a wall of the excavated Palace of Knossos in Crete, believed to be more than four thousand years old. It is identified as the Holy Rose which has been found, still fragrant, in Egyptian tombs. This is the 'rosa sancta', described by Richards in his *Flora of Abyssinia* (1848), where it may have been introduced at the time of Ramses the Great; alternatively it may have been brought from Syria in the fourth century A.D. by Bishop Frumentius for it had been preserved in monastic gardens down the centuries. Indeed, the red rose owes its survival to its ability to grow in the poorest of soils and under the most arid conditions.

The Persian poet Sheik Sadi of Shiraz has given us this description of the gardens of his time and particularly of his own; 'The ground was enamelled with odorous flowers, dewdrops hung on the rose like tears on the cheeks of a maiden; the parterre was covered with hyacinths from whose delicate bells pour forth the most endearing essences.'

The most beautiful poem in the Persian language was written by Sadi in praise of the red rose. It is called *Tales from the Gulistan* or *Rose Garden* and is filled with delightful sentiments:

> Art thou, then musk of ambergris, I said;
> That by thy scent my soul is ravished.
> 'Not so', it answered; 'worthless earth was I,
> But long I kept the roses company;
> Thus near its perfect fragrance to me come,
> Else I'm but earth, the worthless and the same.'

Rose sellers in the streets of modern Persia make their cry: 'Buy my roses. The rose was a thorn; from the sweat of the Prophet it blossomed.' This refers to the miracle recorded by Mohammed: That when it was taken up to Heaven, his sweat fell upon the earth and from it sprang the rose. 'Whosoever would smell my scent would smell the rose,' he said. And, in northern Persia to this day, apartments are fumigated as of old, by burning aromatic gums and fragrant woods; and each Friday, after bathing, the body is purified with sweetly smelling unguents. To perfume the beard, civet is used and musk to give fragrance to various parts of the body.

The Persians, of all eastern peoples, have brought the preservation of flowers to a fine art. To enjoy their roses out of season, when their fragrance is most appreciated, the buds are gathered as they are beginning to open and are placed in earthenware jars sealed with clay. The jars are then buried in the garden, to be lifted when the flowers are required for some special occasion, when they are removed and placed in water in the sun or in a warm room to open and scent the apartment with their perfume. Red rose petals, dried and mixed with eastern spices, are also placed about the home in open bowls and will remain fragrant for many weeks.

The Damask rose is also grown in almost every garden in Syria (hence Damascus) and the country takes its name from the word suri, meaning 'land of roses'. 'Each common bush shall Syrian rose wear,' wrote Virgil, and Sir John Mandeville in his *Voyages and Travels* said: 'No other cytes is like it [Damascus] in comparison, of fair gardens and of fair desportes.'

Herodotus mentions the Damask rose as having sixty petals and surpassing all others in its fragrance. He tells that it flourished in that part of Macedonia where lay the Gardens of Midas, 'in which grew native roses with a scent surpassing all others'.

It was from Macedonia in 333 B.C. that Alexander, son of Philip, marched to defeat Darius III of Persia in battle at Issus in Northern Syria. He came of fighting stock, upholding the Greek warrior tradition. Back in 491 B.C. the Greek armies had defeated the Persians at Marathon in one of the decisive battles of the world, but not until the arrival of Alexander did Greece show a desire for world conquest.

After his defeat at Issus, Darius left in his tent a golden casket filled with precious perfumes which Alexander is said to have removed and replaced with the works of Homer. But after his conquest of Egypt in 332 B.C. during which year he founded the city bearing his name at the delta of the Nile, Alexander became more amenable to the use of perfumes. Athenaeus tells us that wherever he sojourned, he would have the floor of his apartments sprinkled with scented waters, and fragrant resins and myrrh were burnt on censers to impart their aromatic perfume to his clothes.

And, as he was riding his elephant near the borders of Egypt, Alexander is said to have become exhilarated by the sudden smell of spikenard. It would appear, however, that the ancient writers were incorrect in this supposition for the scent, which resembles that of spikenard, would most likely have been released by the Lemon grass (Cymbopogon nardus) which abounds in those parts and which will give off its scent when trodden upon.

The flowering rush of Dioscorides, the 'sweet calamus' of Exodus, used in making the holy anointing oil with which Aaron and his sons were consecrated, was Cymbopogon schöenanthus which grows in Egypt and Arabia and on the hillsides of Western Khandesh. To the oil distillers it is known as 'Motiya' when the inflorescence is young and is of pale blue colouring; and 'Sonfiya' when it has ripened and turned crimson-red.

The oil obtained from the young grass is that most in demand. It has a delicate rose-like perfume and is used in the adulteration of attar of roses. The grass is cut in September and is sold to distillers in the district who set up their stills by the side of streams. The attar which is collected is packed in skins and transported to the markets of Bombay and Cairo where it appears as 'oil of geranium'.

Though known as 'sweet calamus', it should not be confused with the rush, Acorus calamus, a native British plant which was in demand for strewing upon the floors of castle and manor in the Middle Ages. The closely related Andropogon nardus, which is abundant in India and Ceylon, makes an inexpensive distillation and is used extensively for perfuming 'honey' soaps. It has a lemon-like scent and its attar is known as Citronella. It obtained its name 'nardus' from its hairy root which resembles that of spikenard.

In 168 B.C., Jerusalem was once again subjected to plundering and destruction, this time at the hands of King Antiochus Epiphanes, who according to Polybius, the Greek historian, 'left few sanctuaries which were not stripped of their sacred possessions'. The first book of Maccabees says that 'the king sent letters by the hand of messengers unto Jerusalem and the cities of Judah, that they should follow laws strange to the land' and for ten years, until the time of Judas Maccabaeus, the god Zeus was worshipped in the Temple and those who took part in Jewish ceremonies did so under penalty of death.

According to Athenaeus, Antiochus Epiphanes carried his love of sweet scents to extremes. Athenaeus calls him 'Epimanes' or Antiochus the Mad, and in one of the processions for the games held at Daphne in his honour, he ordered that there be two hundred women stripped to the waist and carrying golden sprinklers filled with the most expensive perfumes which were scattered over everyone present. Then came boys dressed in purple tunics, each bearing a golden dish containing frankincense, myrrh and saffron, and following after them came two boys with incense burners 'six cubits in height', made of ivy-wood covered in gold, and carrying a golden altar between them. All who were to take part in the games were anointed with perfume from the golden dishes. Besides frankincense, myrrh and saffron, they contained the precious spikenard and cinnamon which had been brought a thousand miles from the Himalayas. After the events, the guests were sent away with crowns made of interwoven twigs of frankincense and myrrh.

There is another story that the king, when bathing in the public baths at Antioch, was observed by one of his subjects, an old man who smelled the perfumes used to anoint his body. 'You smell in a most costly manner,' he said, which pleased the king so much that he ordered a ewer of unguent to be poured over the man and a multitude gathered about him, to collect all that spilled on the floor.

Xenophanes has given a description of the peoples of Syria and Lydia who were said to be the most effeminate of the East:

> Boasting of hair luxuriously dress'd,
> Dripping with costly and sweet-smelling oils.

Saffron was much used by the Lydians, chiefly to dye the hair a rich golden shade which the women found so attractive. It is the product of the dried stigmata of Crocus sativus which grows in profusion in parts of southern Europe and as far east as Kashmir. It is the Karkon of the Song of Solomon, and is Kirkum in the Indian language. From this, it became 'Crocum' to western Europeans. Linnaeus used the name Crocus for those corm-bearing plants which he grouped under this genus.

The stigmata of Crocus sativus ripen only in hot, dry regions, although, in the fourteenth century, it was cultivated in England, in that part of Essex now known as Saffron Walden, where in 1330 it had been introduced by Sir Thomas Smith, Secretary of State to

Edward III. His idea was to initiate a new industry for the villagers and there it continued to be grown until the beginning of the seventeenth century. Gerard, writing in 1597, said that 'the flower of saffron doth rise from the ground nakedly in September . . . it groweth plentifully at Saffron Walden as corn in the fields'. Once open, the reddish-purple blooms seem unable to close up again. Only in a hot, dry season is it therefore possible to preserve the product for, if allowed to become damp, the stigmata will be spoiled by mildew.

As recently as a hundred years ago, almost 50,000 pounds of saffron were imported into England from Spain alone, its value being estimated at nearly £100,000.

Saffron takes its name from the Arabic sahafarn, meaning 'a thread', because of the thread-like stigmata from which the product is obtained. In an early English vocabulary the name appears: 'Hic crocus, a safarroun', and it is mentioned in a tenth-century Leechbook: 'When he bathes, let him smear himself with oil mingled with saffron.' This was how it was used by the Romans who may have introduced it into Britain. Later, it was valued as a dye in the making of Church vestments as an alternative to gold thread. It coloured the garments worn by Henry VIII's knights at the Field of the Cloth of Gold and it was used by the monks of old instead of gold leaf in the illumination of missals. Hendries' *Translations of Theophilus*, which have come to us from the tenth century, gives these instructions for the illumination of manuscripts: 'If you wish to decorate your work in some manner, take pure tin finely scraped; melt it and wash it and apply it with glue upon letters or other places you wish to ornament with gold. When you have polished it with a tooth, take Saffron with which silk is coloured, moisten with white of egg and when it has stood a night, cover with a pencil the places you wish to guild.'

Saffron was also an important ingredient of cooking, being used to flavour bread and cakes and to give pastry a richer appearance. 'Let me see,' says the clown in *A Winter's Tale*, 'what am I to buy for our sheep shearing feast? . . . I must have saffron to colour the warden pies.' These were made with Warden pears, a popular variety in Shakespeare's day, and saffron greatly improved their flavour.

In the time of Alexander the Great, saffron was distributed

by merchants to all parts of the Macedonian Empire for it filled so many needs. Above all, it was renowned for its medicinal powers, and was used in perfumery. From it unguents and essences were made and prized above all others except perhaps for spikenard. In the Koran, the ground of the Garden of Paradise is composed of pure wheaten flour mixed with saffron and musk. But saffron also had more commercial uses than any plant with the possible exception of flax and, as 70,000 blooms were needed to produce a single pound of the product, it was extremely costly. Only the wealthiest could afford to use it for strewing over the floor of banqueting halls and apartments. Horace has told of its being placed in fountains, to be sprayed into the air for all to enjoy its perfume during banquets in the halcyon days of the Roman Emperors. And during the games, it was sprinkled from the valerium which formed the roof of the amphitheatre. The Romans did things lavishly or not at all.

Sicilian scent
bottle of the
5th century B.C.

Corinthian scent bottle,
650 B.C.

French scent bottles, mid-18th century

French scent bottles in crystal and gold, including a rare double bottle by Mellerio (*top right*), mid-18th century

Chelsea pot-pourri jar encrusted with flowers

CHAPTER FIVE

PERFUMES OF ANCIENT GREECE

The perfumes of Greek mythology – First important work on perfumery – Scents
and their makers – Medicinal properties – Storax and Sweet Flag – The use of
perfumes on special occasions.

THE Greeks ascribed a divine origin to scented flowers and leaves.
In Greek mythology, the invention of perfumes is attributed to the
gods and, according to ancient beliefs, men derived their knowledge
of them from Aeone, a nymph of Venus. It was believed that if the
Olympian gods were to honour anyone with a visit, they left behind
a sweet perfume as a token of their divinity.

Homer and the other contemporary poets, when mentioning the
apparition of a goddess, always refer to her as being accompanied by
clouds of fragrant incense: for instance when Cupid's mother
visits Achilles:

> Celestial Venus hovered o'er his head
> And roseate unguents heavenly fragrance shed.

In one of the tragedies of Euripides, the dying Hippolites cries out:
'O Diana, sweet goddess, I know that thou art near me for I have
recognized thy delicious odour.' And in the *Iliad*, Homer describes
Juno's toilet preparations as she anxiously awaits the arrival of Venus:

> Here first she bathes and around her body pours
> Soft oils of fragrance, and ambrosial showers.

In his account of the life of Ulysses, Homer tells that the famous
leader kept his clothes in a chest made of fragrant wood as was the
custom of the time. He describes the ancient practice of anointing
the bodies of the dead with scented oils:

> Venus, night and day,
> Daughter of Jove . . .
> All the corpse o'erlaid with roseate oil,
> Ambrosial.

65

Homer classified the fragrant oils under the name 'elaion', though the more familiar name for scented oils and unguents was 'myron', probably derived from myrrh which was the most esteemed of all aromatics.

According to Greek mythology, the boatman Phaon, having conveyed a passenger whom he later discovers to be Venus, receives from the goddess, as a special favour, the gift of a divine essence of great power and fragrance which changes his ugly face into one of superlative beauty. Sappho, attracted to his new-found charms but finding him unresponsive, drowns herself.

Homer, describing the wanderings of Ulysses in the *Odyssey* in which he describes the social life of ancient Greece, tells of Penelope who, overcome by the loss of Ulysses, is advised by Eurynome to give an outward sign that she has finally overcome her grief by diffusing 'the grace of unction on her cheeks'. The matron, however, is no willing party to this suggestion, but whilst sleeping, she is visited by Pallas who sprinkles over her a fragrant oil when

> . . . her lovely face
> With such ambrosial unguent first she bathed
> As Cytherea, chaplet-crowned, employs
> Herself, when in the sight-entangling dance
> She joins the Graces.

The ancient Greeks observed a number of different rites in worshipping their deities. Altars were set up for the offerings and no warrior would dare to set off on his journey without first making a sacrifice and asking for a safe return. To Venus, a dove was sacrificed; to Jupiter an ox, which was placed on the altar and covered with fragrant herbs and with frankincense before being burnt. All this was accompanied by the pouring of wine from a patera, a container made in the shape of Aladdin's lamp. The poet Hesiod described such an occasion:

> Let the rich fumes of od'rous incense fly,
> A grateful savour to the powers on high.

But at the celebrations held at Eleutherae which took place in the temple of Jupiter, or those held to honour the goddess Ceres, which took nine days to conclude, things were quite different. Around the altar, smoking with frankincense, were grouped the priests in their purple robes and crowned with fragrant myrtle. On a throne sat the high priest who represented the deity and told the initiates, who had been subjected to the most appalling dangers to test their fortitude, of the pleasure the goddess felt because of what they had undergone on her behalf. In return for their outstanding courage, they could expect favours throughout the coming year. And in the Elysian fields of afterlife they would find a river of perfumes radiating an odorous mist to shed its fragrant dew about them for ever. There they would also find five hundred sweet essences for their daily use.

According to Theophrastus (370–285 B.C.), frankincense reached Greece by way of the Phoenicians who acted as general distributors. During the time of Alexander the Great, who had completed his conquests of the East by 330 B.C., supplies arrived in ever-increasing

Phoenician ointment jar, 1400 B.C.

quantities. Indeed, at the peak of their glory, the Greeks enjoyed the use of a wide range of scents and unguents. So great was their indulgence that Solon published an edict prohibiting their sale but the perfumers' shops continued to be much frequented. Even the unkempt Diogenes made use of them, applying the precious ointments to his feet and legs. 'When you anoint your head with perfume,' he said, 'it flies off into the air and only the birds obtain any benefit. But when applied to the legs and feet, the scent envelopes the whole body and gradually ascends to the nose.'

Athenaeus has quoted freely from the work of Apollonius of Herophila whose *Treatise* on perfumes was the first important work on the subject, and who wrote of those perfumes he considered to be the finest and from where they should be obtained. 'The iris [orris] is best at Elis and at Cyzicus; perfume from roses is most excellent at Phaselis; but that made at Naples and Capua is also good. That made from crocus [saffron] reaches the highest perfection at Soli in Cilicia, and at Rhodes. Essence of Spikenard is best at Tarsus; the extract of the vine at Cyprus. The best perfume from marjoram and from apples comes from Cos. From Egypt comes the best essence of cyperus; the next best is Phoenician and after that, from Sidon. The perfume Panathenaicum is made at Athens and those called Metopian and Mendesian are prepared with the greatest skill in Egypt. The Metopian is made from bitter almonds . . .

'The superior quality of each perfume is according to the purveyors, and to the materials and the artist, not to the place itself. Once Ephesus, as men say, had a high reputation for the excellence of its perfumery, especially of its Megaleion but now it has none . . .

'At one time too, the unguents made in Alexandria were brought to a high degree of perfection for the city enjoyed considerable wealth because of the attention Arisoe and Berenice gave to such matters. The finest extract of roses in the world was made at Cyrene when the great Berenice was alive . . . Syria used to make every sort of unguent admirably, especially that extracted from fenugreek, but this is quite altered now. And long ago there used to be a delicious unguent extracted from frankincense at Pergamus, owing to the invention of a certain perfumer of that city, for no one else ever made it before him, but now none is made there.'

It is surprising that neither Athenaeus nor Apollonius makes any mention of the violet for, at the Games of ancient Athens, the greatly coverted first prize was an award of decorative art, made in the form of a golden violet (the actual flower takes its name from Io who fed on violets after being transformed by Jupiter into a heifer). So much in demand was it for its perfume that, long before the birth of Christ, the sweet violet was in commercial cultivation in Athens and became the symbol of the city. The scent of the violet is due to an attar which may be extracted by maceration; when combined with alcohol, it produces an essence that retains the odour of the flower and is green in colour. Curiously enough, though, violets were most in demand for imparting their perfume to wines; according to Apollonius, the most delicious ones came from Byblos in Phoenicia and were much appreciated by the Greeks.

Theophrastus also wrote a treatise on perfumes in which he categorized those made from flowers, those from stalks and leaves, and those from roots. These last were the most precious of all, being the most powerfully scented, and the roots could be dried and transported to all parts of the known world without any deterioration. In the same way those roots used for food were held in great esteem for they could be cleaned and stored, to be used later whenever required. Ginger was one of the most sought after. It was grown in southern Arabia and was imported into Italy by the Romans; much later, they introduced it into Britain where it became a common ingredient of Anglo-Saxon recipes. In Shakespeare's day, the rhizomatous roots were called 'a race' or 'racine' (in *A Winter's Tale*, the Clown, when he was on the way to the sheep-shearing at the shepherd's cottage, said that he must have mace, nutmegs and 'a race or two of ginger' if he was to make a tasty meal).

In Greece, just as in Egypt and Palestine, unguents were kept in jars made of alabaster and onyx which by their density prevented rapid evaporation and contamination. The name of a perfume usually took that of its maker. Thus Megaleion was the invention of Megallus, a renowned perfumer of Athens in the time of Alexander who set very high prices on his products. Among the ingredients used were the celebrated oil of Balanos, famous for its rejuvenating qualities when applied to the face, also myrrh (hence the high price), cassia, cinnamon and burnt resin.

Another celebrated Athenian perfumer was Peron who had his shop where the King George Hotel now stands. Antiphanes has told of having

> ... left a man in Peron's shop just now
> Dealing in ointment; when he has agreed,
> He'll bring you cinnamon and spikenard essence.

Hipporax says that Baccaris was a favourite current perfume, the principal ingredient being saffron; and Antiphanes has described how the wealthy would use different perfumes to anoint the various parts of the body;

> He bathes
> In a large guilded tub, and steeps his feet
> And legs in rich Egyptian unguent;
> His jaws and breasts he rubs with thick palm oil
> And both his arms with extract sweet, of mint;
> His eyebrows and his hair with marjoram,
> His knees and neck with essence of ground-thyme.

There was a perfume extracted from vine leaves which, if inhaled, possessed the property of keeping the mind clear, whilst the violet essence brought about deep sleep.

In the *Odyssey*, Homer describes the custom of offering aromatics to guests upon arrival, as when Telemachus and Pisistratus are received into the home of Menelaus. First, they are taken to the baths,

> Where a bright damsel train attends the guests
> With liquid odours and embroider'd vests;
> Refreshed, they wait them to the bower of state,
> Where circled with his peers Atrides sate.

According to Athenaeus, it was the custom to fill muslin bags with fragrant flowers and leaves, and to place them beside the guests sitting at table. They were also crowned with sweet-smelling flowers, and vases of unguents were brought to them at table, to be passed around for each to dip in a finger.

A more ingenious method of applying the fragrant oils was that described by Alexis, a comic poet of about 350 B.C.:

> For he to anoint himself
> Dipped not his finger into alabaster,
> The vulgar practice of a former age;
> He let fly four doves with unguents drenched,
> Not of one sort but every bird a perfume bore
> Peculiar; and differing from the rest;
> And they hov'ring round, from their heavy wings
> Showered their sweets upon our robes and trappings.
> And I—be not too envious, gentlemen—
> I was myself bedewed with violet odours.

The method of compounding the celebrated Megaleion has been handed down to us and reveals something of the perfumer's art of more than two thousand years ago. The oil of Balanos was boiled for ten days and nights to drive off any impurities before the 'burnt' resin was added. The myrrh was then pressed for several days, only the oily part known as 'stakte' being used; and this was first mixed with cinnamon and cassia, both of which are closely related botanically. Cassia is the bark of Laurus cassia (cinnamomum cassia) which is found in India and throughout south-east

Asia. One hundredweight of the bark is needed to produce three-quarters of a pound of oil, which is pale yellow in colour, resembling that of cinnamon in its smell and for which it is often used as a substitute when making the less expensive perfumes and soaps. Oil of Cassia would have been used by the Athenian perfumers to adulterate the genuine oil of cinnamon which was always expensive and has a more refined smell. It was called 'cassia' from the similarity of its perfume to that diffused by the flowers of Cassia fistulosa, a tree of the laburnum family widely planted in gardens throughout Egypt and India for its fragrance and beauty.

Like cinnamon, all parts of Laurus cassia are fragrant and are used for the extraction of oil. The bark and twigs, leaves and bud-stalks are treated during its manufacture, nothing is wasted; but it would be the bark and twigs, brought from India by way of Babylon and Syria, on the backs of donkey and camel along the ancient spice road, which reached ancient Greece.

In modern China, the leathery leaves are mostly used in the production of Cassia lignae, for the essential oil has greater purity. The Chinese provinces of Kwang-Si and Kwang-Tung, in the south, are the main centres of production, with stills being set up in the valleys of the Pearl River. In summer, the low-growing shrubs are partly stripped of their twiggy branches and large juicy leaves, which are then tied into bundles and conveyed down to the river-side stills on donkeys and mules, before being boiled in large vessels. From the yellow aromatic juice the celebrated oil of Cassia is obtained, by a most primitive method of distillation.

One of the more popular Greek ointments was Susinum, made from red-flowered lilies. In his *Natural History*, Pliny gives its composition: oil of Ben, an inodorous oil obtained from the seeds of Moringa pterosperma and which does not become rancid, essence of roses, cinnamon, saffron and myrrh, the most precious perfumes known to the ancients. Susinum was the most popular perfume among the fashionable men of Athens, but Crocinum, made almost entirely from saffron, also had its devotees.

Most of the early perfumes were valued for their medicinal properties as well as for their scent, and all were compounded from natural products; the majority included myrrh, used in modern perfumery and the basis of several preparations in the British Pharmacopaeia. 'Megaleion' also possessed healing properties and was rubbed on to the skin so as to bring about a lessening of inflammation of wounds received in battle.

In the temple of Asclepios at Epidauros, sacred to the god of healing, there are a number of recipes for health-giving essences which have been handed down through the centuries. According to tradition, it was here that Asclepios, a child of Apollo and a nymph, was born and Epidauros became the headquarters of all those who believed in the healing powers of the god. It was a city of similar standing to Bath at the time of Beau Nash and was endowed with everything that could be desired of a health resort. There were hospitals and baths, a race-course and a theatre which is the most perfectly preserved of all the ancient theatrical monuments of Greece.

The temple was set aside for intercession with the god, who was said to bestow his healing powers on those who sought his help while they were asleep. That many cures did take place was perhaps due to the position of the resort for it is situated in hilly country in that part of Corinth overlooking the Aegean Sea, where the air is always crystal clear and the ozone invigorating. The geographical position of Corinth ensured a commercial greatness which was achieved early in her history; the population was made up of a large number of Phoenician traders and a high standard of living was enjoyed. Costly perfumes and cosmetics were widely used, and in the British Museum there are a number of perfume bottles, dating from

Corinthian perfume bottle, 800 B.C.

the seventh and eighth centuries B.C. and of Corinthian workmanship, which show their makers to have been men of great artistry for they are of outstanding quality and charm.

Philonides, a Corinthian physician, in his treatise on perfume has said that relief from a headache could be obtained by pressing cool scented flowers against the temples, and Athenaeus tells of the Carmini of southern Greece who, after drinking their toasts, would anoint their heads with unguents made either from roses or from apples. The aroma of apples was believed particularly to refresh the mind and to counteract over-heating and muzziness caused by the wine.

The Greeks, more than any other people, were fond of decorating their heads with fragrant flowers and, according to Sappho, lovers would place a garland on the head of their mistresses whenever they met:

> Twining the tender sprouts of anise green
> With skilful hand; for offerings of flowers
> Are pleasing to the gods, who hate all those
> Who come before them with uncrowned heads.

Crowns of hyacinths when in bloom were worn by Greek maidens who assisted at weddings.

A solemn festival lasting three days was held each year at Amyclae near Sparta, to honour Hyacinthus and Apollo. The first day was spent in mourning for Hyacinthus who had been accidentally killed by Apollo during a game of quoits; no bread was eaten and there was neither singing nor dancing. But the two following days were devoted to the customary games, when heads were garlanded and the heavens made fragrant with incense. Pliny mentions the renowned Greek physician Marestheus, who compiled a number of books on the making of chaplets and garlands, mentioning those that tended to harm the brain, causing depression and fatigue, and those which were famed for their refreshing qualities and brought about exhilaration. The rose, the hyacinth with its balsamic fragrance, and most of those flowers of fruity or spicy perfume will invigorate a tired mind, whereas the lily and narcissus are more oppressive, causing one to feel languid if their scent is inhaled too frequently. And in the *Metamorphoses*, Ovid has described the toilet preparations of a Greek maiden of his time: 'her hair is smoothed with a comb: now she decks herself with rosemary, again with violets and roses; sometimes she wears white lilies, washes her face twice daily in springs that trickle from the top of Pegasean woods; and twice she dips her body in the stream.'

Because so many of the ancient perfumes contained similar ingredients, their inventors coloured them so that they would be more readily distinguished than simply by smell. Megallus used alkenet most to colour his perfume pale pink; and rose perfumes were tinted red, this being the natural colour of the red rose.

Another expensive perfume, mentioned by Antiphanes, was known as 'Egyptian'. It also contained cinnamon and myrrh and was said to retain its strength longer than any other with the possible exception of 'Iris', whose principal ingredient was orris root. According to Theophrastus, a perfumer known to him kept 'Egyptian' in his shop for eight years and 'Iris' for twenty years, saying that at the end of which time they were 'better than when freshly made'. The 'Egyptian' perfume was probably made from a recipe imported from Egypt, where it had been one of the most fashionable perfumes during the reign of Tutankhamen.

In his *Treatise*, Theophrastus was of the opinion that 'Egyptian' and 'Megaleion' were the most lasting perfumes when applied to the skin and that they were used only by those ladies of wealth who could afford and appreciate them. The lighter perfumes, such as Susinum, were most suited to male wearers. He mentions that all solid perfumes last longer if first moistened with wine, but they were also used in the solidified form to impart their fragrance to clothes and vestments, whilst those made into powder were sprinkled about the bed and in this way came into contact with the skin during the night. 'In this way,' wrote Theophrastus, 'the perfume gets a better hold and is more lasting. Men use it thus, instead of scenting their bodies directly.'

Theophrastus, who has been described as the Father of Botany, was born at Eresos in Lesbos in 370 B.C. when the supremacy of Greece was at its height and forty years before Alexander set out on his conquest of the East. He had a knowledge of plants which must have been unrivalled at the time. He was familiar with most of those used in perfumery, and considered that 'the most fragrant come from Asia and the sunny regions. From Europe come none except the iris'. For the making of perfumes, he mentions Cassia, Cinnamon,

Spikenard, Balsam of Mecca, Storax, Iris (Orris), Saffron, Myrrh, Ginger-grass, Sweet Flag, Sweet Marjoram, Lotus and Dill. The Carnation, Narcissus, Rose and Lily were also used, their scent being obtained by the process of maceration or by absorption. If by the former method, the flowers were placed in warm fat, where they remained for two days during which time their otto was extracted. But the odour of some flowers was so delicate that it was entirely destroyed by heat and was extracted instead by placing the flowers on a layer of cold fat or by immersing them in olive oil, which was widely used by eastern perfumers for their concoctions.

Theophrastus recognized that the senses of taste and smell were akin, therefore, he said, 'it is through things which appeal to the taste as well as to the sense of smell, that men try to discover fragrant odours.' He also asked why the odour of certain flowers could be detected from a distance, though the scent of iris (orris) and spikenard, though more powerful, were noticed only at short range. He believed that the perfume of flowers was contained (in the epidermal cells) near the surface of the petals and was released by the warmth of the sun, whereas the scent of roots was released only by the warmth of the body or, as with incense, by fire. He recommended the use of olive oil to absorb the perfume of flowers,

Corinthian perfume bottle, 600 B.C.

not only for its purity but because the scent was so long-lasting when absorbed in oil or fat. But 'best of all,' he wrote, 'is the oil from Egyptian and Syrian balanos, which keeps longest' (he meant that the oil did not become rancid). Oil of Balanos was obtained from the tree Balanites aegyptica, a native of East Africa and also of Egypt. It is thought that this oil was one of the ingredients of the celebrated oil of Spikenard. Both the wood and the greenish-yellow flowers are fragrant and, in India, the wood is used as a substitute for sandal-wood to burn on funeral pyres.

Apollonius believed that 'perfumes were sweetest when the scent comes from the wrist' so that perfumers would apply their scents to this part of the body, as they do to this day. To discover whether or not a perfume suits one's personality, one must 'wear' it rather than smell it from a bottle. Within a few moments of its application, the warmth of the skin brings out the bouquet and then it may be savoured to the full.

'As to the mixing of solid substances in making powders and compound perfumes,' wrote Theophrastus, 'the more numerous and varied the perfumes, the more distinct will be their scent.' Compound perfumes made from aromatic gums were enclosed in a box for several days after which the one with the most powerful smell was removed. The perfumes were then transferred to another box, left for several more days and, again, the most noticeable was discarded. In this way, the smell of no one perfume could overcome that of the others.

One of the most valuable ingredients of the perfumes of the ancient world was the product of Styrax officinale, used by the priests for burning as altar incense and by perfumers everywhere. In modern perfumery, one ounce of Storax dissolved in a pint of rectified spirit yields tincture of storax and enables perfumers to give permanence to those flowery odours obtained by maceration (for instance, jonquil, tuberose and lily of the valley). Benzoin (a product of Styrax benzoin) has a similar effect. Thus, when a perfume is made by a solution of an otto in spirit, it is customary to add a small amount of a less volatile substance such as musk, ambergris, vanilla or storax which 'fixes' or 'holds' a perfume, the ottos being retained in the solution when applied to a handkerchief or to the skin.

Storax is obtained from the outer and inner bark of the tree, which grows in Asia Minor. The outer layer is removed from one side of the branch and is then dried and tied into bundles for use in fumigating churches and dwellings (it was much in demand during plagues). It is the resin obtained from the inner bark which is used in perfumery. This is collected by the natives and stuffed into horsehair bags which are pressed with a wooden lever. Boiling water is then thrown over the bark which is pressed a second time, when most of the resin or oil (yagh) will have been extracted.

Another method is to boil the bark in vats over a low fire. The vats are filled with water and the oil is collected as it appears on the top. It is then run off into casks, to be shipped to the trading centres of the Mediterranean. The odour of storax is similar to that of musk and ambergris. As Professor Johnson has said, 'It is the uniting link between smells we dislike and the odours we enjoy.' In bulk, its smell is unpleasant but, in small amounts, it has something of the scent of the narcissus and tuberose.

Theophrastus also mentions the Sweet Flag, Acorus calamus, which since earliest times has been used in all manner of ways for its scent. It is not really an iris but a rush, a semi-aquatic plant closely related to the arums, with a creeping rootstock and flag-like leaves. The flowers are greenish-brown, covered in a golden mosaic, and they appear in June in a cylindrical spike on stems six feet tall, like church spires. It is known as the Cinnamon iris, for when the stems and leaves are crushed, they release a scent like that of cinnamon.

Though it grows prolifically by the sides of rivers and streams throughout Europe and the Near East, it is rare in England and is found only in the Fenlands of Norfolk and Cambridgeshire where, in mediaeval times, it was used to strew over the floors of the great cathedrals at Norwich and Ely. One of the charges of extravagance brought against Cardinal Wolsey was that he ordered the floors of his palace of Hampton Court to be covered much too often with rushes and flags, since they were expensive and difficult to obtain.

From the long narrow leaves, which resemble those of the water iris, a volatile oil is distilled which is an ingredient of perfumery and is used for making aromatic vinegars; whilst the root, dried and powdered, yields a refreshing talcum powder which the ancient Greeks sprinkled over their beds and clothes. At one time the root was much in demand for imparting its particular flavour to wine and beer and for improving the flavour of gin.

Another volatile oil is contained in the outer skin of the rhizome, but to peel this off before extracting the scent would be wasteful since the most potent part would be lost. Under microscopic investigation, it can be seen that the rhizome is an open network of oil cells, the actual oil when extracted being likened to camphor.

In 1867 Faust extracted from the root of the Sweet Flag the bitter principle Acorin, and from this, at a later date, Thoms obtained the natural resin Acoretin which, when reduced from alkaline solution by nascent hydrogen, gives the essential oil and sugar as final products. After shaking out the acorin with ether, a small quantity of a crystalline alkaloid, soluble in alcohol, is produced, which is familiar as Calamine lotion.

Calamus root, dried and powdered, is also an ingredient of one of the most popular perfumes of the modern world, Chypre. It was widely used at the French court during the reign of Henry IV, and more recently, as the favourite essence of the last Czarina of Russia. The powder was composed of benzoin, storax, calamint, coriander seed and calamus root in about equal quantities. The modern Chypre also includes musk and civet which give it a more powerful and lasting quality.

The value of calamus in the making of perfumes was first discovered by the early Egyptians. It is mentioned in a papyrus found in one of the pyramids at Cheops and was one of the ingredients of the celebrated Kyphi, used in embalming and known to Dioscorides and Plutarch, who said that 'it was made of things that delight most in the night'. Calamus was also part of the famous Egyptian preparation Metopium which was perfumed with almonds and contained, in addition, honey, wine, resin and myrrh.

What the Egyptians developed, the Athenians perfected. The high reputation of the perfumers of Athens is referred to in the writings of Athenaeus. According to him, the best cooks came from Elis and besides their reputation for good cooking, the Eleans were recognized as able administrators and excelled at the art of close weaving. They also supervised the Olympic games.

'From Argos,' wrote Atheneus, 'come the best cauldrons; from Phlius, the best wine; from Corinth, tapestry; from Sicyon, fish;

from Sicily, cheese.' The best eels came from Boeotia, but undoubtedly the best perfumes were made in Athens.

In his play, *The Banquet*, Philoxenus describes how the guests
were treated at the home of a wealthy Athenian family. When they
arrived, slaves brought water for them to wash their hands and
scented clay mixed with the juice of lily flowers which they used to
rub over the hands and arms. To dry their hands, towels of finest
linen were ready and alabaster vases containing 'fragrant ointments
of ambrosial smell' to anoint the hands and face. Finally, each
guest would be garlanded with a crown of violets or other flowers in
season.

Xenophanes, one of the most profound Athenian thinkers, gives a
more detailed picture of an evening's entertainment. After washing

> . . . each guest upon his forehead bears
> A wreath'd flow'ry crown; from slender vase
> A willing youth presents to each in turn
> A sweet and costly perfume; while the bowl,
> Emblem of joy and social mirth, stands by,
> Fill'd to the brim; another pours out wine
> Of most delicious flavour, breathing round
> Fragrance of flowers, and honey newly made.
> So grateful to the sense, that none refuse;
> While odoriferous gums fill all the room.
>   The altar too, which stands
> Full in the centre, crown'd with flow'ry wreaths;
> The house resounds with music and with song.

All manner of perfumes were used at Athenian banquets, not only
for the pleasure they gave but because it was believed that 'the
best recipe for health was to apply sweet scents unto the brain'.
Anacreon recommended that unguents should be applied to the
chest, this being the seat of the heart, which would also benefit from
the gentle massage. The Greeks also believed that, in some
mysterious way, the use of perfumes enabled them to drink more
wine without feeling any ill effects. Wine was flavoured with scented
substances, since it was often of inferior quality. Myrrh was one of
the principal ingredients used, and flowers such as the violet were
infused for several hours before the wine was ready for drinking
(there was a similar custom in mediaeval England and until much

later, when the clove-scented pink, unknown to the ancient Greeks, was infused to impart its rich clove perfume).

Theophrastus mentions a specially prepared wine which was kept for important occasions at Thasos. He says that it was 'of delightful quality', flavoured by dough which had been kneaded with honey 'so that the wine got its fragrance from itself but its sweet taste from the honey'. Pliny the Elder relates that it was the custom at Greek and Roman banquets for the guests to place the fragrant flowers from their chaplets in their wine cups when drinking the health of their friends. To gain his confidence, because he would never eat or drink at anyone's table before a taster had first sampled, Cleopatra had the flowers of Mark Antony's chaplet dipped in poison. Then, as they were about to drink each other's health and were removing the flowers from their chaplets to place in the wine, Cleopatra seized his arm, exclaiming, 'Cure your jealousy, you must now believe that I could not seek the means of your destruction. Could I live without you, Antony?' She then ordered a prisoner to put the flowers in the wine cup and drink; the unfortunate man promptly fell down dead.

Greek glass perfume bottle, 5 B.C.

Though scents were in favour with the wealthy Athenians, the philosophers condemned their use as effeminate. Xenophon tells a story about Socrates who, when being entertained by Callias and offered scents, declined their use, saying that he much preferred the smell of the oils and embrocations used in the gymnasium and at the games. But Socrates also disapproved of bathing.

Leonidas, tutor to Alexander the Great, had on numerous

occasions to rebuke him for his extravagant use of perfumes and aromatics. Once he admonished him for his wasteful expenditure of incense at sacrifices, saying that there would be time for him to worship after he had conquered those parts of the world which produced frankincense. Alexander remembered this gentle reprimand and, after his conquest of the East, sent his old tutor a large consignment of frankincense and myrrh.

But, in spite of the philosophers, cosmetics and perfumes were increasingly used by both men and women. A new fashion was to bathe their faces in rose water and paint their cheeks and lips with red colouring obtained from a root called poederos. This was similar to alkanet, which was used to colour essences. Greek girls would paint their lips red by using a small brush made of goat's hair and with an ivory bodkin would apply soot to shade their eyelids. This they obtained by throwing gum labdanum on to a charcoal fire. The ascending smoke was collected as soot on a plate held above the flame, and the girl, sitting cross-legged on a couch, would apply the scented soot to her eyes by first closing one eye, then, taking the lashes between finger and thumb, rubbing on the soot (modern mascara, which contains wax in place of gum labdanum to make it adhere to the lashes, is applied in exactly the same way).

Greek bronze mirror, 490 B.C.

Greek women rolled their hair and tied it into a knot at the back of the head, in the style known as 'korymbos', a golden clasp in the form of a grasshopper being used for ornamentation. In the 'strophos' style, the hair was allowed to fall upon the shoulders in ringlets but, in some parts of Greece, girls had their hair shorn and it was allowed to grow long only in times of mourning. In the 'mitra' style, of Asiatic origin, the hair was held in place by a cloth band tied around the head; it was of brilliant colouring and was perfumed and powdered. Fragrant oils were also worked into the hair and scalp. The power of Medea rested in her skill as a perfumer and in her ability to turn grey hair black by the use of a vegetable dye. She also improved men's health by placing them in a cauldron filled with water and heated to a high temperature over a charcoal fire. She did this in the privacy of her home and, as there was some element of danger, she soon became notorious for her practices and magic powers, although in effect she was only the inventor of the 'Turkish' bath.

From earliest times, perfumes were also employed by the Greeks in their funeral rites. In the *Iliad*, Homer described Achilles paying the last tributes to his friend Patroclus:

> The body then they bathe with precious toil,
> Embalm the wounds, anoint the limbs with oil.

Warriors considered themselves duty-bound to grant the same honours even to the enemy, and Achilles had the body of Hector, the Trojan leader whom he had slain in battle, perfumed and anointed before being returned to his father Priam for burial.

The ancient Greeks burned the bodies of their dead on a pile of fragrant juniper wood, upon which friends and relations of the deceased threw incense and aromatic gums and poured libations of wine. Afterwards, the ashes were collected, mixed with precious spices and placed in funeral urns on which were depicted scenes of battle and pleasure. In the *Odyssey*, Agamemnon explains to Achilles exactly how the ceremony is performed:

> ... when the flames your body had consumed,
> With oils and odours, we your bones perfumed,
> And washed with unmix'd wine.

It was also the custom to strew fragrant flowers on the graves of the dead, a practice which has been maintained to this day in all civilized countries, Christian or otherwise. Alexander is believed to have paid this mark of respect to Achilles when visiting his tomb at Troy.

Anacreon, however, preferred to have perfumes and scented flowers to enjoy during his life-time. He asks in one of his Odes:

> Why do we shed the rose's bloom
> Upon the cold insensate tomb?
> ... I ask no balm to steep
> With fragrant tears my bed of sleep;
> But now while every pulse is glowing,
> Let me breathe the balsam flowing.

Even so, perfumes were considered so essential a part of the last rites, to accompany the soul on its heavenly journey, that if they could not be afforded, scent bottles were painted on urns and coffins in the expectation that these would perform the same duty.

CHAPTER SIX

ROMAN PERFUMES

Aromatics for religious offerings – Perfumes for personal cleanliness – The satirists and the lavish use of scent – Beauty preparations – Public bathing – Use of perfume by the early Christians – Frangipani, first of the well-known perfumes.

THE first Romans burnt twigs and branches of fragrant woods like myrrh, cypress and juniper (savin) in order to appease their gods. They were, for instance, strewn over stone altars set up in the fields where, after the corn had been harvested, the people gave thanks to Ceres for a bounteous crop. Ovid has written that

> The simple savin on the altars smoked,
> A laurel sprig the easy gods invoked . . .
> Ere stranger ships had brought from distant shores
> Of spicy trees the aromatic stores . . .

The goddess Flora, who from earliest times was an object of religious veneration amongst the heathen nations, was worshipped by the Romans at the time of Romulus in about 750 B.C. Every spring a festival was held in her honour when there was rejoicing at the appearance of the first flowers. Five centuries after the founding of Rome, it was ordained that the feast of Flora should be celebrated each year on April 28, four days before the May Calends, when the goddess was invited to give her blessings for a fruitful season. The same festival was introduced into Britain by the Romans at a later date and is the origin of the May Day celebrations, 'when once the May-pole o'erlook'd the Strand' and, in 1515, Henry VIII accompanied by his Queen and court attendants rode a'Maying from Greenwich to Shooter's Hill. It was the day on which garlands of fragrant flowers were placed on the doors of every house as an offering to Flora, in thanks that the winter had passed and the season of plenty was about to begin.

Though the ancient Romans had no knowledge of eastern

aromatics, they appreciated flowers from an early date. Pliny refers to the plaiter of chaplets and garlands who was in as great demand by the fashionable as the couturier is today. The Roman women's knowledge of floral arrangement was in fact derived from Glycera, who was so ingenious in the art of making garlands as to win the attention of Pausius, the most eminent painter of his day, who delighted in portraying Glycera and her confections. These paintings were still well preserved in Pliny's time.

In his treatise, Cato says that the gardens of ancient Rome were planted only with those flowers which were of use for making garlands; and from Pliny we learn that the garden was tended by the women of the household who grew and prepared the vegetables and made the flowers into chaplets and wreaths.

The violet could be seen in every garden, and the Imperial Crocus (Crocus imperati) which grows in the Alban hills, near Rome and as far south as Naples, opening its scented flowers of lilac-mauve early in January, also found a prominent place. The flowers were dried and the petals used for filling cushions and pillows; and Roman women bathed their bodies in toilet water made from the flowers. The saffron crocus was also cultivated, as the stigmas produced a dye which turned hair a rich golden shade.

In emulation of the women who garlanded their heads with flowers (these not only improved the appearance of the wearer but acted as a substitute for perfume as it was scarce or too expensive), the Roman generals took to crowning themselves with laurel when they returned from victorious campaigns. Laurus nobilis, the Sweet Bay, derived its name from the Latin word laudare, to praise, whilst the word 'bay' comes from an Anglo-Saxon word meaning 'crown' or 'chaplet'. The phrase 'keeping at bay' is also connected with the plant as the aromatic perfume of the leaves was believed to counter-act the plagues. For this reason the Emperor Claudius moved his court to Laurentinum, so named because there the Bay Laurel grew in profusion.

The Romans, when returning from battle, would place Bay leaves in their baths, to give comfort to their aching limbs and, with their fragrance, pleasure to a tired mind. As Laurus nobilis was an ever-green, there was always a plentiful supply of leaves available and much later, during Elizabethan times, they were strewn over the floors of the homes of the wealthy; when the leaves were trodden underfoot, the aromatic fragrance released would have counteracted the musty atmosphere inevitable in the days when houses were built without a damp course.

Not until the Romans began the conquest of their own country—a process which included first the annexing of the provinces of southern Italy then held by the Greeks in the name of Magna Graeca—did they adopt the customs of the Greek peoples who at an early period in their history had been familiar with the use of all the costly aromatics of the Near East. Wall paintings and objects found at Herculaneum, and at Pompeii, reveal something of the Greek influence in the Romans' mode of worship and in their use of perfumes. The early Romans buried their dead but later cremation on a funeral pyre of scented woods was the custom, the bones and ashes were gathered up and mixed with perfumes before being placed in a decorated urn. The wealthy built family sepulchres where the urns containing the remains of each member of the family were in turn deposited.

Religious offerings were made from ornate altars, set on four tapering legs on the top of which was a bronze cauldron, ornamented with the heads of cats or tigers. The altars were placed in the temples and were so numerous that they were fed by an incense chariot, a square box made of copper and mounted on four wheels which was pushed from one altar to another, providing each with a continuous supply of aromatics.

Believed to be the most ornate of all the altars of ancient Rome was the sumptuous Altar of Victory which the Emperor Augustus brought from Tarentum. It was placed in the Senate House which, though not consecrated ground, enjoyed a position similar to that of the temple. Here, in the world's first house of parliament, the Senate met shortly after sunrise and, before commencing the business of the day, each member would approach the Altar of Victory and sprinkle particles of incense over the glowing charcoal. Incense for sacrifices was kept in a bronze casket, known as an 'acerra', and in the temples and homes of the wealthy, aromatics would burn continuously in a bronze censer. This was known as a 'turibulum', and was suspended from the roof by chains.

By 450 B.C. the use of perfumes for personal cleanliness and for pleasure had become widespread. At this time Ticinus Menias, a native of Sicily, introduced the practice of shaving, establishing a

Roman scent bottle, 600 B.C.

chain of barber's shops near the temple of Hercules. Here, the élite of Rome called for their daily shave which was performed with a razor made of sharpened bronze. Afterwards, the somewhat sore face would be covered with hot towels, and then massaged with scented unguents; the hair would also be treated with perfumed pomades of which the most popular was Susinon, made to a Greek prescription and containing oil of ben, saffron, calamus and oil of lilies. Nardinum, made from myrrh and spikenard, was also popular, so much so that spikenard became the most sought-after of all the aromatics. Horace mentions that an onyx box of the precious ointment was worth the value of a cadus of wine.

Before the battle of Actium, in which he defeated Mark Antony to establish himself as ruler of Egypt and of the whole western world, Augustus had been obliged to hasten to Spain, to quell the rebellion in the Roman province of Calabria. The successful crushing of the rebellion is celebrated by Horace in an ode in which he bids the people to look for perfumes and tells the beautiful Neaere to do up her scented hair into an elegant knot and make herself presentable for the general's return.

Pliny tells of the discovery, in that part of Spain visited by Augustus and which bordered the Bay of Biscay, of the clove-scented pink, which from the time of its introduction into Italy until late in the eighteenth century, for almost two thousand years, was in greater demand than any other flower for flavouring wine. The plant was originally called Cantabrica after the place where it was found, and did not receive its more familiar botanical name of

Dianthus until Linnaeus compiled his binomial system of plant classification. As late as the mid-sixteenth century, Dr. Turner, a close friend of Bishops Latimer and Ridley and himself Dean of Wells, called the plant Cantabrica gelouer in his *New Herbal*. He was the first to use the derivation from the French word for a clove-tree, *giroflier*, thus denoting its spicy scent, and this caused the writers of Elizabethan and early Stuart times to add the prefix 'gilly' to all those flowers of clove-like perfume. Thus, Hesperis matronalis was Dame's Gillyflower and the yellow wall-flower was the Yellow Stock Gillyflower. Chaucer, in his Prologue to *The Canterbury Tales*, uses the French spelling *girofleur* when in the tavern yard, before setting out on the pilgrimage to the tomb of Thomas à Becket at Canterbury, his party gather together for a mug of wine or ale.

In the 'Tale of Sir Topaz', he tells of

> ... many a clove girofleur,
> And nutmegge, to put in ale,
> Whether it be moist or stale ...

for the plant was to be found in tavern gardens everywhere, being affectionately known as 'sops-in-wine', the 'sops' being the wet flowers. In *The Shepherd's Calendar*, Edmund Spenser implores the nymphs to

> Bring Coronations and sops-in-wine,
> Worn of paramours.

After the defeat of Hannibal at Carthage in 202 B.C. when the Romans became undisputed leaders of the Mediterranean, they began to import large quantities of aromatics for their personal requirements, and the myrepsi or perfumers soon formed a flourishing section of the community; the élite went so far as to anoint themselves with perfumed oils and unguents three times daily. Three categories of perfumes came into general use: solid unguents, known as 'hedysmata'; liquid unguents or 'stymata'; and powdered perfumes or 'diapasmata'. Simple unguents were flavoured with perhaps a single odour, like malobathrum which was obtained from Cinnamomum cassia. The compound unguents, such as Susinum and Nardinum, were the most costly, and indeed one, originally prepared for the king of the Parthians at great cost and known as the Royal unguent, contained twenty-seven of the most expensive ingredients.

Roman scent bottle, first century A.D.

But it was the solid unguents which were the most popular. These were applied to all parts of the body, but the most wealthy imitated the Greeks by using a different unguent for each part and even rubbed the costly materials into the coats of their dogs and horses. Indeed, the use of exotic perfumes was carried to so great an excess during the time of Julius Caesar that he issued an edict fobidding the use of all those which were imported from the East.

Suetonius tells of the Emperor Otho who, when embarking on a military campaign in 69 A.D., had prepared for him costly essences and cosmetics which were placed in a 'beauty' box to accompany him on his journey. The satirist Juvenal lampooned his effeminacy:

> A looking glass must load th' imperial car,
> The most important carriage of the war . . .
> But as a courtier used the nicest art
> To keep his skin from tan; before the fight
> Would paint and see his soil'd complexion right.

The 'beau' of ancient Rome also came in for considerable ridicule. Martial says that 'he that smells always well, never does so', and on another occasion he remarks that

4*

A beau is one who with the nicest care
In parted locks divides his curling hair;
One who with balm and cinnamon smells sweet
Whose humming lips some Spanish air repeat.

Martial was well aware of the moral degradation of his countrymen
that was to be the main contributory factor in the rapid extinction
of their once mighty empire. At every opportunity, he warned
them of the consequences of their depravity but his advice mostly
went unheeded.

But the women were just as bad. So lavish in their use of cosmetics
were they in fact that Juvenal reproached them, saying that their
husbands rarely saw their faces at home since they applied pastes and
'packs' which remained on throughout the night and at all times
during the day when they were indoors.

Pliny has given us some idea of the various ingredients which
went to make up a 'face pack'. Pea-flour or barley meal, moistened
with egg, wine and honey and the secretion from narcissus bulbs was
a widely used preparation thought capable of removing age-lines and
blemishes.

Ovid, in a book on perfumes, of which unfortunately only a small
fragment has survived, advised his readers to learn from him how to
give a dazzling whiteness to the complexion: 'Take two pounds of
barley brought from Libyan fields, add an equal quantity of bean-
flour and mix with ten eggs. Dry in the sun and add to it a sixth of a
pound of hartshorn. Reduce to a powder and complete the preparation with the juice from two narcissi bulbs pounded in a mortar;

*Roman flask, second century
A.D.*

two ounces of aromatic gums; the same of Tuscan seed; and eighteen ounces of honey.' He believed that 'every woman who spreads this on to her face will render it smoother and more brilliant than her mirror'.

To remove blemishes from the skin, Ovid suggested using the famed Egyptian treatment of steeping lupin seeds in water and applying them to the face and other affected parts. But for a more permanent cure, he advises pounding lupin seeds which have been roasted with beans, red nitre and orris root, and making the concoction into a paste by mixing it with honey. Honey was the principal ingredient of all facial 'masks' and is considered by modern beauticians to be one of the finest of skin foods.

For tinting the cheeks, Roman women used fucus, a red colouring matter like rouge; and Egyptian kohl to shade the eyes. Another aid to beautifying the skin was ass's milk, and Poppaea, Nero's wife, who bathed each day in ass's milk, obtained permission to take with her fifty animals for this purpose when she was exiled from Rome because of her extravagance.

In his golden palace, the ruins of which are still to be seen near the Colosseum, Nero displayed a thousand statues removed from Grecian temples, and installed warm baths fed by Mediterranean waters for the use of his friends. In the state dining-room, fragrant flowers continually rained down on the guests from a ceiling which opened at a signal from the Emperor, whilst movable ivory covers concealing silver pipes, showered scented waters on those who sat at table. It is said that every room in the palace was covered with red rose petals to a depth of several inches, and at Poppaea's funeral, Nero burnt more incense and fragrant gums than could be produced in the whole of Arabia in one year.

Unlike the Greeks who made little effort to keep themselves clean, the Romans were the world's greatest bathers, not only because of the cleansing powers of the warm water but for its health-giving qualities. The baths or thermae of ancient Rome were the most important feature of the city's social life and, like the perfume shops of Athens, were the meeting place for the fashionable coteries of the day. Though most Emperors built their own public baths and made use of them daily, mingling freely with the people, the finest were undoubtedly those erected by the Emperor Caracalla, who succeeded his father Septimius Severus in 211 A.D. and reigned for seven years. Caracalla ordered his great baths to be built on the outskirts of the city near the Caelian Hill, not far from where the animals were caged for use in the Colosseum; now they are used each summer for an operatic festival.

The 86th letter of Seneca describes the Plebeian's bath of the time, saying that 'the walls were ablaze with precious marbles, the chambers adorned with gorgeous mosaics, whilst the water was discharged into marble basins from silver taps'. The public baths were divided into three main compartments, the central area being the Tepidarium or warm-lounge in which the bathers warmed themselves in the vapour before moving to the Calidarium or hot-room which contained the hot water baths; the Sudatorium was hotter still. But first, having undressed and handed in their clothes to be looked after by the capsarii, they would wash in the Frigidarium which usually had a swimming bath attached. After washing, they would then go to the Unctuarium and here they received a massage of cheap oil. The oils and ointments were kept on shelves in jars of alabaster and terra cotta, and it was in the Unctuarium that the aliptor carried out his duties of scraping the skin with the stigil and massaging the body with oil after the bathing had been completed (these were sometimes performed by the bather's slave); so that the oils could be handled more easily, a quantity was placed in a small jar known as an ampulla.

The walls of the baths were covered with mosaics, and statues filled the niches around the rooms which, with their graceful arching roofs, more resembled temples than public wash houses. There were also separate rooms for discussion and for exercise; indeed, the toilet requisites of an intellectual and wealthy people were well catered for in every possible way.

Caracalla's baths measured 675 yards in length and were 550 yards wide with accommodation at one time for more than two thousand bathers, each of whom was provided with a seat of polished marble. On one side were the temples of Apollo and Aesculapius; on the other were those of Hercules and Bacchus. One part was set aside for the women but few of them came to the public baths, preferring to complete their toilet in the privacy of the home— possibly because their faces were so often encased in beauty masks. The most wealthy were attended during their toilet by numerous slaves, in the style of the ancient Egyptians. These were known as cosmetae and were overseen by the ornatrix, or mistress of the toilet. Each performed a given task in turn, beginning with the hair which was styled and dyed and treated with fragrant oils. The face was then massaged, the cheeks were painted with fucus, the eyes shaded. Finally the neck and shoulders were massaged with fragrant oils and the rest of the body washed in rose water. Saffron would be sprinkled about the clothes and over the floors of the apartment, whilst sweet-smelling saffron water ran from the mouths of statues and was sprinkled over the guests.

In a Roman banqueting room, fragrant vines were allowed to grow about the roof which was usually constructed of wooden beams, open to the sky like the flower-covered pergolas which were a feature of southern gardens as they are to this day. They adjoined the main house, and the overall effect resembled the courtyard of a modern terraced house. No meal was provided unless accompanied by fragrant flowers and waters, and in one of his humorous epigrams, Martial complains to his host that he has provided him with more perfumes than meats:

> Who not feeds, but is anointed,
> Lives like nothing but the dead.

Martial was forever satirizing the effeminacy of the men of his time. Of a member of the senate who frequently resorted to dyeing his hair, he asks how it is that 'he who was a swan before, had now become a crow'. Ovid, also, reproaches the maiden in one of his elegies for having destroyed her flowing locks by the use of dyes.

To dye the hair a sandy colour, the Romans imported from Mattium (Marburg) in Germany a 'soap' made of goat's fat and wood ash. Martial referred to it as 'Mattiac balls' since the soap came in small cakes of about the size of a golf ball. Known to the Romans as sapo, it is the first mention of soap that we have.

Roman ladies also paid large sums for blonde wigs obtained from Gaul whose people were noted for their fair hair. 'The golden hair that Galla wears is hers,' noted Martial acidly. Later, they adopted Grecian hair-styles. Young girls tied their tresses into a bun and fastened it with perfumed bands. Older women drew their hair up at the back and held it in place with a gold pin called an acus. But for special occasions, the hair was transformed into long flowing curls which hung down to the shoulder in a style called 'the nimbis', which also necessitated the hair at the back being brought to the front of the head and also being curled.

In Ovid's time, Rome had almost as many perfumers, the unguentari, as Athens, and they occupied that part of the city known as Vicus Thurarieus. The best known of these was Cosmus, whom Martial often mentioned in his *Epigrams*, and his preparations were particularly popular with the wealthy. In Capua, in southern Italy, which was noted for its luxurious living, the perfumers occupied a whole street of the town. They grew and extracted many of their floral essences but most were imported from Egypt and Arabia, some being so expensive that the slaves who worked in the laboratories concocting the perfumes were stripped and searched each evening before being allowed to leave.

Roman perfume lamp, second century B.C.

At the games, fragrant gums were burnt on altars and in lamps, placed at intervals around the arena. Pliny the elder records that it was considered so essential to maintain an atmosphere refreshed by the scent of aromatics that the air of the amphitheatres in and around Rome was kept fragrant by fountains which 'played' scented waters on all important occasions. This was necessary to counteract the warm, sultry atmosphere of a Roman summer, especially oppressive when a crowd had gathered together for the games or to see a play.

The first Christian Emperor of Rome, Constantine the Great, provided fragrant oils and incense to be burnt in the church of St. John-in-Lateran, once the Lateran Palace of his wife Fausta but which was to become the first church of Christendom. It was to be the home of the early Popes for a thousand years and Constantine filled it with silver and gold and ordered scented wax candles to burn continually. By 330 A.D., when he moved the central government to Byzantium to found the new city of Constantinople, Rome was as thickly populated as it is today and almost a thousand public baths provided for the ablutions of the people. It was the most affluent society the world had ever known. But, under Constantine, the Christian Church at last found the peace denied her for three centuries and places of worship for those of her faith sprang up everywhere. St. Paulinus of Nola, a contemporary observer, tells how in his day scented wax tapers and candles were burnt in every church, and he also comments upon the brilliancy and fragrance of the lamps and waxen tapers, fed with fragrant oil, which were to be seen at the festivals of the martyrs and saints, 'shedding perfume round from fragrant wicks'.

Branched candlesticks, highly ornamented, held the fragrant candles. One of these is depicted on the Arch of Titus, erected in Rome in the first century A.D. shortly after Titus had returned from Palestine after the sacking of Jerusalem. He is shown in triumph, bringing with him the tabernacle and the seven-branched golden candlestick which held the perfumed candles. Exactly what became of these priceless relics, no one knows, but even to this day no Jew will ever walk beneath the Arch.

The tradition of scents being used in Church ritual remains. In accordance with the custom which has been handed down since earliest times, the Pope each year blesses the Golden Rose, made of pure gold and anointed with balm and myrrh, to commemorate the gifts of the three kings to the infant Christ. It is said originally to have consisted of a single rose, but it later became more ornate; from a single stem there rises a 'bush' consisting of numerous roses, held on thorny stems, an allusion to the Passion. In the sacristy of St. Mark's at Venice can be seen an outstanding example, presented to the cathedral in 1833 by Pope Gregory.

One of the most popular of all perfumes owes its origin to a famous Roman family, several members of which served in the Papal army at the time of the Italian Renaissance and whose forebears had held special office in the Catholic Church, supplying the holy bread, the wafer, at important ceremonies. It was the Marquis de Frangipani (the name means 'broken bread'), marshal of the armies of Louis XIII of France during the regency of Mary of Medici, who created the perfume bearing his name.

It is distilled from the flowers of Plumeria alba, which grows on several of the West Indian islands, and its scent was first brought to the attention of Europeans by Mercutio Frangipani, a botanist of renown, who accompanied Columbus on his voyage to the New World in 1492, and took part in the discovery of Jamaica.

As Columbus first approached Antigua, those sailing with him noticed a delicious scent in the air which Mercutio said came from some sweet-smelling flower. On landing, they found the island filled with small trees bearing white flowers which became known as the Frangipani, to commemorate the man who had first recognized the perfume. It was later named by Tournefort, Plumeria alba, to honour the French botanist and Franciscan monk Fr. Charles Plumier, who died in 1706. The White Frangipani, as it is called by the islanders of Antigua, grows fifteen feet tall and has long brittle leaves which curl inwards at the margins. The flowers are of purest white with a long in-curving tube, and the scent they diffuse is similar to that of white jasmine.

Also to be found on Antigua is the species Plumeria acutifolia which makes a crooked tree with knotty branches and has scented flowers. It blooms almost the whole year round, and is planted near every Buddhist shrine in Burma and Cambodia where it has become known as the Pagoda Tree. It is regarded as a symbol of immortality for it will continue to bloom even if lifted from the ground with its roots. Day after day it drops its waxy white petals over the hallowed ground and they continue to release their glorious perfume even when dying. From the flowers, the perfume champac is obtained.

The Frangipani perfume is, however, made from Plumeria rubra, which grows mostly on the islands of Jamaica and Martinique and is known there as Red Jasmine; the native women adorn their hair with the flowers and place them amongst clothes for, like those of the Red rose, the petals retain their perfume for several months after drying. The flowers are crimson-red and the perfume they emit is less heavy than that of the flowers of the Pagoda Tree. Typically with that species, its perfume is most pronounced at night-time when it may be detected from a distance of several miles off-shore.

The original Frangipani perfume may have been made to a recipe resembling the scent of the dried flowers brought into Europe by travellers to the West Indies during the early years of the seventeenth century, for Martinique, the chief supplier, was part of the French colonial empire when the Marquis de Frangipani first made his perfume. One of the ingredients of the original scent was the bark of Cascarilla gratissima which also went into the toilet

Wedgwood pot-pourri vases in the Adam style

Modern Pomander in Crown Staffordshire

'Pot Pourri' by George Dunlop Leslie R.A.

Chelsea scent bottles of the 18th century

water known as Eau à Brûler. Cascarilla is Spanish for 'little bark' and alludes to the short curled pieces of bark which are stripped from the branches and burnt to fumigate apartments. The plant was renamed Croton eleutheria after Eleuthera, the island in the Bahamas where it was found. It is a member of the Euphorbia family and releases a thick balsam-scented juice when the stems are broken. The bark, which is known to the natives as 'sweet-wood', has been shipped to the perfumers of Europe since the beginning of the seventeenth century. The leaves also are scented and are used by the islanders for placing amongst clothes.

The Marquis de Frangipani was the first to use the preparation to perfume his gloves, and the idea was quickly taken up by the fashionable of the time. It was prepared from a grease or pomade which was then rubbed into the gloves and thus absorbed by the hands. Ménage, who was Frangipani's contemporary and met him in Paris on several occasions, alludes only to the perfuming of gloves, though the scent was later prepared as an essence and as a powder. Another contemporary, however, speaks of the Marquis inventing 'la composition du parfum et des odeurs', from which one may infer that his preparation had been made in various forms, perhaps following the popularity of his perfumed gloves. Esprit de Frangipani was one of the most famous scents made by Charles Piesse, the celebrated perfumer of Nice during the second half of the nineteenth century.

As early as 1190, it is on record that there were perfume sellers in Paris, and their fraternity was established at St. Anne's Chapel in the Church of the Innocents. The arms of the French perfumers were first registered by letters patent granted in 1426 by Henry VI of England and France, but the popularity of gloves scented with Frangipani was such that under further Letters Patent, dated March 26, 1656, Louis XIV gave recognition both to the glovemakers and to the perfumers of Paris, in which the glovers are styled 'Les marchants Maîtres Gantiers Parfumeurs'. As glovers, they now had the right to make and sell gloves and mittens in all kinds of materials, whilst as perfumers they not only enjoyed the privilege of perfuming gloves but also of selling perfumes of all types. They also imported skins from Italy to make perfumed pouches and purses, which were bought by the 'dandies' of France and Italy, often for quite large sums.

Though scented gloves were known in England during Elizabethan times, it may be said that modern perfumery in France and Italy began with the introduction of the Marquis de Frangipani's famous scent. Ménage, in his *Origini della Lingua Italiana*, published in 1685, noted: 'Da uno di que' Signori Frangipani furono chiamati certi quanti porfumati, Guanti di Frangipani.'

One important ingredient of Frangipani powder was orris root, dried and finely ground, which had been part of all the best perfumes in ancient Athens and Rome. It is still used today in talcum and sachet powders. Orris is the dried root of the Florentine iris, I. florentina (its pale blue flowers have been the symbol of the city of Florence since its foundation). Resembling the violet in perfume, the roots are lifted in alternate years, the lower part being cut away and the leaves trimmed back. The upper part of the rhizomatous root is replanted and will flourish with increased vigour, but it will grow best in a poor, gravelly limestone soil such as found in the Florentine hills, where the people chew the dried roots to sweeten the breath. They also burn it on the fire in winter-time to scent their houses.

When grown commercially, the roots are spread out to dry, the soil being scraped away and the fibrous roots removed. Sometimes the roots are baked over a fire, and girls will make scented beads from the pieces, and weave them into necklaces.

Like spikenard, the drier orris root becomes the more pronounced is its perfume, so that it is not used for its essence until it is at least a year old. The roots are then crushed and dissolved in rectified spirit. After standing for a month, the extract is ready to remove and is then used for mixing with other materials to form the basis of a number of well-known perfumes, chief amongst these being Jockey Club, very popular a hundred years ago. The odorous principle is due to a ketone named Irone which is freely soluble in alcohol. The violet scent, however, is more noticeable in the dried root, though by distillation its otto exactly resembles the violet fragrance, a scent which was greatly esteemed by the Athenian and Roman perfumers.

Orris also figured in the 'sachet powder' made for Queen Isabella of Spain, and in the powder used by Henry IV of France to perfume his household linen. It was, with sandalwood, the principal ingredient of Maréchale, the most popular powder of the French

Orris, Iris Florentina

Regency, whose other ingredients included the dried petals of red roses, cloves, cassia bark and grain musk which were pounded together in a mortar before being placed in silken bags.

In its more romantic name of Florentine Iris, orris essence is used in modern perfumery, to include in those light Bouquets so popular with the women of Italy and France.

CHAPTER SEVEN

PERFUMES OF THE EAST

Mohamet's love of perfumes – The first distillations – Beauty preparations of eastern women – Perfumes for religious rites – Perfumes of Hindu mythology – Indian scents – Perfumes of the Chinese people.

AFTER several centuries of unrivalled splendour, the Roman Empire began to crumble before the barbaric hordes of northern Europe, and the appreciation of perfume and luxurious living once again moved eastwards. On the Byzantine domes of Constantinople, the Crescent replaced the Holy Cross, the followers of Mohamet bringing with them a love and knowledge of the aromatic gums of Arabia, where the prophet was born and where he died. By the tenth century Muslim suzerainty stretched from Araby to Byzantium and as far east as the valley of the Indus, encompassing almost the whole of Alexander's Macedonian empire.

Mohamet, who founded his religion upon the right of all men to enjoy material pleasures, delighted in the company of children and women, but next to these pleasures came his love of perfumes about which he made no secret. Amongst many delights promised to Muslim believers is the Garden of Paradise, Djennet Firdous, where, according to the prophet, the most exotic perfumes are to be found. The Koran says that all who have passed over Al Sirat, a bridge as narrow as a razor's edge, may drink in the pool of Al Cawthar, the waters of which are whiter than milk, more perfumed than musk and which will quench their thirst forever.

They will then enter Paradise, in the Seventh Heaven, under the throne of God and walk on ground made of wheaten flour mixed with saffron and musk and covered with stones of fragrant hyacinths and pearls. But of all the attractions, none will surpass the black-eyed houris who will welcome the faithful to the fragrant bowers, waving before them embroider'd scarves 'whose motion gave forth perfume'. In 'Lalla Rookh', Moore has described the state of ecstasy into which the faithful will be transformed, after being welcomed by nymphs created entirely out of sweetly smelling musk. For the Arabs, musk is the most pleasantly scented of all perfumes. It is a curious fact that the warmer the climate, the more appreciated are those perfumes which emit a powerful, almost oppressive aroma. In Arabia and the Near East, frankincense and myrrh are most in demand, whilst the Indian peoples love champac and patchouli. But to the followers of Mohamet, musk was considered to be above all others, chiefly because it was the most endurable and, in the Garden of Paradise, its perfume would never fade. For this reason, the mosque at Kara Amed, built by a wealthy merchant, and known as Iparie, meaning musk, was so called because seventy juks of musk were mixed with the mortar used in its construction. The mosque of Zobiade at Tauris is also scented with musk, the mortar having retained its perfume right up to the present.

To Avicenna, an Arabian doctor practising in the tenth century, goes the honour of being the first to obtain the volatile oil of flowers, the attar, by distillation. Until then, the only known perfumes were the exudations of sweet gums and those obtained from the bark and twigs of trees and shrubs, known in perfumery as resins and spices; though flowers had since earliest times been used for scenting clothes and for flavouring wine and food. Not until the experiments of Avicenna, however, were the fragrant volatile oils obtained and so made permanent. The learned doctor, who in a lifetime of almost sixty years found time to write nearly a hundred volumes on the general knowledge of his country, is believed to have used the rose of a hundred petals, Gul sad berk, in his experiments, but Father Catron, in his *Histoire de Mogol*, gives another version of the origin of attar of roses. This was that the Princess Nourmahal ordered a large tank, on which she and the Great Mogul were rowed, to be filled with the water of red roses; when the heat of the sun caused the oil to separate and float on the surface, it was immediately collected. This story, however, may well be apocryphal.

In his works, Avicenna has faithfully described the method by which he distilled the attar from the rose, and Arabian writers on chemistry confirm that his ideas soon came into general practice. When Saladin, the chivalrous enemy of the early Crusaders, entered Jerusalem in 1187, he ordered the floor and walls of Omar's Mosque to be washed with the perfume of the rose.

In the Near East, rose water was sprinkled—from a gulabdan, a container with a narrow spout—over every guest upon entering the host's apartments, as a mark of esteem. Niebuhr, in his *Descriptions of Arabia*, adds the information that, when it is time for the visitors to leave, a censer is brought out and the incense is directed on to beards and garments as a parting gesture. Censers in Arabia are made of wood and are handsomely covered with plaited cane, but the gulabdan is usually made of glass, chased in silver or gold if it happens to belong to a person of wealth. The Beduin tribesmen always add otto of roses to their coffee, and later, as a sign that the evening's entertainment has ended, will pass round a bowl containing glowing charcoal on which incense is thrown and around which garments are wrapped. The guests depart, blankets smelling of incense are spread over the floor of the tent, and all is quiet.

Persian incense burner,
A.D. 1250

Sadi, the most widely read of Persia's poets, has described the burning of fragrant woods on braziers in the homes of the wealthy which is a common practice in the Muslim world:

> The aloes-wood, from which no fragrance came,
> If placed on fire, its inodorous state
> Will change, more sweet than ambergris.

Sadi also tells how, after spending the night in his garden with a friend, he decided to write a poem. When morning came his friend gathered some scented flowers and placed them in the folds of his garments. 'Throw them away,' said Sadi, 'for I am going to compose a Gulistan [a poem about a garden of roses] which will last for

eternity, whilst your flowers will live but for a day.' And he pro-
ceeded to write the most beautiful of all Persian poems.

The rose has always been a particular favourite in the Arab world.
The Kalif El-Mutawekkel had every rose bush, for miles around,
dug up and re-planted in his palace gardens, and, every hour of the
day, had the rugs of his apartments sprinkled with rose water. 'I am
the king of all Sultans and the rose is king of sweet-scented flowers,'
he declared.

In Turkey, most apartments are fumigated with pans of burning
incense or fragrant woods and, after bathing, unguents are rubbed
into the body. The Turks took their love of bathing from the Romans
and introduced into their country the idea of steam-heated baths—
which later they passed on to the West. The sweating caused by the
heat opened the pores and rid the skin of its impurities. The body
was then washed with scented soaps and massaged with oil. Sadi,
in his time, must have been familiar with this form of bathing:

> 'Twas in the bath, a piece of perfumed clay
> Came from my loved one's hand to mine one day.
> 'Art thou then musk or ambergris?' I said,
> 'That by thy scent my soul is ravish-ed?'

Oriental women, obsessed with the sole idea of pleasing their
menfolk, attend to their toilet as their most urgent occupation and
love to be always in an atmosphere redolent with fragrant odours.
Indeed Sonnini, in his *Travels*, was of the opinion that nowhere in
the world do the women pay greater attention to their cleanliness than
in the East, bathing frequently and massaging all parts of the
body with perfumed oils: 'nowhere are the women more uniformly
beautiful, nowhere are they better skilled or more practised in the
art of arresting or repairing the ravages of time.'

A French beautician of the last century described the method by
which the women of Morocco and Tunis make their kohl for
darkening the eyes. First, they remove the inside of a lemon and fill
it with plumbago and burnt copper, placing it on a charcoal fire
until it is carbonized. They then pound it in a mortar and add to it
some pieces of coral and pearl, some sandalwood and ambergris to
perfume it, and a bat's wing, all first having been burnt to a cinder
and then moistened with rose water.

In the harems, a complexion powder known as batikha, used for whitening the skin, is made by pounding in a mortar cowrie-shell and borax, white marble and rice, eggs, lemons and the seed called helbas. The whole is then combined with the meal of peas, beans and lentils and placed inside a melon, to be mixed in with the pulp. This is left in the sun for several days until the whole concoction becomes dry and has disintegrated into a fine white powder ready for use.

To colour the hair black, gall-nuts are fried in olive oil and then added to a mixture of cloves, burnt copper, various herbs, gum-arabic, henna and flowers of the pomegranate, pounded in a mortar. This gives a jet-black preparation, resembling walnut oil, which is massaged into the hair each day. Sadi ridicules the vogue amongst older women for using it to dye their grey hair:

> . . . thy hair with silver bent
> May cheat us now; yet, little mother; say,
> Canst thou make straight thy back, which time has bent?

Lady Mary Wortley Montague tells, in letters describing her travels in the East, of a hairstyle adopted by the women. One side of the head was covered with a talpock, a small velvet cap, and on the uncovered side, jewels of all descriptions, made to resemble the most highly scented flowers, were fixed in the hair. 'It is hard to imagine anything more beautiful,' she wrote, 'the hair hangs at its full length behind, divided into tresses braided with pearl and ribbon.' And Robert Browning in *Paracelsus* tells of the lavish use of perfumes used by Hindu women to dress their hair:

> Heap cassis, sandal-buds and stripes
> Of labdanum, and aloe-balls,
> Smeared with dull nard, an Indian wipes
> From out her hair.

But of the famed Balm of Mecca, used by all wealthy women of the East to preserve their youthful complexion, Lady Mary wrote in the utmost disgust: she tried it and, instead of the expected improvement, her face became red and swollen and remained so for several days, causing her great indignation. It was the same sub-stance as that carried into Egypt by the merchants who came upon Joseph and, though it was even then a great rarity, Piesse tells that, by the end of the seventeenth century, the Amyris opobalsamum

from which it is obtained was to be found only in one small planta-
tion near the rock city of Petra, built by the Romans on their way to
southern Arabia in the hope of capturing the spice trade; and that
the plants yielded only about three pounds annually. To protect it,
the resin was originally kept in shells found by the shores of the Red
Sea. This was how the Arab traders transported all their resins. The
Greeks and Romans also used shells to store their ointments where
boxes of onyx and alabaster could not be afforded. Horace alludes to
this method, advising his friend to 'pour out the perfumed ointment
from the capacious shell'.

Along the north African coast, from Alexandria to Casablanca, the
scent of spices and resinous gums pervades the Arab markets and
their purchase takes pride of place, to burn as incense, to fumigate
clothes, and to anoint the body. The Arabs consider fragrant substances to be amongst their most prized possessions, and these
really take the place of laundries and dry cleaning establishments in
the Western world.

Because of the continual shortage of water in those lands occupied
by the Arab peoples, modes of bathing were practised by them which
purified the body without using water at all.

Until recently Sudanese women practised a most primitive method
of bathing. First, they made a hole in the sand in which was placed an
earthenware pot filled with burning charcoal on to which were then
thrown aromatic woods and resins. The women then removed their
underclothes and crouched over the pot, drawing around them a
cloak to keep in the fumes. This caused sweating and cleansed the
pores, in addition to fumigating the lower parts of the body with
scented smoke. Afterwards, fragrant oils were rubbed over the skin.
This acted as a cleanser and gave a valuable tonic to the skin, its
effect being similar to a Turkish bath followed by a gentle massage.

The love of perfumes became an essential part of the life of the
peoples of India at an early period in her history, since fragrant
plants have always abounded throughout the country. Kalidasa, a
Sanskrit writer of Cleopatra's time, mentions them in his dramatic
poem *Sakoontala*, or *The Lost Ring*, saying that perfumes were used
both for personal and for religious rites. Sacrifices, consisting of
fires of scented wood, were offered in the temples of Brahma,
Vishnu and Siva, and the flames were fed with a consecrated

ointment and ringed with leaves of the sacred herb 'rusa'. This is Andropogon nardus which, when dried and crushed, releases the scent of spikenard.

There are said to be more than three thousand temples in India sacred to the Brahmins, whose faith became established almost four thousand years ago. They believe in a Supreme Spirit or 'Essence' called Brahm who is present in everything and has placed his three great gods, Brahma, Vishnu (whose many incarnations included Krishna, Rama and Buddha) and Siva, in control of the world.

In the grounds of the great Hindu temple at Tanjore in Madras with its tower of pyramidal form, can be seen a huge bull more than twelve feet high, sculptured from a solid block of black granite. Each day it is anointed with perfumed oil so that, beneath its canopy of carved stone, it shines like polished marble and scents the air around. And at Orissa, incense is offered daily by the priest to the god Siva.

In his poem, Kalidasa tells of Sakoontala who is about to be married, and of her father who invokes the blessings of the gods upon her with an offering of wreaths of upward-curling smoke from burnt oblations. When attending to the bridal preparations of Sakoontala, Anasuya, her handmaid, compounds unguents with a consecrated paste and rose-grass, to anoint the limbs of her mistress, whilst a hermit brings presents for Sakoontala, including 'a roseate dye [henna] wherewith to stain the lady's feet', as was the custom of the times.

At wealthy Hindu marriages, it is usual to erect a silk canopy over the bride and groom beneath which burns the sacred fire or oman alluded to in 'Sakoontala'. This is kept alight with sandalwood and aromatic gums which, during the ceremony, fill the 'tent' with their delicious fumes. At a Brahmin marriage, saffron and rice are thrown over the shoulders of the couple, to consecrate the union, and the ceremony ends with the husband presenting his wife with a small golden image which she wears for ever around her neck. Amongst the other gifts a bride receives from her husband at her wedding is a toilet or beauty box containing attar of roses; some rose water and a bottle to sprinkle it; a spice box; a box of powder called soorma to blacken the eyelids; and another for kohl to darken the eyelashes. A comb for the hair is also included.

Sandalwood, so important in Hindu marriage ceremonies, is

mentioned in the 'Nirukta', the oldest of the Vedic commentaries, written in the fifth century B.C. It was one of the principal commodities conveyed from India to the Middle East. In India, the wood was used chiefly in the construction of Hindu temples, especially for entrance gates such as those at Somnath, erected about A.D. 100 and which are still in existence.

In religious festivals for the god Vishnu, those taking part rub their bodies with saffron ointment and go around collecting alms, in return for which they distribute sticks of scented sandalwood. It is the white wood of Santalum album, which more correctly should be called 'Santalwood', and is used in perfumery, the odour assimilating so well with the rose that at one time its essential oil was used to adulterate attar of roses. When dissolved in 'spirit' its extract was employed in the composition of a number of perfumes, to impart to them something of its 'heavy' eastern quality. Once, Santalum album grew in dense forests in northern India, Burma and China, but such vast quantities were used in the building of temples, for houses and for making caskets and wooden ornaments, that its numbers were greatly reduced and it had to be imported from Indonesia and the islands of the Timor Sea. Being parasitic, it attaches itself to the roots of other trees and will eventually reach a height of forty feet or more.

Not only is the highly scented wood a principal ingredient of incense but it is one of the few woods immune to attack from the white ant, which is extremely common in China and India and devours every living thing it comes across; for this reason alone sandalwood was employed for building. And from the chippings collected during the felling of the trees, an otto is obtained, about one hundredweight of wood yielding thirty ounces of otto. It is always mixed with rose otto and on April 12, the last day of the Birman year, women throw rose water mixed with essence of sandalwood over everyone near them, to wash away the sins which have been committed during the year and to enable them to begin the new year purified in body and soul. To facilitate the extraction of the otto, sandalwood shavings are placed with the flowers, so that Hindu perfumes carry the 'heavy' scent of the wood by which the perfumes of the Orient are so readily recognized.

In Hindu mythology, there are five heavens, each presided over by a different god. That of Brahma is on Mount Meru; those of

Vishnu, Siva, Kuvera and Indra are on summits of other Himalayan mountains where scented flowers are amongst the chief delights. It is on Mount Meru that the blue-flowered Champac, which is in fact unknown on earth, is supposed to be found; it has the delicious fragrance of the yellow-blossomed Michella champaca with which Hindu maidens decorate their jet black hair. The real Champac is a low-growing evergreen tree bearing pale yellow funnel-shaped flowers with a jasmine-like scent which are used in the manufacture of expensive perfumes, and yield a fragrance resembling that of the Ilang-Ilang of the Philippine Islands.

In Indra's garden of Paradise, the flowers not only enchant the senses of those who breathe their sweet scent but have the power to grant their every wish.

Kama, the god of love of Indian mythology, is always depicted with his cupid's bow and five arrows, each of which is tipped with the blossom of a fragrant flower and which pierce the heart through the five senses. One of the flowers is the Jasmine, in Arabic 'Ysmym', in Persian, 'jasemin'. This is not the yellow-flowered species to be found growing against many an English cottage wall but the white jasmine, J. officinale, native of Persia and Kashmir and well known to Tudor gardeners. So delicious is its perfume that Edmund Spenser could think of no more appropriate flower with which to compare the attractive body of his young wife:

> Her breasts, like lilies, 'ere their leaves be shed;
> Her nipples, like young blossomed jessamines;
> Such fragrant flowers do give most odorous smell
> But her sweet odour did them all excel.

From these flowers and from those of Jasminum sambac, perfume is made by means of enfleurage, a process which involves embedding the fresh flowers in fat from which the scent is then extracted.

Near Grasse, the centre of the French perfume industry, the plants are grown as shrubs in the open and in well-cultivated ground, and their flowers reach several times the size of jasmine growing in English gardens. They yield as much as two hundredweight of blossoms each day during July and August, when the flowers are harvested during sixty or so consecutive days so as to provide the best jasmine fat. A thousand plants will yield about half a hundred-weight of flowers each year. They are gathered at dawn by women and children, each having strapped to his or her side a wicker basket in which the blossoms are conveyed to the laboratory as quickly as possible.

Extract of jasmine is prepared by pouring rectified spirit on to the fat and allowing it to remain for a fortnight in the heat of summer. After straining, the pomade is re-melted and used for the fixation of the hair and in face creams, as it still contains the perfume of the flower. Jasmine is the most difficult of all scents to extract and to imitate.

The essence of Jasminum sambuc, which the Hindus make so well and is the most popular of all Indian perfumes, is mostly produced around Ghazepore, situated on the left bank of the Ganges above Benares, the Holy City which all Hindus hope to visit at least once to ensure salvation in the life hereafter, and to die there and be cremated on a pile of fragrant sandalwood is thought to make salvation sure beyond all doubt. To extract the essence, the flowers are placed in stills with twice their weight of water and exposed to the air. Next day, the otto appears on the surface and is removed by skimming. More flowers and more water are then added, and the process is repeated until the entire crop has been harvested.

India has a unique number of 'holy' cities and each is in some way connected with an event in the life of a Hindu god. Brindaban, for instance, is famed for the deeds of Krishna whose sacred plant, the Holy Basil (Ocymum sanctum) or Tulsi, named in honour of the nymph Tulasi, is to be found in every Hindu home where it is nurtured and watered daily and worshipped by the entire household. The plant is also sacred to Vishnu whose followers wear necklaces made from the stems. In Deccan villages, the Brahmin mother, having completed her toilet, walks round the pot of Holy Basil, asking for heaven's blessing for her family and freedom from malaria and other dangerous diseases. The plant inhabits dry places and is a short-stemmed woody perennial, its leaves and stems being covered in purple hairs. It is closely related to Ocymum gratissimum which grows to a height of six feet and is planted in the gardens belonging to Hindu temples because of its refreshing smell of ripe lemons.

Shelley's 'sweet basil and mignonette' refers to Ocymum basilicum, to be found on arid hillsides in Persia and Afghanistan. His coupling of the two fragrant plants is of interest, for French perfumers consider that the essential oil of the Sweet Basil so closely resembles the scent of mignonette that the two are often mixed together. Mignonette, a native of Egypt and North Africa, gives little essential oil, but the smooth oblong leaves of Sweet Basil do yield one which, when crystallized, becomes the inhalant known as basil camphor.

Foremost amongst the perfumes used by Indian women is Abeer (or Abir), a scented talcum powder which is sprinkled on clothes and linen. It is made from sandalwood, aloes, rose petals, zedoary and civet, pounded together in a mortar and brought to a fine powder.

Zedoary is the tuberous root of Curcuma zedoaria, a plant of the ginger family, native of China and Bengal. The roots constitute one of the most important articles of native perfumery and from them the women extract a colouring matter which imparts a lively tint to their naturally dark complexions as well as a delicious fragrance. Curcuma takes its name from the Persian, Kurkum, their name for saffron, which it resembles in colour. The plant is surpassed by few others in beauty, the highly scented pale pink flowers forming a spike twelve inches long.

Cucuma zerumbet is another species, whose roots are used in Indian perfumery. The Hindus know it as Kuchoora and its ovate tubers, greyish-yellow in colour, release an agreeable camphor-like smell when dried and powdered, resembling that of the cardamon. And from the roots of Alpinia officinarum the peoples of the East obtain the celebrated Galanga perfume. Its name is derived from Kau-liang, which is the ancient name for the Chinese province of Kwangtung where the plant abounds. To the people of Arabia it is Khulanjan; to the Persians it is Khusrodara. It was in common use throughout the East in the early fifteenth century. Saladinus, physician to the Princes of Tarentum in 1450, believed it to be one of the most important of all commodities and it was to be found in the shop of every aromatarius.

Western perfumers believe that one of the ingredients of the scent Abeer is the powdered root known as Kapur-Kachri. This is the dried root of Hedychium spicatum and is used in many eastern perfumes. It takes its name Hedychium from two Greek words meaning 'sweet snow', an allusion to the pure white flowers which are so sweetly scented. The plant is found amongst the snow-covered mountain ranges of Nepal, to a height of at least 8,000 feet.

The reddish-brown root is marked with white rings and, when dry, has a powerful violet-like scent, more pronounced than that of orris root. In Indian markets, the roots are sliced into rings which are dried and powdered or placed amongst clothes. Dr. Thresh in the *Pharmaceutical Journal* tells of having extracted the essential oil which, when a few drops were placed on clothes, 'rendered them highly odorous for a considerable length of time, or in a room, it pervades it with an odour like that of hyacinths.' All these scented roots are burnt in the temples as incense and in the homes of the wealthy, so as to cool the oppressive heat and counteract unpleasant smells.

A sweet ointment or oil known as Urgujja, composed of similar ingredients but with oil of jasmine added to give it a smooth consistency, is used for massaging into the body. Another perfumed oil is made by placing gingelly-oil seeds, in alternating layers with fresh flowers of outstanding perfume, in a container which is then closed. After several weeks, during which time the flowers are frequently renewed, the seeds are pressed, and the oil exuding from them is found to be impregnated with the perfume of the flowers. The scented oil is used to massage into the skin.

When they marry, Muslim women colour their teeth black, using a preparation called munjun, which is a mixture of burnt almond shells, tobacco leaf, black pepper and salt, pounded in a mortar. And, in their religious ceremonies, they burn an incense composed of benzoin, aloe wood, sandal and patchouli, which is placed in a censer and lit at the feet of the dead so that the soul may be wafted upwards to heaven in the perfume of the incense. Sandalwood ointment is also used to rub over the bodies of the dead and, in cremation, the wealthy use aloe and sandalwood to be consumed with the remains. The poorer, however, burn juniper wood, and the Nepalese and Tibetans also normally use it as incense and on funeral piles. The Tibetans burn incense at the initiation ceremony of a monk, and a daily offering was at one time made to the Lamas in every monastery. Because of their belief that it will guard them against evil spirits and from bodily harm, the priests place incense in the amulet boxes they carry on their belts.

Nowhere on earth are more plants with scented attractions to be found than in India, and the people make the fullest use of them. One, which abounds in northern India and Tibet, is Aucklandia costus, known there as Costus or Koosht. The roots have the violet-like scent of orris and, when dried, they are burnt as incense; an excellent tincture may also be distilled from them, which, a century ago, found favour with Western perfumers. Another highly esteemed plant is Vetiveria zizanioides, belonging to the grass family, which forms a thick rhizomatous root, and releases the same violet scent as orris root. When powdered, it is known to the natives as 'vetivert' or 'kus-kus'. From the roots, the Eastern perfume Mousseline is made, taking its name from Indian muslin which at one time was treated with the perfume before being despatched to European markets.

There is a delightful custom, practised in India and Malaya, of incorporating the roots in the sun-blinds. When they are watered in the heat of the sun, as is done throughout the day, they release the violet perfume which is enjoyed both inside and outside, while the watering helps to cool the apartment. The thinner roots are used to weave into baskets which, when damp, give constant pleasure to those carrying them. At one time the dried roots were imported into Europe and, after being cut up and steeped in rectified spirits for two weeks, produced essence of Vetivert which was extremely popular as a perfume in late Georgian times.

One of the better known Eastern perfumes is Patchouli, obtained from the nettle-like leaves of the labiate, Pogostemon patchouli, a member of the lavender family and found near Silhet in Bengal. Its odour is the most powerful of all scents derived from the botanical kingdom, and in its unadulterated form smells extremely unpleasantly of goats. But when the otto is diluted with attar of roses and is dissolved in rectified spirit, it has a most pleasing quality. A hundredweight of leaves will produce about twenty-eight ounces of otto, which is dark brown in colour and oily to the touch.

Patchouli first became known in Britain in about 1820 when it was used to impregnate Indian shawls which became so fashionable that the designs were copied by the Paisley weavers for export to many other parts of the world. They were unable to sell them, however, if not scented with Patchouli. In the East, the perfume is used to scent linen, and the leaves when dried and powdered are packed in muslin bags to place amongst clothes and to make pot-pourris. The odour of patchouli is also present in Indian ink, for the plant is used in its making.

Patchouli, Pogostemon patchouli

Almost as powerful is the perfume obtained from the flowers of Pandanus odoratissimus, known as Pandang and used by Hindu women for toilet purposes. Dr. Roxburgh, writing in the last century, said that it was the male flowers which gave the most powerful scent. Both male and female flowers are present on the same plant, the former appearing above the latter in a dense cylindrical spike and opening first; their pollen is carried by the wind on to the female flowers below and on to the inflorescences of other plants. The Pandanus is one of the most primitive of plants and is known as the Screw Pine from the screw-like formation of the leaves as they develop from the main stem. Its leaves, which are long and narrow and sharply pointed, appear in tufts at the ends of the branches and from a distance resemble small palm trees. The Pandanus is a water-loving plant, found on beaches in western India and on most islands in the Indian ocean.

But, above all other plants esteemed for their perfume, there is the rose, which abounds in Kashmir and northern India, and whose attar is considered to be of the finest quality, comparable to Bulgarian attar. This is not surprising for, in the cool, dry climate of the Himalayan foothills, the fragrance of the rose excels.

To collect the oil, a quantity of rose water, already twice distilled,

5

is allowed to run off into an open vessel which is left overnight in a cold stream. In the morning, the oil is found floating on the surface in minute specks and these are carefully removed with the tip of an iris leaf. When cool, the oil sets quite hard and is dark green in colour. About five hundred pounds of flowers are required to produce one ounce of attar.

The Provence and Damask roses are those most widely cultivated for their perfume. In Turkey and Bulgaria, where the roses are gathered during May and early June, before the weather becomes too warm, the blossoms are removed at sunrise whilst the petals are still covered with dew and are placed in baskets and sacks to be removed to the distilling plant without delay. The distilling operation is simple. The roses are placed in a copper alembic and a fire lit beneath. To every twenty-two pounds of flowers are added sixteen gallons of water, and the fire drives off the steam into a vat where it condenses and runs off into a receiving flask, which is connected to the vat by a small glass tube known as a 'worm'. This quantity of flowers will produce two one-gallon flasks of rose water which are then re-distilled together with others to make eight gallons of rose water. From these, a single flask of distillate is obtained and, when cool, the otto rises to the top and is collected in a small ladle, shaped like an inverted cone or dunce's cap. The oily liquid which quickly solidifies is placed in a collecting flask from which any surplus water is allowed to drain.

About seven thousand rose plants are required to plant an acre of ground which, in an average season, will produce a weight of about five thousand pounds of roses. The plants, if well looked after, will be profitable for ten years.

The Hindu perfumer takes up his position in the bazaar with his richly painted boxes around him, each filled with powders and scents, in the midst of which he sits, dispensing to his patrons. There will be those who take their own bottles to be filled with rose water, and some will buy the barks and roots to compound the powders to their own particular liking. The barber is usually at hand and also attends to his customers in the bazaar, handling his scissors with dexterity, but no Mohamedan will ever allow them near his beard, which he retains in memory of the Prophet. His head, though, will be shaven, except for a few strands of hair which will provide him with the means of being hauled up to the heavenly Paradise at the appointed hour.

There is a proverb attributed to Confucius which says; 'Incense perfumes mitigate bad smells, candles lighten men's hearts'; and he has left it on record that, in his time, scented flowers were scattered about on all Chinese festive occasions. On New Year's Day, house-boats on the Yangtse and temples throughout the land were hung with the fragrant blossoms of the peach and magnolia, the jonquil and jasmine. This was followed, on the first full moon of the New Year, by the Feast of Lanterns.

Joss-sticks of incense, usually placed in a censer at the feet of the idols, were offered morning and evening in the temples, and at one time the consumption was so great that, in the province of Canton alone, there were ten thousand people employed in its making. In the Hall of Ceremonies at Peking, incense burned continuously in twelve large urns, as an offering to the memory of and as a thanks-giving for the lives of past emperors, while in the home, the incense burner remained an indispensable item of furniture.

'Ancestor worship' has always been foremost amongst the religions of China, and incense is burned at the deaths of parents and grand-parents. First, the body is washed and perfumed and is clothed in the finest garments left by the deceased, while incense burns from a small censer placed in the centre of the room. Then, after the procession led by the eldest son has formed up, the mourners carrying lighted incense sticks precede the body on the way to its last abode.

Since earliest times, China has been famed for her appreciation of scented flowers, and the earliest known treatise written on flowering plants was that of Chi Han of the Tsin dynasty in the third century A.D. In this work he recorded those plants growing in south-western China at the time, including the scented jasmine, Yeh-hsi-Ming; a Chinese work of the ninth century describes it as being native of Po-szu, or Persia, and it must therefore have reached China very early in her history, possibly during the period of Persia's greatness when, under Darius I, her empire extended from the Nile to northern India and beyond. At approximately the same time, Confucius began to spread his religion.

Chi Han also mentions the Sambac jasmine Mo Li, which was once cultivated for its perfume from Pekin to Canton. Until recently, there were gardens in many parts of China which were devoted solely to its cultivation and, each day, the unopened buds were taken to the cities to be sold for decorating the hair of Chinese girls, and to impart their fragrance to tea. During the eighteenth century, at Foochow in Fukien Province, it was estimated that at least three million pounds of jasmine buds were produced each year for this purpose alone, and the jasmine gardens in Kwangtung province extended for miles along the banks of the Pearl River.

In *An Account of the Interesting objects in Kwangtung Province* by Li T'so yuan, written in 1777, there is a delightful picture of jasmine buds being used to decorate the hair. The flower buds which blossom after dusk are suitable for that very night. After the fragrant buds are placed in the hair, they begin to open, becoming brighter and more beautiful under moonlight and more fragrant with human warmth, lasting for the whole night, their scent lingering until dawn.

At the flower farms, the unopened buds would be collected at daybreak and placed in a wet cloth in which they would be taken to the city flower sellers to string into garlands for the ladies to wear in the evening. The ability of jasmine flowers to 'cleanse' an oppressive atmosphere also made them much in demand for draping over the bed at night (in Europe, lavender is placed in the sick room for a similar purpose, as it gives off more ozone and cleanses the air more effectively than any other flower). In China, jasmine 'balls' were given to guests departing from dances and banquets, for the flowers cleared the head of muzziness. They were also used to flavour wine, and their fragrant oil was massaged into the body after bathing.

In the *Floricultural Cabinet* for May 1846, Carl Thunberg, the Swedish explorer, tells a charming story about the Batavian women, who tie up their hair (which is anointed with scented oil and is not powdered) into a large knot on the crown of the head and adorn it with wreaths of fragrant flowers of Nyctanthes sambac, which are run upon a thread and brought to the towns each evening for sale. Thunberg said that 'the smell of them is inconceivably delightful, like that of orange flowers. The whole house is filled with the scent, enhancing if possible, the society of the fair sex'. The Nyctanthes is a small tree, native of the Indonesian islands, and bears a profusion of white star-like flowers which open in the evening, diffusing the rich perfume of honeysuckle. The petals fall at sunrise but, like the Persian red rose, retain their scent, and are collected by the women to make pot pourris.

The delightful custom of decorating the hair with scented flowers is followed throughout south-east Asia and especially where the natives follow the Hindu religion. On the island of Bali, the women and children spend much of their time in prayer and make offerings of incense and flowers in the numerous temple courtyards. It is an enchanting sight to see them attired in costumes of the most brilliant colours and balancing on their heads baskets of sweet-scented flowers.

The women of Thailand, Land of the Free, also adorn their heads with fragrant flowers, which form a natural enfleurage in the oil of the hair and give it a perpetual fragrance. At one time, the head of a well-born girl was cropped short except for a few strands of hair gathered into a knot on top of the head and held in place by a golden pin. This was surrounded with a small wreath of fragrant flower buds, freshly gathered each day.

From Thailand and the Indonesian islands comes the finest benzoin, which is employed in perfumery to give 'body' and permanence to an odour. It was used in the manufacture of Chinese joss-sticks and pastilles for burning in a sick-room and fumigating apartments. Benzoin is a resinous gum obtained by 'tapping' the tree Styrax benzoin when it has attained six years of age. The white

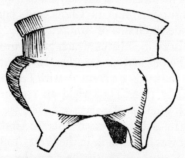

Chinese incense burner, A.D. 960

resin is similar to that of the rubber tree and each will produce about three pounds. Benzoin, or benjamin as it is called in perfumery, is used as incense in Buddhist and Hindu worship, and also burned by the wealthy in their homes.

In Burmese temples, where Buddha is worshipped, incense is burnt throughout the day and night. On the steps of the Shwe Dagon pagoda in Rangoon, 370 feet high and covered in sheets of pure gold, there are stalls filled with the scents of frangipani and

jasmine and with wax tapers and incense sticks made from sandalwood, which are purchased by those who have come to this most
famous of all Buddhist shrines. Inside, the air is thick with the
smoke of incense, and the people kneel in prayer among heaps of
scented blossoms.

In Japan, too, the aromatic sandalwood and jinko wood are burned
in shrines to Buddha, and this practice has influenced the Shinto
religion in the burning of incense and aromatic gums on all ceremonial
occasions, and during funeral rites, when the body is placed on a pile
of fragrant woods. These are set alight by the youngest member of
the family and all present throw scented gums and oils on the pyre.

Today, western perfumes are appreciated in the East but Ilang-
Ilang, the Flower of Flowers, distilled from Cananga odorata,
remains as fashionable as ever. The Cananga is a small, twiggy tree,
native of Burma, Malaya and south-east Asia, and from its incon-
spicuous dull yellow flowers a perfume is obtained with the scent of
Champac. It has the same spicy undertones present in the flowers of
the stock and pink and, for this reason, it is usually blended with otto
of pimento (allspice). Cananga oil is also used in the famous Macassar
oil which imparts its pleasing scent and fixative qualities to the hair.

Another favourite perfume in China and Japan is Ambrette,
known to the trade as Grains of Ambrette. The 'grains' are merely
the seeds of Hibiscus moschatus which grows in many parts of the
tropics of both the old and new worlds. It makes a dense bush six
feet tall, but only the seeds are scented, with a pronounced musk-like
perfume when fully ripe. They yield an essential oil which also
contains Farnesol, smelling of cedarwood. The seeds are ground into
a powder for use in sachets to place amongst clothes and, when the
powdering of hair was fashionable in the West, Ambrette powder was
mixed with starch to shake on the hair for the sake of its pleasant
perfume.

The Tagal women of the Philippine Islands pay particular
attention to their hair which is long and jet black and unusually
glossy, because they treat it daily with coconut oil to which is added
an essence of fragrant flowers. The women of Tahiti also use coconut oil, scented with sandalwood or with the extract of a heavily
scented root called Toromeo. Like most women of the South Pacific
islands, the tall, graceful Tahitians decorate their hair with fragrant
flowers, having a special fondness for the jasmine-scented tiare of

which the word tiara is a corruption. The islanders also rub over their bodies an oily preparation which they call monoi, which keeps the skin subtle and smooth and always sweet-smelling in the tropical heat. And the inhabitants of the Marquesas Islands have a great fondness for perfumes. Both sexes freely anoint themselves with scented oils or with papaya juice which similarly preserves the smoothness of the skin. Carved pins and earrings made from fish bones complete the coiffures of the women.

Where water and sanitation is limited, the eastern peoples have, since earliest times, made use of the natural scents which abound as nowhere else on earth. It is as if a benevolent Providence has made up for deficiencies in other ways, with the greatest generosity.

CHAPTER EIGHT

PERFUMES OF EUROPE—
FROM CHARLEMAGNE TO NAPOLEON

Charlemagne – The early French perfumers – First alcoholic perfume – Carmelite water – Beauty preparations of Italian women – Luxuries of the French court – Master Alexis and his creations – Napoleon and his love of eau de Cologne.

AT the height of her power, Rome received large quantities of perfumes and cosmetics from Gaul and sent her perfumers there to learn and to teach. With the expansion of the Roman Empire northwards, her knowledge and use of cosmetics and perfumes came to be copied by those they had conquered, for in the more northerly countries scented flowers and aromatic gums were a rarity. Gregory of Tours tells how Clotilda sought to increase her attractiveness by the use of balsams and unguents, and mentions that both the Franks and the Gauls made artificial wines from fragrant gums. Matthew de Courcy relates that, at a banquet given by Philip the Good of Burgundy, there was on a nearby table a bronze figure of a child from which spouted scented rose water.

When Clovis, first Christian king of France, was baptised at Rheims on Christmas Day, 496, incense was burned in the cathedral and fragrant tapers were lit and held by those in attendance. And from the *Chronicles* of William of Malmesbury, who was active at the end of the eleventh century, we learn that Hugh the Great, King of the Franks, after asking King Athelstan for the hand of his sister in marriage, dispatched to his majesty such magnificent presents 'as might gratify the most boundless avarice'. Amongst them were 'perfumes, the like of which had never been seen in England before; jewels, more especially emeralds; many horses with their trappings and champing their golden bits; an alabaster perfume vase so exquisitely chased that the cornfields really seemed to wave and the vines to bud'. In addition, the French king sent Athelstan several of his most prized possessions, guarded day and night by his trusted knights. These included the sword of Constantine the Great; an iron spike used for the crucifixion of Our Lord; and Charlemagne's spear. Athelstan was pleased to give the precious gifts to his favourite abbey of Malmesbury and it was, as William has said, 'that by these gifts, the place now flourishes.' Hugh did eventually take Athelstan's sister in marriage which turned out to be one of great happiness.

Charlemagne (768–814), who emerged from the dark ages and by his strength of character welded the barbaric hordes into a united Europe, was a particular lover of perfumes and of good living. He was crowned Emperor in Rome by Pope Leo III on Christmas Day, 800, and soon afterwards the Caliph Harun al Raschid sent from Baghdad to his court at Aix-la-Chapelle presents of the most costly perfumes, together with a magnificent white elephant. The early French kings imitated the Egyptians in having scents placed around them at their burial. Cedarwood boxes filled with fragrant gums and resins were laid in the coffin and the boxes left open so that the fragrant gums could perfume the body.

When, in 1140, Matilda, daughter of Henry I and rightful heir to the English throne following the death of Henry's son William, married Geoffrey, Count of Anjou, she received from the French people a magnificent silver peacock, its train set with pearls and precious stones, and filled with rose water. It was placed on the dining table and had a more utilitarian purpose than that of sprinkling the scented water on the guests for, after the meal, those who took part could rinse their hands in the perfumed water, a necessary ablution when it is remembered that food was eaten entirely with the hands. Forks were not invented until the middle of that century and it was not until the reign of James I that they were first used in England in the houses of the wealthy.

As long ago as 1190, just before the start of the Third Crusade, the perfumers of Paris were granted arms by Philip Augustus, who fully recognized their contribution to society. That perfumes were considered to be an essential part of Western culture was by then apparent and, in 1250, it was decreed that the Doge of Venice 'might receive no presents and no gifts from anyone, except offerings of rose water, and scented leaves and flowers and sweet herbs' (oddly, in the event of marriage he might receive only the gift of food).

5*

The first alcoholic perfume was obtained from a distillation of rosemary, which grows wild in southern Europe and particularly on the Mediterranean coast of Spain. These initial experiments were made in Hungary, in 1370, from a recipe given to Queen Elizabeth of Hungary by a hermit who told her that it would preserve her beauty until her death. The story appears in Beckmann's *History of Inventions*, a translation of a book published in Frankfort in 1639, and from it we learn that the hermit's recipe for beauty must have been highly successful for, at the age of seventy-two, the queen received an offer of marriage from the King of Poland. It may truly be said that hers was the first act of seduction by alcoholic perfume.

One hundredweight of rosemary will yield about twenty-four ounces of otto, and with its aromatic scent it is the most refreshing of all perfumes. It is used in Eau de Colognes which are of more complex blending, whereas the ingredients of Hungary Water, with the exception of the otto of lemon peel, may be obtained from ordinary garden plants. Its composition consists of a gallon of grape spirit; two ounces of otto of rosemary; one ounce each of otto of balm and lemon peel; a half drachm of otto of mint; and one pint each of extract of rose and orange flower. Should the orange flower extract prove difficult to obtain, it can be omitted and the esprit de rose increased to two pints. Hungary Water may be applied to the handkerchief and will refresh a tired mind, but its primary use is as a face wash or to add to bath water, when it will act as an invigorating tonic.

A toilet water possessing similar qualities was prepared by the nuns of the Carmelite abbey of St. Just, who took care of Charles V, King of France in 1379, when he was in advanced senility and shortly after the people of Brittany had risen against him. He apparently used the water in his daily bath and inhaled it to refresh his once-vigorous intellect during his declining years. So renowned did the water become that the nuns were requested to send samples to all parts of Europe, and their monastery achieved wide fame. The distillation became known as Carmelite Water and was an important addition to the toilet preparations of cultured men and women of mediaeval Europe. Its principal ingredient is balm, Melissa officinalis, which grows wild in central and southern Europe and which has become naturalized in the hedgerows of southern England. It was grown in every cottage garden in Elizabethan times, as its lemon-scented leaves were used for strewing and released their refreshing perfume when walked on, whilst the stems were woven into chaplets for ladies to wear.

Carmelite Water is made by taking two pounds of fresh balm leaves; a quarter of a pound of lemon peel; two ounces each of nutmeg, cloves, coriander seed, some cinnamon and angelica root. These are placed in a still with half a gallon of orange-flower water and a gallon of alcohol and slowly distilled until a gallon of the celebrated water is obtained.

The early French perfumers, to make their distillations, found use for all the fragrant leaves that grew wild and, by the fifteenth century, they had attained a position of standing. By patents granted on July 20, 1426 by Henry VI of England, who during the wars with France had also assumed the kingship of that country, the arms of the perfumers were registered in the Armorial General of France as 'Argent, three gloves [scented?] gules, chief azure, charged with a scent-box of gold'.

At the beginning of the fifteenth century, however, it was Italy rather than France which had become the centre of the perfume industry in Europe, and Venice in particular, with its palaces occupied by princely merchants and teeming with the luxuries that only wealth could buy. Some of the most expensive aromatics of the East reached the city through its trading connections with Constantinople, and the Venetians adopted all manner of preparations in their toilet and to improve their appearance. A book which appeared under the auspices of the Countess Nani contained many curious recipes, one of which described a method of dyeing the hair so that it would take on the glorious golden shade so much admired by Raphael and Titian. The colour was obtained by washing the hair with water distilled from a mixture of honey, alum and black sulphur; and Cesare Vecellio, Titian's cousin, has left us with a detailed explanation of how it was applied.

The ladies first soaked their heads in the preparation and then retired to the terraces of their houses for several hours to sit in the sun and allow the colouring to become thoroughly fixed. To protect the complexion, they would put on a straw hat which had a wide brim but no crown so that the hair was allowed to fall around the brim until it was quite dry.

Venice was to remain one of the most fashionable centres of

artistic development until the end of the sixteenth century. Writing in 1558, Matthiolus, after whom the Night-scented Stock is named, gives an account of the belladonna plant and of how the ladies would distil from it a water which dilated the pupils, making the eyes appear considerably larger. It was used at the French court during the seventeenth century and until the Revolution, though its application is believed to have resulted in several cases of blindness.

In Rome, the most popular perfume was Neroli, a distillate of the orange flower, prepared from the fresh blossoms of the bitter orange, the bigarade, one of the principal ingredients in Eau de Cologne. The plant first reached Europe in the twelfth century, brought by Portuguese sailors from the East Indies, and it is believed that the first orange to be planted in Rome was by St. Dominic in the year 1200. In France, the oldest known tree was raised from seed sent to the Queen of Navarre in 1421, and it grew in a tub in the orangery at Versailles until a century ago.

Neroli perfume derives its name from Flavio Orsini, Prince of Nerola, a member of a wealthy Roman family who in the sixteenth century took as his second wife Anne-Marie de la Trémoïlle-Noirmoutier. The distillate was greatly to her liking and she used it for scenting her bath and to perfume her gloves, copies of which became known in Rome as Guanti de Neroli. These gloves were famed throughout Europe and it is recorded that, in 1625, on his first visit to Rome, Nicolas Poussin the celebrated painter was entrusted by a M. de Chanteloup to procure for him a pair of the scented gloves, which he duly obtained from the shop of Signora Maddelena, then the most widely patronized of Roman perfumers. Poussin was so delighted with Rome that when he was recalled to France by Louis XIII in 1640 to decorate the Long Gallery of the Louvre, he was so unhappy away from his beloved Italy that he returned two years later, and there he remained until his death in Rome in 1665.

Since early in her history, Florence was famed for her perfumers and beauticians, and when Catherine de Medici made the journey to France to become the wife of Henry II in 1533 she took with her a Florentine skilled in the art of concocting perfumes, a man named René who opened a shop in Paris on the Pont au Change which soon became the meeting place of the fashionable. Also in Catherine's entourage was an alchemist, Cosimo Ruggiero, who made up her powders and possibly her poisons, for it was believed that she had prepared for Jeanne d'Albret, mother of Henry IV of France and Queen of Navarre, as a pledge of safe conduct, a pair of perfumed gloves which were also impregnated with a deadly poison and which the unfortunate woman was wearing at the time of her death.

The luxuries of Renaissance Italy had, however, reached France long before Catherine became queen, for in 1516 Leonardo da Vinci had arrived at the Court of Francis I whose dream it was to recreate the enlightened age of Charlemagne. Leonardo found Diana de Poitiers firmly installed there as the king's mistress at his official residence, the Chateau of Amboise on the Loire, and she was perhaps the leading patroness of perfumes of her time. The preservation of her beauty until old age enabled her to outstay her rivals in the king's affections until his death in 1547. A French writer of the time said that she had 'preserved in the autumn of her life, all the graces of her sex in its springtime' and, when Henry II ascended the throne, he too was to take as his mistress the ever-youthful Diana. Finally, though, she tired of her association with the French kings and, to console himself, Henry turned to more strenuous occupations, agreeing to take part in a tournament during which he was killed on July 29, 1559.

During the reign of Henry III, the amount of perfumes squandered at court was so enormous that their users, or abusers, came in for ridicule from the satirists. In his *Miroir des François*, published in 1582, Nicolas de Montaut reprimands the ladies of court for their extravagant use of 'all sorts of perfumes, cordial waters, civet, musk, ambergris and other precious aromatics to perfume their clothes and linen; even their whole bodies'.

Henry himself was a lover of perfumes and had prepared a violet-scented powder, consisting mainly of orris, to place amongst his linen and clothes. Other ingredients were the dried leaves of red roses, sandalwood, benjamin, storax, calamus root, cloves, ambergris, coriander and lavender which were powdered and mixed together and made into sachets.

Before the preparation of perfumes from scented flowers began, most of the substances used in perfumery were those which released their fragrance when dry; scented leaves and the bark and roots of trees were mixed with them. The clove, the dried fruit of the tree Caryophyllus aromaticus, native of the Molucca Islands, was included in most scented powders not only for its sweet aromatic perfume but for its germicidal qualities. It was believed to have the properties of warding off the plague and, indeed, Professor Chamberlain has discovered that the essential oil of cloves was able to destroy the typhoid bacillus within thirty minutes, and cinnamon within half that time.

The production of cloves was for long a monopoly of the French and their culture was introduced into the islands of Mauritius and Bourbon at an early date; the Swahili word for the clove, 'garafe', is a corruption of the French 'giroflier' or gilly-flower. From Bourbon, with the help and permission of the French, the culture of the clove spread to Zanzibar, which has supplied the bulk of the world's clove requirements during the past two centuries.

The clove tree will attain a height of about fifty feet, its spreading branches shading the ground about, and it can remain in bearing from five to a hundred years. The picking of the buds begins in August and continues until the end of the year, each tree being gone over once a month. The unexpanded buds are pinkish yellow when gathered and later turn dark red as they are spread out on mats to dry. 'Zanzibar red-heads' are the finest of all cloves, being much in demand for mixing in sachet powders, and their essential oil is entirely without the 'hot' taste and smell which is a characteristic of cloves of inferior quality.

The earliest book on perfumes, written in French, and entitled *Les secrets de Maistre Alexis de Piedmont* appeared in 1580, and it contains many strange ideas for making pomatum; pomanders to ward off the plague; odorous resins for burning in apartments; scented pastes for perfuming gloves; and numerous suggestions for dyeing the hair and making cosmetics. To concoct a toilet water guaranteed to make the ladies 'beautiful for ever', Master Alexis advised one 'to take a young raven from its nest, feed it on hard boiled eggs for forty days, kill it, then distill it with myrtle leaves, talcum powder and almond oil'. From which it would appear that the writer was more of an alchemist than a perfumer, and possibly obtained his recipes from Cosimo Ruggiero who was still an active member of Catherine de Medici's court.

Not all the recipes of Master Alexis were of such an eccentric nature. To perfume an apartment he suggests a 'Damask' scent made up of musk and ambergris, five grains of each; civet, two grains;

fine sugar four grains; benzoin, one grain; and storax, calamus and aloes-wood, three grains each. These should be powdered and placed in a perfume pan. Cover with Damask Rose Water 'as will be two fingers high' and place the pan over a low fire so that it will slowly simmer and release its delicious perfume about the apartment. Master Alexis says that when the rose water has evaporated, the same quantity may be used again and again to fill up the pan, over a period of several days.

Another way of perfuming a room was to make small scented 'cakes' to place on a low fire 'when you use or occupy the room, for it will make a singular good odour in the place where you burn it'. For this, his recipe consisted of five ounces of willow ash; one ounce each storax, calamint, benzoin and aloes-wood beaten into a powder and made into a paste with Aqua-vitae. The mixture is then made into a number of small cakes and allowed to dry hard, when they will burn slowly and fill the room with an aromatic fragrance. Where there was no fire in the room, a recipe was given for blending aromatic gums to burn over the low flame of a perfume lamp, so that the smoke would fill the room with 'a swete odour'.

To perfume chambers and garments 'belonging to any Prince', take citron-peel and civet and heat them on some coals—'but better if you add ambergris and musk'. The same aromatics, said Master Alexis, may be made into pills to place amongst linen and clothes.

To ward off the plague, the house should be fumigated with all manner of fragrant substances including rosemary, cloves, nutmeg and sage, aloes and juniper wood. The master perfumer also suggested the inclusion of 'pitch' which, in addition to the other ingredients, would create a pungent smell possessing powerful germicidal qualities. Pitch was frequently burnt in the streets of Paris to guard against plague.

To make little cushions of perfumed roses to place beneath the pillow, take and dry a quantity of red rose leaves, orris root and calamus, and pound with two grains each of ambergris, civet and musk, into a powder. The cushions are then filled with dried Damask rose petals and the powder sprinkled over them before the cushions are sewn up.

Alexandre Dumas gives an interesting account of René's perfume shop at the time of Catherine de Medici's death. It was then situated on the Pont Saint-Michel, one of a row of dwelling houses constructed entirely of wood, the lower façade being painted blue with mouldings of gold leaf. It was in the shop on the ground floor where the sale of perfumes, unguents and cosmetics took place. These were 'the articles of a skilful chemist' and from a staircase in the shop, leading to the first floor, a door opened to a small chamber which contained a stove, alembics, retorts and crucibles, the necessary tools of an alchemist's laboratory.

In the front part of the room were ibises from Egypt; mummies; death's heads with eyeless sockets. From the ceiling hung a stuffed crocodile. Behind a curtain were all manner of curious boxes and vases. The room was lit by two silver lamps supplied with fragrant oil which cast their yellow flame over the eerie place and its contents. Yet, in spite of its connections with witchcraft and sorcery, René's shop continued to serve the beaux and belles of Paris for many years, at least until the end of the seventeenth century. Even so, with the death of Henry III in 1589, and the extinction of those patrons of luxurious living the House of Valois, the use of perfumes and cosmetics gradually declined.

During the reign of Louis XIII and his queen, Anne of Austria, little interest was taken in perfumes at court. But though he was firmly opposed to the use of perfumes by others, Cardinal Richelieu delighted in having his room fumigated with perfumed powders applied by bellows and he is said to have been a firm believer in the use of perfumes to counteract the unpleasant smells of the sick room.

To make a powder for bellows, Philbert Guibert, Physician Regent in Paris, gives this recipe in *The Charitable Physician* (1629): Take iris root of Florence, half a pound; roses, four ounces; cyprus root, marjoram and cloves, one ounce each; yellow sanders and benjamin, of each four ounces; storax one ounce and beat them into a powder. The same may also be made into sachets to place amongst linen and was a favourite recipe of the royal household of the time.

Louis XIV, however, reversed the trend. He was dubbed the 'sweetest smelling monarch that had yet been seen', and was so fond of perfumes and luxurious living that he would insist on being in attendance on his perfumer while his scents were made up to his own requirements. This we learn from a rare book, *Le Parfumeur François*, published in 1680, which mentions that 'his Majesty was pleased to see Mons. Martial compose in his closet the odours which he wore on his sacred person'.

Dr. Theodor's *Medicinal Councels*, written during the lifetime of the king, describes the method of perfuming his majesty's shirts, which he would always insist upon having done and would not consider wearing if they had not been so treated. The relevant mixture, 'Aqua Angeli', consisted of aloes-wood, nutmegs, cloves, storax and benzoin, boiled in rose water 'of a quantity as may cover four fingers'. This was simmered over a gentle flame for a day and a night. Then the water of jasmine and orange flowers and a few grains of musk were added and the shirts were rinsed in the sweetly scented water.

So great was his love of perfumes that Louis arranged for a pavilion in blue and white to be built at Versailles, which he had filled with the most deliciously scented flowers, including orange blossom and the tuberose, stocks and white jasmine; in the short intervals between his love-making, Louis would be found amongst his favourite flowers, filling his lungs with their satisfying odours and perhaps gathering his strength for further amorous onslaughts.

Under Colbert, the Sun King's political adviser and the influential mind behind the expansion of French commerce in the seventeenth century, the 'parfumeurs-gantiers' obtained additional patents registered in the Parlement, which gave further proof of the important position they had by then acquired. And perfumes continued to increase in favour with the accession of Louis XV. Court etiquette demanded that, on each day, a different scent was to be worn, so that Versailles became known as 'la cour parfumée'. At Choisy, where Madame de Pompadour maintained a standard of elegance never before attained amongst the court favourites of Europe, perfumes were consumed on a stupendous scale and were the main item in the household expenses which usually amounted to more than half a million livres per annum. The Marquise sought to increase her powers of seduction by the use of the beauty spot, a tiny patch made of black or purple material which was first dipped in scent then stuck on the cheeks or breasts with gum. Later, facial ornaments consisted of half-moons and stars, and certain ladies of the court were known to have had a silhouette of a coach and horses fixed to the forehead. These artistic patches were first mentioned by Bulmer in 1650 in his book *The Artificial Changeling* and the idea was rapidly taken up by the beauties of the French courts, especially by those who had some small skin blemish to cover. Louis' favourite pastime was apparently to search for these beauty spots, which the Pompadour delighted in fixing on the most alluring parts of her body, and he derived much satisfaction from finding the hidden treasure.

Ladies kept their beauty spots in 'patch' boxes usually made of ebony or tortoise-shell and inlaid with mother of pearl to the design of flowers and fern leaves. These were about two inches square and one inch deep, so that they would fit into a reticule. The boxes were divided into three compartments, two of which held the patches, while there was also a brush made of badger's hair to remove any powder from the face before applying the 'spots'. In the lid was a small mirror which allowed the ladies discreetly to replace their 'spots' when the need arose, without leaving the room. These charming little patch boxes have now become collector's pieces, those commanding the highest prices being made in the mid-eighteenth century, during the reign of Louis XV, by Mathieu Philippe of Paris.

Scent bottles of exquisite taste also littered the boudoirs of every lady at court, as they had since early in the sixteenth century when the Duc de Nevers inaugurated the French glass-making industry, setting up a factory at Nevers where the making of scent bottles was a speciality. Later, at Orléans, Bernard Perrot made scent bottles of blue glass, embossed with the fleur-de-lis motif in gold.

Under Louis XIV scent bottles were made of imitation ivory or opaque glass and encased in hundreds of tiny glass beads to give the appearance of being covered by needlework. But by the reign of Louis XV they were usually made of clear glass, mounted in gold or in porcelain. The best examples came from Saint-Cloud which, before the founding of the Meissen factory, was the only porcelain manufactury in Europe.

This was the time when pot-pourri and perfume jars of exquisite workmanship were the principal attraction in the royal palaces and in the homes of the wealthy. Madame de Pompadour had made, for her private apartment in the Château de Bellevue, a pair of ormolu-mounted Japanese lacquer pot-pourris jars, which can now be seen in the Louvre; and in the Museum at Hamburg there is a most elegant two-handled Ludwigsburg pot-pourri jar, highlighted with rococo moulding and decorated in the style of Watteau, which gives some idea of the richness of eighteenth-century craftsmanship.

From the soft-paste porcelain factory of Chantilly, with its 'hunting horn' mark in red or blue, came some of the finest examples of the artist's creations in pot-pourri vases and incense burners. The incense containers were modelled in the style of tree trunks with a base of gilded bronze and were decorated with encrustations of foliage or flowers. The smoke rose from holes in the lid which was also of gilded bronze, topped with a motif of a spray of flowers or leaves.

Several of the German factories made their incense burners from hard paste, and these found their way into many European homes during the eighteenth century. In the collection of Mrs. K. Berger of New York there is a delightful example from the Bavarian Nymphenburg factory, made shortly after it had opened in 1755. Of rococo style and modelled on the small circular burners of Grecian days, the cap from which the smoke issues is hinged with gilded mounts which allow it to be opened for the incense to be placed inside. Set on three feet, it is a dainty and perfect example of the fine quality china which the factory produced.

It was considered necessary to beautify and make fragrant court apartments with sweetly scented flowers for hygiene was far from being adequate in keeping the rooms free from unpleasant smells.

The most fashionable flower of the French Court was the hyacinth, especially the double varieties which Madame de Pompadour decreed should be used indoors during winter and spring, a time when few other scented flowers were in bloom, and soon the double hyacinth, with its sweet balsamic perfume, had achieved as much notoriety for inflated prices as the streaked tulips.

The first double hyacinth had been raised in Holland by Peter Voerheim early in the eighteenth century and was named Mary, but it was soon lost to cultivation. Others followed in quick succession, as much as £200 or its equivalent in francs being paid for a new variety. These hyacinths had a rosette-like centre, tightly packed with petals so that they retained their beauty and perfume for many weeks. They were grown and brought into bloom entirely without soil, the bulbs being grown in handsome dishes made of pewter or porcelain, and made so that the base of the bulb was touching water. After keeping them in the dark for several weeks, they were introduced to the warmth of the apartments and soon came into bloom. James Justice, who introduced the pineapple into Scotland, wrote in 1754 a description of the new variety, Assemblage de

Beauté, which was then so popular with the French Court: 'its stem is not very high but is adorned with bells, some of which are broader than an English crown piece, erect and well reflexed, displaying a large heart [rosette centre] charmingly mixed with violet, scarlet and carnation [pink] colours . . .' Their culture was extremely simple. All that was necessary was to ensure that the base of the container was filled with water.

The French perfumers of the time sought to increase the sale of their products by making use of itinerant vendors who toured the country, visiting the larger towns with a horse and cart stocked with favourite perfumes and aids to beauty. Others dispensed their wares in the streets of Paris, from trays held by twine tied around the neck. Usually they sold quack medicines with their other wares and all kinds of pills and elixirs to cure every ailment under the sun. Jars of perfumed wax to rub on furniture and cheap soaps were popular lines. But these strolling perfumers became such a nuisance that, in the years immediately before the Revolution, the court physician asked the king to have them banished from the streets, and the perfumer's shop became a place of respectability once again.

The use of hair powder was very much in vogue at this time. The idea is believed to have been introduced by a lady of the court whose hair had turned prematurely grey and who may have wished to set a new fashion by introducing to court procedure an order that all should follow her example. The powders were scented, and were applied with bellows after the hair had been made up. This operation was usually carried out by the lady's maid or by her husband, standing on a stool so that the powder would reach all parts of the head. To make the powder stick, the hair was treated with macassar oil, then covered with buckwheat flour before the perfumed powder was blown on. To prevent the powder from being inhaled, it was usual to make a dunce's cap out of a sheet of paper which was held over the face. Afterwards, the powder was wiped from the shoulders. Powdering of the hair gave a pleasing softness to the features but it is not recorded how redheads reacted to the idea. In France and in England, the wealthy had special powder closets built, so as to prevent the powder from being blown about the rest of the house.

Powdering the hair remained in fashion until the end of the nine-teenth century and received fresh impetus in 1860 when, for the first time, the Empress Eugénie appeared at the Festival of Boeuf

Gras, her hair a mass of golden spangles. Poudre d'or, which consisted of minute particles of crushed gold leaf, created a new wave of fashion in hair decoration, and those who could not afford to use gold leaf used a powder made of coarse bronze.

Rouge was also used in large quantities by the fashionable, as indeed it has been since Jezebel painted her face to attract Jehu. In his *Decline and Fall of the Roman Empire*, Gibbon describes how the Emperor Elagabalus, on first entering the eternal city, had his eyebrows tinted black and his cheeks painted with red. And the first present given to Catherine de Medici by the Dowager Queen of France upon her arrival at court was a pot containing rouge, to give colour to her lifeless complexion. Rouge was intended to impart the colour of the much admired red rose and was so popular a facial decoration during the reign of George III as to suffer Swift's biting sarcasm. It was at this time that the famous French carmines were replaced in English beauty salons by the red clay obtained at Rugeley in Staffordshire.

When, in 1770, Marie Antoinette became the wife of the future Louis XVI, she set a new fashion by her love of the more natural perfumes, distilled from the violet and rose, neglecting the heavier Eastern scents. In court circles, the fragrant bath became an important part of a lady's toilet and endured sarcastic treatment from the pen of Voltaire. Mme Tallien went so far as to bathe in crushed strawberries when in season, and like Nero's Poppaea washed herself in perfumed milk. Not unnaturally, at the time of the Revolution little interest was taken in the use of perfumes but, when Bonaparte was crowned Emperor in 1804, his love of sweet-smelling substances gave perfumery a new popularity.

In the records of Chardin, his perfumer, there is an amount for a large bottle of Spanish jasmine which the Emperor may have purchased as a gift for his wife Josephine, since his own preference was for Eau de Cologne which he used extravagantly throughout his life. He appreciated its cooling qualities and, after washing, would pour it over his neck and shoulders. Mme de Rémusat states that he had a standing order with his perfumer to deliver fifty 'rouleaux' (bottles) a month. A quarterly bill for 1806 shows that Chardin supplied 162 bottles of Eau de Cologne costing 423 francs; twenty-six pots of almond paste for 355 francs; and twenty sponges which cost 262 francs. Another quarterly account for 1810 shows that he had been supplied with 144 bottles of Eau de Cologne. Later, there is a bill for supplying 108 cases, each of six bottles, of an 'improved' quality, which may mean that it had been made specially to his requirements and was stronger than normal. Napoleon greatly loved the scent of rosemary which is present in Eau de Cologne; he knew it well since it abounds along the cliffs and scrubland of southern Europe and on his native island of Corsica.

Eau de Cologne consists of the otto of neroli and other orange ottos, mixed with otto of rosemary and bergamot and dissolved in spirit. Bergamot was produced in Lombardy, from plantations of the Bergamo orange which grew near the city bearing that name. During Napoleon's lifetime, the demand was such that the perfumers of Paris could never obtain enough. The greenish-tinted otto has a refreshing smell, like that of rosemary, and is obtained from the rind of the pear-shaped fruit. Mixed with rectified spirit, it forms 'extract of bergamot', which was once widely used on handkerchiefs.

The finest French product, like the best Cognac, is made with grape spirit, which gives the true Eau de Cologne its own particular scent (due to the oenanthic ether it contains). It is essentially a man's perfume, used in modern 'after-shave' lotions, hence its appeal to Napoleon.

Eau de Cologne began as 'Aqua Admirabilis' at the beginning of the eighteenth century when the brothers Johann Maria and Johann Baptiste Farina moved their business from Santa Maria Maggiore in Italy to open a fancy-goods business in Cologne. The cordial water they made achieved considerable popularity during the Seven Years War, the troops quartered in Cologne taking away supplies for their families at home when peace was eventually declared. By the middle of the century, the Farina brothers' elixir had become world-famous and was known as Eau de Cologne after the city of its origin. It has retained its popularity ever since.

After his return from exile in Elba, Napoleon transferred his business to Jacques Tessier at the Sign of the Golden Ball in the Rue Richelieu and once more resumed his orders for his favourite perfume and for the white Windsor soap which he used throughout his adult life. This also contained rosemary, in addition to otto of caraway, thyme and clove, all plants which grew in the south of France or in French possessions overseas.

Perhaps the almond cream which figures in several bills for

perfumes was for the use of Josephine, the creole daughter of an Orléans merchant who had settled in the French colony of Martinique where the natives had a fondness for the fragrant oils and creams of almond and coconut which they continually massaged into the skin. Josephine was already the leader of Paris society when she married Napoleon, in a civil ceremony in 1796. In 1810, her marriage was declared null and void and thereafter she lived at Malmaison, where she died four years later. She delighted in the scent of violets, using the perfume whenever possible. Napoleon had her grave covered with the plants and, shortly before he was finally exiled, picked flowers from it, which after his own death were found in a locket he always wore around his neck.

Josephine also followed the fashion of keeping pots of scented flowers in her rooms. She was particularly fond of hyacinths and of mignonette with its violet-like scent. Napoleon sent her some seed of this plant direct from Egypt, its natural home, where he had collected it during his campaigns, and it soon became a popular flower with the French aristocracy. It was grown in the nursery gardens around Paris, not only to make posies for evening wear but also to fill pots for placing on verandahs for the perfume was so powerful it obliterated the offensive odours of the streets. The French named it 'Little Darling' because of its sweet scent and the plant became as popular in England as it was in France. Writing in 1830, Henry Phillips said that even those who considered the fragrance of the flower too powerful to have in the home 'must be delighted with the scent it throws from the balconies into the streets, giving a breath of garden air to close-pent man.'

CHAPTER NINE

THE SCENTS AND SMELLS
OF EARLY ENGLAND

The refined tastes of the Romans – Incense and the early Church – Rushes for strewing – To fumigate apartments – Perfumes of Elizabethan times – Pomanders – Elizabeth and her scented gloves – Early scent bottles.

THE toilet of the ancient Britons consisted of painting the body as a protection against adverse weather and as a means of distinguishing a freeman from a slave. Later, when the freeman carried arms, they transferred the designs from the body to the shield, which may be the origin of family arms and armorial design.

The first occupants of northern England were the Picts (from the Latin 'picti', painted), a people famed for the remarkable decorations of their bodies. Like the Gauls, they dyed their breasts red so as to deceive the enemy into thinking that they had been wounded. In his *Natural History*, Pliny speaks of Glastrum, a plantain with which the Gauls and ancient Britons stained their bodies. And Diodorus Siculus says that hair dyes were known in early Britain and tells that the naturally auburn hair of the people was made redder by frequent applications of boiled lime water.

The Roman conquest of Gaul and Britain brought with it the civilized manners of the Romans with their love of scents and cosmetics, their graceful clothes and luxurious bathing; but this lasted only during the time of their occupation. As there were few scented flowers and leaves growing in the British Isles, it was left to the Romans to introduce the plants which grew in the warmer climes of southern Europe, and which were used by the inhabitants to flavour food and drinks, and to make toilet waters for body cleanliness. Saffron in particular was well known to the Romans for it was the principal ingredient of their most celebrated fluid unguent, Susinum, and either the plant or the finished product would most surely have been imported at the time of the invasion, to be re-introduced for its commercial attractions during the reign of Edward III. Saffron is mentioned in an Anglo-Saxon leechbook—'when he bathes, let him smear himself with oil mingled with saffron'—and this was the method employed by the wealthy Romans to keep their bodies subtle and sweet-smelling.

To make toilet waters, which the Romans used on a lavish scale, the Red Rose (Rosa gallica) and lavender, which they took with them into Gaul, would most certainly have accompanied them to Britain, maybe first as dried leaves and petals, later as plants, for they are known to have been grown in Britain since very early in her history. With the leaves and stems of the lavender steeped in water, the Romans freshened their bodies; and so popular was lavender water for washing clothes that, at an early date, a laundress was known as a 'lavendre'. Keats's Madelaine slept between linen that had been 'smoothed and lavender'd', and in southern Italy today, the house-wife will hang her washing on bushes of rosemary and lavender which impart their aromatic fragrance to the clothes whilst drying.

In *The Garden of Health* (1579), William Langham wrote, 'Boil it in water, wet thy shirt in it, dry it again and wear it'; and because of its fresh sweet smell, lavender was grown in every countryman's garden until the beginning of the nineteenth century. Dr. Turner, Dean of Wells, suggested the delightful idea of placing the dried flowers and leaves in the front of one's cap 'to comfort the brain', in the same way that, in warm weather, the smell of lavender on the handkerchief will, in Parkinson's words, 'pierce the senses' in a most refreshing manner. In *A Winter's Tale* Shakespeare referred to 'hot' lavender, mints, savory and marjoram, all these being plants of southern Europe valued for their invigorating qualities in warm weather.

Mint, too, was introduced by the Romans and was used in much the same way, to wash the body and to impart its keen, piercing smell to clothes when rinsed in its water. Both lavender and pepper-mint were made into bunches and placed in bedrooms because of their ability to absorb heat by their odorous vapours; they kept a room cool and fragrant in summer, and masked insanitary odours.

Izaak Walton has painted a delightful picture of the 'honest ale-house' of his time, where he found a clean room to his liking with lavender on the sill, for it was the custom to have pots of lavender and rosemary, and scented leaved plants, growing in the window of every village inn. On another occasion during his angling expeditions, he wrote: 'Let's go to that house for the linen looks white and smells of lavender, and I long to be in a pair of sheets that smell so.'

'Buy my sweet lavender, two bunches a penny' was one of the cries of old London and every part of the bunch was made use of, even the stems which, when dried and set alight, burn slowly for hours releasing the familiar smell about the sick room. In early Roman history, the stems were burnt as incense, to honour the deities, and lavender may have been 'the incense' referred to in a riddle which appears in the Anglo-Saxon Exeter Book which begins:

> I am much sweeter than incense or the rose,
> That so pleasantly on the earth's turf blows . . .

Since the beginning of the Christian Church in England, incense and fragrant flowers have played an important part in the ceremony of worship on all special occasions. When Edward the Confessor's first abbey of Westminster was consecrated on December 28, 1065, incense was burned and hyssop was strewn over the floor whilst in the wardrobe accounts of Edward I for the Feast of the Epiphany, January 6, 1299, there is an entry for gold, frankincense and myrrh, offered by the king in his Chapel Royal. Incense and fragrant tapers burned in religious places everywhere. Erasmus, who visited the shrine of Our Lady at Walsingham in 1511, said: 'There is little or no light in it but what proceeds from wax tapers yielding a most pleasant and odoriferous smell . . .'. And in the *Historie de Episcopis*, Wharton says that when Roger de Walden was made Bishop of St. Paul's in 1405, he was crowned with a garland of scented red roses.

The garden attached to the abbey church was under the care of the sacristan whose duty it was to provide flowers for feast days throughout the year. In the accounts of 1483 for the church of St. Mary-at-Hill, London, where beneath the altar is buried John Brand, the antiquary who spent most of his lifetime describing the interesting customs of his beloved England, there is an item 'for garlandes' on Corpus Christi Day amounting to 8½d. In the same accounts, there is an item for woodruff for St. Barnabas' Day, to decorate the church, for as Gerard said, 'it does make fresh the place, to the delight and comfort of such as there are therein.' The fragrant leaves of agrimony and woodruff were also used for filling pillows and cushions for their fragrance increased the drier the leaves became.

In a similar way, dried hops were also used for, besides their pleasing fragrance, they have a slight narcotic effect, encouraging sound sleep. It is said that George III always slept on a hop pillow.

Incense continued to be burnt in churches until the Reformation when, officially, it was prohibited though numerous extracts have survived which tell that in several churches its use continued uninterrupted. In Malcolm's *Londinium Redivivum* (1603) it is recorded that two pounds of frankincense were burnt in the church of St. Augustine, Farringdon-Within, and in George Herbert's *Priest to the Temple*, the writer mentions that amongst the duties of the wardens was to 'keep the church clean without dust or cobwebs and that at festivals, it must be strewed and stuck with boughs, and perfumed with incense'. On such occasions, it was usual for the lord of the manor, his lady and members of his household to be in attendance, and to counteract the musty smell of the stone floor it was covered with fragrant rushes and leaves.

Pegge's *Curalia* records that at the Court of King Stephen, and in the homes of his knights upon occasions of feasting, the floors were strewn with flowers and rushes, and that when Thomas à Becket was made Archbishop of Canterbury, he ordered his hall to be strewn each day, in spring with fresh May blossom; in summer, with sweet-scented rushes '... that such knights as the benches could not contain, might sit on the floor without dirtying their clothes'. The reason for May blossom being thought to bring misfortune when taken indoors is because of its unpleasant smell after the fertilization of the flowers; this is due to trimethylamine (which smells like decaying fish) which is present in the early stages of putrefaction. 'The Hawthorn has a deathly smell,' wrote Walter de la Mare, and to Thomas of Canterbury it certainly brought great misfortune.

Germander and hyssop were amongst the most common plants then used for strewing and, in the wealthiest churches, 'rushes' were also used. As has already been noted, these were the stems and leaves of the Sweet Flag, Acorus calamus, which grew only in the fenlands of Norfolk and Cambridgeshire and in low-lying areas of Europe, because of which they were obtained at great cost. At the church of St. Mary Redcliffe, Bristol, which Queen Elizabeth I described as 'the fairest, goodliest and most famous parish church in all England', the strewing of rushes on Whit Sunday is a custom maintained to this day.

The stems and leaves of the Sweet Flag, known to the Saxons as the Beewort, release a refreshing lemony smell when trodden on, and its roots, dried and crushed, were once used in England as a toilet powder after its essential oil had been combined with a farinaceous substance. For this reason, it enters into the composition of modern sachet powders for placing amongst linen and clothes. The essential oil, which was also used to flavour snuffs, has an aromatic camphoraceous smell which is highly persistent. To the druggists it is known as radix calimi aromatici.

All plants with sweet-smelling leaves and stems were used to strew over the floor of church and manor, since buildings had no damp courses in mediaeval England and rooms usually had a musty smell about them. Herbs and rushes were also used for the servants to sit upon for only the lord of the manor and his family were privileged to eat at high table. There are records of payments made in 1226 for the sum of 'twelve pence, to provide rushes for the baron's chamber' and, in 1516, for 'flowers and rushes for the chambers of Henry VIII'. Robert Herrick wrote of 'Green rushes then and sweetest bents to re-adorn the house.' Later, a pleasing custom of the time was to strew scented flowers and leaves in those church pews used by the lord of the manor and his household; this is alluded to in a play, *Apius and Virginia*:

> Thou knave but for thee 'ere this time of day
> My lady's fair pew had been strewed full gay
> With primroses, cowslips and violets sweet,
> With mints and marigold, and marjoram meet.

It was Thomas Tusser, an Essex man who as a boy sang in the choir of old St. Paul's, who gave the most practical instruction on the growing and strewing of all plants with scented leaves. Tusser was born at Rivenhall in Essex in 1525 and was educated at Eton College and Cambridge from where he 'came to Court' and remained there for ten years. He then took a farm at Cattiwade and in 1557 published his *One Hundred Points of Good Husbandry* in which he gives advice on garden cultivation, on housekeeping; how to keep Christmas; and how to treat one's wife and servants. Later he enlarged on his original work which now became known as *Five Hundred Points of Good Husbandry* and was published in 1573. He died in 1580 and was buried in St. Mildred's in the Poultry. Fuller said of him: 'Whether he bought or sold, he lost . . . yet hath he laid down excellent rules in his book of husbandry and housewifry. He spread his bread with all sorts of butter, yet none would stick thereon.'

Amongst twenty plants he recommended for strewing to release their refreshing perfume when trodden upon were basil and balm; camomile and costmery; lavender and hyssop; sage and thyme. Surprisingly he makes no mention of meadowsweet which Elizabeth I most enjoyed to have on the floor of her apartments. So desirous was the Queen of having a regular supply of herbs for strewing, that a woman was appointed to her household with a fixed salary and for the sole purpose of having suitable plants in their season always in readiness. To this day one can see at Greenwich a bill paid by Elizabeth which includes the sum of 1s. 4d. for 'strewing herbs' and 6d. for 'flowers for pots in the windows of the houses', placed there to give a special welcome to the bands of the City who were to entertain Her Majesty with a special display.

Of meadowsweet, Gerard said that 'the leaves far excell all other strewing herbs to deck up houses, to strew in chambers, hall and banqueting houses in summertime, for the smell thereof makes the heart merry and joyful and delighteth the senses'. Parkinson, who dedicated his *Paradisus* to Queen Henriette Maria, enjoyed its 'pretty, sharp scent' and said that 'a leaf or two in a cup of wine will give as quick and fine a relish thereto as burnet will'. Both the leaves and flowers were used in pot-pourris to scent a room for they will retain their aromatic perfume for many months and this actually increases in strength as they dry.

Parkinson also said of wild thyme that 'there is no herb of more use in the houses of high and low . . . for bathing, for strewing and to make sauces for fish and flesh, whilst Marjoram', he said, was much in demand by the ladies 'to put in nosegays and to use in sweet powders, sweet bags and sweet smelling waters'. Of these plants, Parkinson wrote: 'We preserve them with all the care we can for the sweet and pleasant smells they yield.'

'To use in nosegays', the Wallflower was one of the most beloved of plants. 'The sweetness of the flowers causeth them to make nosegays of and to deck up houses,' wrote Parkinson and, because the flowers were carried in the hand for smelling, it was given the name Cheiranthus, hand flower. To earlier gardeners it was called

chevisaunce, an Anglo-Saxon word meaning 'Comforter' for it
brought comfort to a weary mind. Edmund Spenser wrote of 'the
pretty paunce [pansy] and the chevisaunce'. The Sweet William,
too, was used in a similar way, and like the Wallflower may have
reached England with the Conquest for it grew on rocky outcrops in
Brittany and Normandy. Gerard said that it was 'not used either
in mete or medicine but as esteemed only for its beauty and scent,
to deck up gardens and the bosoms of the beautiful.'

In his *Description of England*, William Harrison mentions a Dr.
Lemnius, a Dutch physician who, when on a visit to this country in
1560, told of the great pleasure he had from seeing the fine furniture
which he found in so many homes, and said that 'their chambers and
parlours strewed over with sweet herbs, much refreshed me'. The
doctor also mentioned the pots of lavender and rosemary he saw
suspended from the walls and ceilings in several homes, there for
their cooling qualities rather than for their perfume.

The furniture Dr. Lemnius so enthused over would have had
their brilliant gloss and sweet perfume from constant rubbing with
balm. This was not the celebrated Balm of Gilead but the juice of
Melissa officinalis, the herb used in the making of Carmelite
Water. In *The Merry Wives of Windsor*, Shakespeare alludes to the
practice of rubbing the juice on furniture when, in the final scene
in the Great Park, Mistress Page gives her famous 'Garter' speech:

> The several chairs of order look you scour
> With juice of balm, and every precious flower:
> Each fair instalment, coat, and several crest,
> With loyal blazon, evermore be bless'd;
> And nightly, meadow fairies, look, you sing
> Like to the Garter's compass, in a ring.

The seeds of Sweet Cicely or Sweet Fern, a perennial plant of
northern European pastureland, were also used to rub on furniture
and to polish oak floors and panelling, to which they would impart a
glossy 'finish' and a myrrh-like scent. The leaves were used in
salads, to which they imparted a sweet, aromatic taste.

The obnoxious smells of badly drained streets, and of houses in
which there was little sanitation by modern standards, compelled
the use of herbs for strewing until the end of the eighteenth century;
but in the more important religious festivals and on other special

occasions, herbs were strewn more to perpetuate a custom than to suppress unpleasant odours.

At the time of the accession of James II, one Mary Vowle was appointed 'strewer of Herbs in Ordinary to His Majesty' and, before the coronation ceremony in Westminster Abbey, she received instructions from the Lord Almoner to spread two breadths of blue broadcloth from the stone steps in the hall to the foot of the steps in the choir, 'which cloth is to be strewn with nine baskets full of sweet herbs and flowers.'

Rue was much in demand for strewing since it kept away fleas which were thought to be carriers of plague. As a reminder of this, boys of Christ's Hospital each year walk before the Skinners' Company carrying bouquets of scented flowers and leaves. The ceremony takes place on St. Matthew's Day (September 21), when at eleven o'clock at St. Sepulchre's, Holborn, a service is held attended by the Lord Mayor, Sheriffs and Aldermen, together with the Bluecoat Boys from the famous Horsham school, and twenty-five girls from the Hertford school. After the service, the procession of 300 pupils, headed by the school band, marches to the Mansion House where each boy receives a gift from the Lord Mayor.

Bouquets of fragrant flowers and sweetly scented herbs are also carried at the Road Sweeping ceremony of the Vintners' Company which takes place in July. Following the installation of the new Master of the Vintners, the procession goes from the Vintners' Hall to the Church of St. James's Garlickhythe, it is headed by the Wine Porters in their white smocks who, with their brooms, sweep a passage clean for the members of the Court who carry bouquets 'lest they do slip in mire or their nostrils be offended by mal odours'.

In 1750, rue was used to strew the dock of the Central Criminal Court at the Old Bailey as protection against jail fever which at the time was raging in Newgate Prison, and the custom continued until the present century. Today in the London criminal courts, judges are still sometimes presented with bouquets of wild flowers, whilst aromatic leaves are strewn over the tables as a reminder of the days when judges everywhere were given sweetly scented flowers to counteract the unpleasant odours of the prisoners. And the aldermen who walk in procession to elect a new Lord Mayor of London carry bouquets of flowers.

In the coronation procession of George III, the King's groom of the vestry appeared dressed in scarlet and holding a perfume pan in which were burning aromatics 'as at previous coronations'. The perfume pan contained any of the resinous gums and preparations that would burn readily and provide a pleasing fumigation. The pastilles made for this purpose were for many years known as 'osselets of Cyprus' because, during the Crusades, Richard I had proclaimed himself King of Cyprus and, for some considerable time afterwards, a number of fragrant gums were brought into England from the Mediterranean island, for burning in perfume pans in church and manor.

Dr. Turner, a Northumberland man born at Morpeth, who at one time was physician to the Protector Somerset, gives in his *Herbal* (1551) many delightful instructions for scenting a house. The learned doctor says that if southernwood is burnt in a room, it will not only make the room fragrant with its pungent smoke but will 'drive away serpents' lurking in corners. This may be taken to mean frogs and toads and other unsavoury creatures which often sought shelter from the heat of the day within the damp, dark walls of castle and cottage.

Ben Jonson, in his masque *Chloridia*, asks: 'Have you smelled the bud of the briar or the nard on the fire?' Here, the reference would be to any of the sweet-smelling woods or roots which, when dry, were thrown on a low fire to scent a room. Most of these fumigants were to be obtained from the countryside at little or no cost, and even the cottager could scent his humble abode. A plant which was a particular favourite was Inula conyza. Both its flowers and leaves emit a refreshing perfume, but it was for the burning of its roots that it was most esteemed, and because of their scent the plant came to be known as Ploughman's Spikenard. In Scotland where the Scots Pine grew everywhere, the Highlanders cut the roots into thick 'candles' which, when lighted, burnt with a low flame, providing both light and a sweet aromatic fragrance to the cottage home.

Seeds of several plants readily obtainable from hedgerow and field were also used for burning and would diffuse their aromatic scents about the home. In his *Calendar for Gardening* (1661), Stevenson suggests that one should 'be sure every morning to perfume the house with angelica seeds, burnt in a fire-pan or chafing dish of coales'. This handsome herb, Angelica officinalis, native of the northern hemisphere, has purple stems covered in a grape-like 'bloom' and, if cut when young, they will impart a musky flavour to stewed apples or rhubarb. From the seeds, an essential oil is obtained which has a similar musk-like smell and is used by the monks of La Grande-Chartreuse in making their celebrated emerald liqueur. 'The whole plant, leaf, roots and seed is of an excellent comfortable scent, savor and taste,' wrote Parkinson.

A recipe to make 'an odoriferous perfume for chambers' appears in a small book by an unknown writer entitled '*A Queen's Delight*'; it was published towards the end of the year in which Charles II married Catherine of Braganza and the recipe is believed to have been used to scent her apartments. It consists of a glassful of rose water to which clove powder is added 'little by little until it is all consumed when you shall make a perfume of excellent good order'. Mary Doggett, in her *Book of Receipts* (1682), suggests warming rose petals with orris root, to scent a room. The flowers of the red rose, which increased in perfume as they became dry, possessed similar properties to herbs and so were usually included in all herbal pot-pourris.

Another recipe was given by Mary Eales, Confectioner to Queen Anne. It is to take three spoonfuls of dried rosemary and as much sugar as half a walnut beaten into a powder. Then place this in a perfuming pan upon hot embers and the room will be filled with a sweet aromatic perfume. Queen Anne is said to have particularly loved the smell of rosemary.

Robert Burton, in his *Anatomy of Melancholy* (1676), said that the smoke of juniper wood was in great demand with the students at Oxford 'to sweeten our chambers'; and Ben Jonson, some years earlier, also found the wood excellent to fumigate a room. Of the attentive husband he says: 'He doth sacrifice twopence in juniper to her every morning before she rises to sweeten the room by burning it' and the expense must have been considered well worth while. Later, the resinous juniper wood was used for making spoons and forks, to impart its sweet, aromatic scent to food.

To provide night warmth, a glowing fire kept alight with fragrant woods burnt throughout the hours of darkness in the bedrooms of the wealthy. Here, in the privacy of his room, the King would often attend to affairs of state until the early hours. In the second part of Shakespeare's *Henry IV*, while his subjects were fast asleep, the King sends his page to summon the Earls of Surrey and Warwick
6

to hasten to his perfumed chamber, wondering why he is so troubled
with the affairs of state that

> Nature's soft nurse . . .
> . . . no more wilt weigh my eyelids down
> And steep my senses in forgetfulness.

During the brief reign of Edward VI, his apartments were always
kept pleasantly scented. First the foul air was cleared away by
burning juniper or cypress wood; then the room was made to smell as
though it were filled with roses by burning over hot embers 'twelve
spoonsful of red rose water into which is added the weight of a
sixpence of fine sugar'. Fragrant woods and roots were also used to
impart their perfume to clothes and linen. 'Now are the lawn
sheets fumed with violets,' says Marston in *What you Will*, and here
the reference would surely be to burning elecampane roots. The
elecampane is a handsome native plant which bears a bloom like
that of a sunflower and has orris-scented roots. When dry and
burned, they do indeed release a violet-like perfume.

During Elizabethan times, servants were employed for the sole
task of fumigating rooms—which, in the many-roomed castles and
manor houses, fully occupied their time. Professional perfumers also
travelled the country, calling at the homes of the wealthy to carry
out the task of fumigation; 'Selling rotten wood by the pound, like
spices, which gentlemen burn by the ounce,' according to Beaumont
and Fletcher in *Wit Without Money*. In Shakespeare's *Much Ado
About Nothing*, upon being asked how he comes to be in the palace,
Borachio replies that he was 'being entertained for a perfumer. As
I was smoking a musty room, comes me the prince and Claudio,
hand in hand in sad conference'. Rooms that had been closed up for
any length of time, and were to be re-opened for a guest, would
usually require fumigating before being made ready. In his *Delights
for Ladies* (1594), Sir Hugh Platt, 'Knight of Lincoln's Inn, Gentleman,' gave details for retaining the scent of rose water and for
retaining the perfume of a pot-pourri: 'you should hang your pot in
an open chimney or near a continual fire so that the petals will keep
exceeding fair in colour and be most delicate in scent.'

The returning Crusaders brought back with them from the Near
East many fragrant roots, seeds and gums, amongst which were
seeds of the Love-in-a-Mist, which takes its name from the manner in

which the grey-blue flowers are surrounded by a feathery green ruff. Nigella sativa is an annual plant with seeds smelling like nutmeg. If placed in a muslin bag by a fire, they will release their spicy scent for several weeks, after which the seeds should be renewed.

Love-in-a-Mist is one of the oldest plants known to man still in commercial use. In the time of the Pharaohs, the seeds were added to bread and cakes, as they are to this day in Eastern countries; and in classical Rome, they were used to impart their nutmeg flavour to cheese. Apothecaries extracted a fragrant oil from the seed which was used in unguents as a substitute for the more expensive spikenard. The ladies of ancient Egypt consumed the seeds in large amounts, in the belief that they would bring about the much desired plumpness to their breasts; and in Tudor times, the powdered seed was rubbed into the hair, since lice could not abide its spicy scent.

The ancient Eastern custom of sprinkling one's clothes with rose water was also prevalent in the sixteenth century, and in Marston's play, *Antonio and Mallida*, a dashing young gallant enters holding a 'casting' bottle filled with sweet perfume which he pours over his head and clothes. Later in the play, mention is made of a 'barber's casting bottle' which was used by those who followed this trade, to scent the hair after its cutting. The bottle was made of porcelain and around the top were a number of small holes so that it resembled a sugar caster. In a play called *The Fancies*, John Ford, the last of the great Elizabethan playwrights, introduces a dandy who sprinkles scented water on to his hair and continually looks at his face in a mirror, which he carries fastened to his girdle.

Sir Hugh Platt gives, in his *Delights*, instructions for sweet water for a 'casting bottle'. To rose water he suggests adding three drams of spikenard oil; one dram each of oil of thyme, lemon and cloves, together with a grain of civet, which must be shaken well together before being placed in the bottle.

In Elizabethan times, it was a common practice to sprinkle rose and other fragrant waters on the floors of apartments whenever necessary. In Marlow's *Doctor Faustus*, Pride complains, 'Fye, what a smell is here, I'll not speak another word for a king's ransom, unless the ground is perfumed.' And in *A Winter's Tale*, the beggar Autolycus sings out a list of the wares he carries around the countryside to earn a few pence and which he takes from door to door according to the custom of the time. He has arrived at the shepherd's cottage and, amongst other things to sell, he has

> Bugle-bracelet, necklace amber,
> Perfume for a lady's chamber:

This would be a cheap scented water to sprinkle over the floor, possibly made from the roots of native plants which were readily available about the countryside. One of these was Sedum rhodiola, known as Roseroot since its roots yield the fragrance of the rose. It grew in every cottage garden and on old walls and cliffs.

Tinkers included amongst their wares bracelets and necklaces made of scented gums which, after setting hard, were threaded on to lengths of twine. In a manuscript in the British Museum, Mary Doggett says that the 'beads' should be made as large as nutmegs and coloured with lamp-black. As the 'beads' were being fashioned, oil of jasmine was poured on to the hands and this gave the 'beads' a brilliant gloss.

Pomanders were also carried by the tinkers during Shakespeare's time. Autolycus says, 'I have sold all my trumpery; not a counterfeit stone, not a ribbon, glass, pomander, brooch, ballad, knife, tape, glove . . . to keep my pack from fasting.' They first came to be used in France, possibly as a protection against the plague. Henry V, victor of Agincourt, carried with him 'a musk ball of gold' which he may have obtained during his French campaign. This was a ball of musk-smelling amber (pomme d'ambre), which was later replaced by dried oranges stuck with cloves, like the one which Cardinal Wolsey carried with him on his visiting days, tied to his belt. George Cavendish, usher to the Cardinal, who was so devoted to him that he continued to serve him even during the period of the Cardinal's disgrace and until his death, has left a graphic description of Wolsey and his pomander which, near the end of his term of office, was filled with a sponge soaked in scented vinegar. This was to give protection 'against the pestilent airs, the which he most commonly smelt unto, passing among the press, or else he was pestered with many suitors'.

In the well-known portrait of Sir Thomas Gresham by Sir Antonio More, the sitter holds in his left hand an orange pomander; and in the Wallace Collection in London there is a painting by Cornelio de Vos which depicts a Flemish lady of wealth holding a pomander in her hand. In the entrance room of the Shakespeare Museum at Stratford-on-Avon, hangs a portrait of a gentleman which clearly shows an orange pomander suspended from his belt, which would have been stuffed with cloves and other spices. These were carried and frequently smelled by those, such as doctors and priests, who came in direct contact with the poor; and, when removed from the belt indoors, were hung up in the bedroom or sitting-room, which would soon become filled with their aromatic fragrance.

Elizabeth I usually carried with her a pomander made in the shape of a ball composed of ambergris and benzoin, and showed her obvious delight when once presented with 'a faire gyrdle of pomanders' (this was really a number of small pomanders, strung together and worn around the neck). Later, pomanders were made of silver or gold and worn as a pendant to a lady's girdle. They were constructed with a central core around which were grouped six orange-shaped segments held in place by a ring fastened to the top of the column. When the ring was lifted, the segments opened, each being attached to the base of the column by a hinge. Along the top edges of the segments were slides which opened to allow each one to be filled with a different perfume.

An earlier type of pomander, shown in an illustration for the 'Boat of Foolish Women', one of a series of five caricatures published in 1502 by Jodocus Badius, was perforated with small holes. It was similar both in size and shape to the pomanders of glazed porcelain and those made in the traditional blue jasper ware of Wedgwood design which are obtainable today from the perfume shops of London and New York. These are filled with sweetly scented herbs and can be suspended by a golden hanging cord from the ceiling.

Queen Elizabeth's favourite pomander can be seen at Burghley House, seat of the Marquis of Exeter. Here, in the bedroom used by Elizabeth on her first visit to the home of her Lord High Treasurer, shortly after the completion of the house, is to be found a small table on which rests her thimble, note book and pomander. The room, with its ancient bed and hangings of dark green velvet on a ground of gold tissue, is in its original state, just as it was when prepared for the Queen. Mary, Queen of Scots' pomander may be seen in Holyrood House, Edinburgh and is similar to that used by

Elizabeth. It is made of silver and was suspended from her belt by a silver chain.

A writer of the Elizabethan age said that, to make a good pomander, 'take an ounce of garden mould and steep it in rose water for several days. Then take the best labdanum, benzoin, storax, ambergris, civet and musk, mix together and add to the mould'. The recipe concludes by assuring that it will make one smell 'as sweet as any lady's dog'—which often had the same ingredients rubbed into its coat before being carried around by its owner when making social calls.

In England, perfumes did not come into general use until the sixteenth century, with the beginning of the Tudor dynasty, the transitional period between the Middle Ages and the Renaissance. During his reign, Henry VII encouraged private enterprises and greatly increased the wealth of his country. His rule also ushered in a period of peace and scholastic learning and, when Henry VIII ascended the throne, he introduced into England much of the Frenchman's appreciation of perfumes. The recipe for Henry's own particular perfume is given in a manuscript now in the Ashmolean Museum at Oxford. It says: 'Take six spoonsful of rose oil, the same of rose water and a quarter of an ounce of sugar. Mix well together and add two grains of musk and one ounce of ambergris, then boil slowly for six hours and strain.' The result would be a perfume of great richness.

During Elizabeth's reign, perfumes were in demand to place amongst clothes and linen, to sprinkle over the floor and to fumigate apartments; but, for the first time, they also began to be used for personal cleanliness and even merely for enjoyment. Howe, who continued Stow's *Chronicles*, stated that no expensive washes or perfumes were made in England until about the fifteenth year of the Queen's reign. Then, in 1573, Edward de Vere, Earl of Oxford, brought from Italy 'perfumed gloves, sweet bags, and other pleasant things' which were greatly appreciated by Her Majesty whose sense of smell, it is said, was keenly developed. In the same year, the Queen had made a pair of perfumed gloves, trimmed with four rows of coloured silks.

Nichols in his *Royal Progresses* writes that once 'three Italians came to the Queen and knowing her liking for scented gloves, each presented a pair to Her Majesty'. On another occasion, when she was

on a visit to the University of Cambridge, the mayor and towns-
people presented her with a pair of her favourite perfumed gloves
and, being so pleased with them, she put them on at once; to the
delight of those who were present. In the Bodleian Library at
Oxford there is a pair of the Queen's scented gloves, believed to be of
Italian origin. In several portraits she is seen wearing them and the
scent with which they had been impregnated was known for some
time afterwards as 'the Earl of Oxford's' perfume.

Ambergris and civet were used in most glove perfumes, which
accounts for the many highly derogatory allusions to the latter by
the literary men of the times. Philip Massinger, the dramatist
who collaborated with Fletcher in at least thirty plays, makes one
of his characters say:

> Lady, I would descend to kiss thy hand,
> But that 'tis gloved, and civet makes me sick.

In *As You Like It*, there is the humorous dialogue between Gorin
and Touchstone in which the pastoral life of the countryman is
adversely compared to that of the courtier. 'Those that have good
manners at the Court are as ridiculous in the country as the behaviour
of the country is most mockable at Court,' says Corin. And later,
'Our hands are hard. They are often tarred over with the surgery
of our sheep; would you have us kiss tar? The courtier's hands are
perfumed with civet.' Again, in *A Winter's Tale*, Autolycus says
that he has gloves for sale 'as sweet as Damask roses'.

In England, as in France, scented gloves were made and sold by
milliners, who lived and worked alongside the herbalists in that part
of London known as Bucklersbury, situated between the Mansion
House and Cheapside. Earlier, it had been the home of the pepperers
and grocers; Sir Thomas More lived there for a time and his
daughter Margaret was born there. Shakespeare knew the district
well for it was but a short walk to London Bridge and across to
Bankside and the Globe Theatre. In *The Merry Wives of Windsor*,
Falstaff is using every device he knows to make love to Ford's
wife but, after making little headway, he says, 'Come, I cannot cog,
and say thou art this and that, like many of these lisping hawthorn-
buds, that come like women in men's apparel, and smell like
Bucklersbury in simpling-time. I cannot, but I love thee; none
but thee.'

During Elizabethan times, herbs were known as simples and at the height of the harvesting season, Bucklersbury was redolent with the scent of lavender and rosemary. It was perhaps these delicious smells which persuaded Sir Thomas More to make plantings of lavender and rosemary in his garden when he moved to Chelsea, for rosemary was said to 'gladden the spirits' of all who inhaled its perfume. 'As for rosemarine,' wrote More, 'I let it run over my garden walls, not only because the bees love it, but because it is the herb sacred to remembrance, to love and to friendship.' In *Hamlet*, Ophelia says 'There's rosemary, that's for remembrance', and each year on April 23, St. George's Day and also Shakespeare's birthday, the people of Stratford-on-Avon walk in procession through the town, wearing sprigs of rosemary and carrying posies of fragrant flowers and leaves, preceded by a band and the town beadle dressed in crimson livery. They make their way to the Church of the Holy Trinity where Shakespeare was baptized and where he is buried, and there place on his grave rosemary and the posies which they have carried around the town.

Both in France and in England at the time, it was customary to decorate the bodies of the dead with rosemary as it will remain fresh and fragrant longer than any other herb and because it was a herb of perpetual remembrance—hence the saying, 'keeping the memory green'. Back in the fourteenth century, it was the favourite scent of Philippa of Hainault, wife of Edward III and mother of the Black Prince. To commemorate her name and her love for rosemary, each year at Christmastime a sprig is used to decorate the boar's head carried into hall at Queen's College, Oxford. A manuscript in the library of Trinity College, Cambridge, sent by the Countess of Hainault to her daughter the Queen, describes the virtues of rosemary in numerous ways. Its scent was said to 'uplift the spirits', acting in the same way as smelling salts, and a sprig was always carried by the Queen to be inhaled when oppressive conditions caused her distress.

'To preserve youth,' wrote William Langham, whose *Garden of Health* appeared during Shakespeare's lifetime, 'make a box of the wood and smell it.' Rosemary seeds were placed in muslin bags and hung about a bedroom because they were thought to bring on sound sleep. And Thomas Newton, in *A Butler's Recipe Book*, suggested distilling the seed or the flowers, when the water 'drunk morning and evening, first and last, will make the breath very sweet'. It was also used to rub into the hair to promote its growth, and clothes and linen were washed in its water. The principal ingredient of Eau de Cologne, rosemary water, was once believed to be the 'elixir of life', a cure for all ailments.

Shakespeare alludes to the city milliners and their love of scented powders in *Henry IV*, Part I. The king, together with Northumberland, Hotspur and others, is discussing the events which have recently taken place at Homedon. Hotspur cannot contain his anger at the indifferent attitude shown by his prisoners:

> I remember, when the fight was done,
> When I was dry with rage and extreme toil,
> Breathless and faint, leaning upon my sword,
> Came there a certain lord, neat and trimly dress'd,
> Fresh as a bridegroom . . . perfum'd like a milliner;
> And 'twixt his finger and his thumb he held
> A pouncet-box, which ever and anon
> He gave his nose, and took 't away again;
> Who, therewith angry, when it next came there,
> Took it in snuff . . .

The pouncet-box was made of scented wood, and filled with perfumed powder which was used as an inhalant as well as a snuff (this was before the introduction of tobacco early in the seventeenth century).

Sachet powders were popular with Elizabethan housekeepers, to place amongst clothes and to keep away moths. The violet scent of orris root was much in demand, also the dried leaves of mint and thyme, rosemary and lavender. Few actual flowers retain their perfume when dry, and only Red and Damask roses were used, the petals being powdered in a mortar and afterwards sifted. Sir Hugh Platt made a sweetly scented powder by pounding and mixing together orris, calamus, cloves, storax and rose petals, and it would retain its perfume for a year or more.

A hand water for use at table was one of the refinements of a more enlightened age. Rose water was placed on the dining table for washing and perfuming the hands. In *The Taming of the Shrew* there is a reference to the custom, when the lord returns from hunting to find Christopher Sly in a drunken stupor by the alehouse door:

6*

O monstrous beast! how like a swine he lies!
Then take him up ...
Carry him gently to my fairest chamber,
Balm his foul head in warm distilled waters,
And burn sweet wood to make the lodging sweet:
Let one attend him with a silver basin,
Full of rose-water.

In all wealthy men's houses, silver bowls were kept in the bedrooms and were filled with rose water to be used for washing the hands and face and to sprinkle over clothes. Sir Hugh Platt gives a recipe for making a scented water consisting of lavender, a few cloves, orris powder, together with four ounces of benjamin, 'a little of which will sweeten a basin of fair water for your table.' Sir Walter Raleigh had a cordial water made from wild strawberry leaves and enjoyed having his rooms filled with the scent of a dry pot-pourri made with Damask roses and orris powder.

The cassolette or printanier was a popular device for diffusing perfumes and was introduced towards the end of the sixteenth century. In the British Museum there is a manuscript containing a recipe for 'a paste for a cassolette' made to the requirements of the Duchess of Braganza. It suggests mixing together two drachms each of ambergris, musk and civet, to which is added a little oil of cloves and three drachms of essence of citron. The whole should be made into a paste with rose water and placed in the cassolette, a small box made of ivory, silver or gold, its lid being perforated with holes through which the scent of the paste could be inhaled.

Clothes were kept in coffers made of fragrant wood such as juniper, cedar or sandalwood which impregnated the clothes with a pungency much appreciated in an age when dry cleaning was unknown. But alcoholic perfumes for applying to the body as 'scent' were unknown during Elizabethan times, and the use of perfume was confined to fragrant powders and water. Elizabeth's love of clothes and perfumes was the only feminine weakness she allowed herself for, as Queen, she had sacrificed the majority of those things a woman most enjoys so as to remain master of herself and of her kingdom. In addition to her liking for scented gloves, she is said to have had her shoes made of perfumed leather, which was imported from Spain until the time of the Armada. Among other agreeable

things, brought from Italy by the Earl of Oxford, was a perfumed
jerkin made of suede which was presented to Her Majesty, and she
was very fond of a cloak made of perfumed leather which she wore on
all special occasions. Some idea of its cost may be obtained from
Charles Piesse's book, *The Art of Perfumery*, published in 1880, in
which he mentions that peau d'Espagne was then sold by the Bond
Street perfumers at a shilling a square inch.

The skins were first steeped in an otto made up of the oils of
neroli, rose, sandalwood, lavender and verbena, to which was added
a small quantity of the oils of clove and cinnamon. All this was
added to a half pint of spirit in which four ounces of gum benzoin
were dissolved. The skins were left in this mixture for a day or so
and were then dried by exposure to the sun and air. Next, a paste
was made by rubbing together in a mortar one drachm of civet and
one of musk, with gum tragacantha to give a spreading consistency,
and into this was mixed the residue of the otto in which the skins
had been soaked. It was spread on the skins which were then placed
together, one above another like a sandwich, and over them were
placed several sheets of paper. The skins were then pressed with
weights for several days, during which time they became so saturated
with the perfume that they retained it permanently. The strips of
leather, known as peau d'Espagne, were used as book marks and for
bindings as well as for numerous objects of clothing.

One of Queen Elizabeth's perfumers was Ralph Rabbards who
edited Ripley's *Compound of Alchemy* and who concocted a number
of perfumes for the Queen's use, made to his own secret formula. In
a letter to the Queen, Rabbards said that he had many 'rare inventions, as I have for long studied and with practice found out', and
he extols the virtues of a number of his perfumes 'of odours
most sweete and delicate'. He suggested for Her Majesty's use his
renowned 'water of violets' and his gillyflower water which would
not 'retain their own proper odours, except they be distilled very
cunningly'. He also had the audacity to suggest to the Queen,
towards the end of her reign, that she make use of some of his
special waters, 'to clense and keepe brighte the skynne and fleshe
and to preserve it in a perfect state'—which would have greatly
appealed to Elizabeth's vanity when she was young but hardly at
this time of her life. She spent large sums on perfumes and cosmetics
and her annual expenses for the year 1584, according to Peck's

Desiderata, included the sum of £40 (a considerable amount in those days) for the services of John Kraunckwell and his wife as 'stillers of sweet waters'.

The Elizabethans kept their scented waters in small bottles of chastened silver, one of the finest examples of which, dating from about 1565, is to be seen in the Victoria and Albert museum. It may have been made by Robert Danby (or Danbe) whose speciality was making communion cups and who was a member of the select and powerful silversmith's guild which up to that time had provided the city of London with seventeen lord mayors. This charming piece of Tudor refinery is only four inches tall and is fitted with a silver base which enables it to stand upright when not in use. A silver chain fastened to the shoulders allows the bottle to be suspended from the girdle.

Towards the end of Elizabeth's reign, the first glass scent bottles were made in England, and Shakespeare mentions one in his fifth sonnet:

> Then, were not summer's distillation left,
> A liquid prisoner pent in walls of glass . . .

The playwright would possibly have been familiar with their manufacture, which was in the hands of those Huguenots who had fled from France after the Massacre of St. Bartholemew and who had set up in business at Crutched Friars in London. This was at about the time Shakespeare took lodgings in Silver Street. One of them named Jean Caré, following protests by English glass makers resentful of the competition, was compelled to move his business to Stourbridge. Shortly after, a Venetian, Jacopo Verzellini, began making glass wine and scent bottles in the Venetian style and persuaded Elizabeth to prohibit the importation of all foreign glass.

But it was not for another two hundred years that scent bottles came to be manufactured on any considerable scale, when the exquisite blue bottles with golden floral sprays began to be made at Bristol, by William Lowdin and his successors at their works known as Redcliffe Backs. The bottles, which were only three inches high, were also produced in green and amethyst, though the most handsome of all were those made in opaque-white with paintings of flowers by Michael Edkins. Several of these delightful bottles have survived and are eagerly sought after by collectors.

In the London Museum there are a number of scent bottles in gold and enamel, fashioned in the most exquisite style, less than two inches high and mounted with rubies and diamonds. They date from late Elizabethan times and may have been made by one of the many jewellers of Cheapside who, during the seventeenth century, performed the additional duties of bankers. They also sold snuffs and perfumes to fill the elegant 'toys'. The British Museum possesses a trade card belonging to one of them, Richard Boult by name, a goldsmith and jeweller whose premises were at the Blue Anchor and Star, opposite Wood Street in Cheapside, and who advertised, 'at the lowest prices', snuff-boxes, sponge-boxes and smelling bottles as well as watch chains, trinkets and, surprisingly, fountain pens.

CHAPTER TEN

THE STUARTS, THEIR PERFUMES AND SNUFF-TAKING

The early distillation of flowers – Lavender – Perfumes of the Restoration – Beauty patches – Snuff – Early snuff-boxes – The vinaigrette – Early pastille burners – Pot-pourris – The House of Yardley – The first perfumery shops.

THE distillation of flowers and leaves was one of the chores in all large houses from the beginning of the sixteenth century. The household books (1502) of the 5th Earl of Northumberland contain the names of 'herbes to stylle', to make sweet waters to use for personal cleanliness, in cooking, and for medicine. Balm and sage, marigold and tansy were amongst the most widely grown plants for distillation, and every garden had its rosemary and lavender bushes. All large houses possessed a room for the drying of herbs and another for their distillation where the ladies took lessons in the art of making sweet waters. These were given as presents at Christmas or for birthdays, just as the more sophisticated perfumes are given today. Nichols' *Royal Progresses* mentions that, at Hawkstead, the still-room was a prominent feature of the ground floor, and here the ladies of the court amused themselves in the making of sweet waters.

The distillation of lavender, which began early in the seventeenth century, was the first attempt at any form of commercial scent production in the British Isles. Mitcham in Surrey was the home of lavender growing, and its climate and soil produced the world's finest lavender water. Later, lavender was grown and distilled at Hitchin in Hertfordshire, in Norfolk, and at Market Deeping in Lincolnshire where a number of ancient distilling plants can still be seen; but it is at Mitcham that most of the lavender water is manufactured today. It is estimated that half a hundredweight of lavender flowers will yield about sixteen ounces of essential oil. It is, however, not from the actual flowers that the oil is obtained but from the tiny green bracts which enclose them, as the flowers of lavender and all the labiates are entirely devoid of perfume. In the finest ottos, the stems are excluded because, though useful for burning indoors, they yield little essential oil.

To plant an acre of ground, 3,500 plants are required and, at their fourth or fifth year, these yield about six quarts of otto. After six years, the plants are taken up and burnt and the delicious scent spreads for miles around. The lavender is harvested in August and September, when it is cut with a sickle and placed on mats for conveying to the still-house. The otto is grouped into 'firsts' and 'seconds', the latter being the end of the distillation and used for perfuming soaps. The finest lavender water is made by the distillation of the essential oil with rectified spirit and rose water, the final product being pure white.

The earliest recipe for English lavender water is from a manuscript of 1615 which directs that the flowers be distilled with canella bark, wallflowers and grains of paradise; and the distillate could be taken internally as well as being used as a perfume and for toilet water. Lavender water was the favourite scent of Queen Henrietta Maria. In the garden of her manor of Wimbledon grew large borders of 'rosemary, rue and white lavender', which is believed to yield the most pleasing of all lavender water. The Worcestershire pastoral poet, William Shenstone, in 'The Schoolmistress' tells of that particular lady's fondness for lavender, having bundles of it hung about her home and using the perfume on her handkerchief:

> And lavender, whose spikes of azure bloom
> Shall be, ere-while, in arid bundles bound
> To lurk amidst the labours of her loom,
> And crown her 'kerchiefs with mickle rare perfume.

During the seventeenth century, perfumes were used to ward off the plague and Rushworth mentions the recipe of a doctor who advised eating apples roasted with cloves or frankincense. Most medical practitioners of the time carried, at the end of their walking stick, a cassolette filled with aromatics which they held to the nose as inconspicuously as possible when visiting the sick. A writer on medicine recommended fumigating with those things 'which abound in subtle volatile parts which they exhale into the air', and he suggested burning benzoin, storax and any aromatic roots and woods which would take away unpleasant smells.

During the plague of 1603, when the Court moved to Wilton House, near Salisbury, the Lord Mayor of London commanded that pitch and faggots be burnt in the city and Londoners were ordered to place wood outside their homes for that purpose. During the Great Plague, sulphur, saltpetre and ambergris were used for burning in the streets and resin was burnt on coal fires indoors. Fires were lit in the open every twelve hours and at night were kept burning by watchmen. At this time, the Deanery of St. Paul's was fumigated twice weekly with frankincense, and angelica root, powdered and steeped in vinegar, was placed in a pan over hot embers, so that the fumes could impregnate any clothes hung above them.

Though many of the ideas for fumigation were strange in the extreme, there may have been some value in several of them, for in the nineteenth century, at the Pasteur Institute in Paris, it was discovered that the micro-organisms of yellow fever were readily killed by the essential oils of cinnamon and thyme, also by angelica and sandalwood, the bacteria being disposed of in less than an hour and, in some cases, after only a few minutes.

From his experiments on the bactericidal properties of essential oils, Professor Omeltschenki concluded that the bacillus of typhoid fever was killed within forty-five minutes in air containing the vapour of oil of cinnamon, and that tuberculosis bacilli were killed within twelve hours when exposed to the vapour of oil of lavender.

In his *Essay on Health* Sir William Temple recommended that, though the use of scent is rarely practised in modern physic, it could well be with advantage, seeing that some smells are so depressing and others so reviving. He remembered once walking in the gardens of India House in Amsterdam among nutmegs, cloves and other spices, and being completely refreshed in humour and in health by their aromatic scent.

Writing in 1656, William Coles said: 'Herbs do comfort the wearied brain with fragrant smells which yield a certain kind of nourishment'; and, in *The Country Housewife*, Lawson suggested dividing the garden into equal halves, one to contain those flowers which are suitable for making nosegays and garlands, such as violets, pinks and lily of the valley; the other to be filled with sweet herbs for distilling.

Perfumery made little headway after Elizabeth's death until the

One of a pair of Louis XV ormolu pot-pourri bowls sold at Christie's for 14,000 guineas

(*Above*) Two Bilston scent bottles, early 18th century
(*Below*) Two Chelsea scent bottles, *c.* 1760

Pair of Louis XVI ormolu-mounted 'Porcelain de Paris' *brûle-parfumiers*

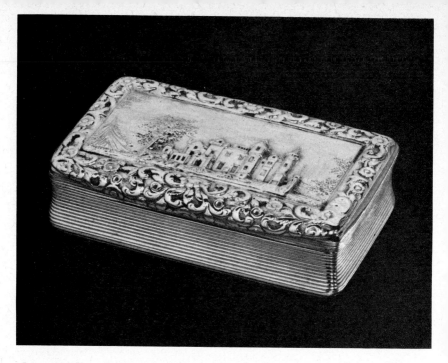

Snuff boxes: (*above*) William IV silver snuff box by Nathaniel Mills,
(*below*) snuff box in gold and enamel by Christian Gottlieb Stehl of Dresden

Restoration of the Monarchy in 1660. Charles II returned with the Frenchman's love of luxury, and perfumes and cosmetics were once again in favour at court. It quickly became fashionable for ladies to paint their faces and to wear patches, a form of facial ornamentation noticed by Pepys who revealed in his *Diary*, for April 26, 1687, that the Duchess of Newcastle was 'wearing many black patches because of pimples about her mouth'. These may have been caused by the Duchess's remarkable prescription for improving the complexion, by rubbing oil of vitriol on to the face to remove the skin so that a new layer might take its place. In her *Poems and Fancies*, the Duchess also recommended cleaning the teeth with china clay or pumice and, to improve the appearance of the eyebrows, removing those at the edges, so that only a thin row was left. It was then modish for both sexes to darken the eyebrows with lamp black. Thomas Shadwell, in *The Humorists*, alludes to this practice: 'Ah! your black eyebrow is your fashionable eyebrow. I hate rogues that wear eyebrows which are out of fashion.' And in another of Shadwell's plays *The Virtuoso*, there is an interesting description of the stock-in-trade carried by a perfumer of Charles II's time, though the author satirizes the quest for the preservation of lost beauty for which all manner of weird concoctions were used including a mixture of mercury and hog's bones.

Among the perfumes which were popular at the time, Shadwell mentions Orange, Genoa, Romane, Frangipani, Neroli, Tuberose, Jasmine and 'Marshall', while, for the toilet, the perfumer had a 'good choice of [scented] gloves in addition to frowzes, combs, all manner of washes; almond water for the complexion and the best pomatums in all Europe'.

About this time Gervase Markham's famous skin lotion, probably the first beauty preparation to appear commercially, was creating considerable interest. It was distilled from rosemary, featherfew, fennel, violets and nettle leaves and applied to the face after its dilution with milk. This was a natural herbal recipe, introduced at a time when white lead and lime to whiten the skin were in daily use, often resulting in lead poisoning and permanent disfigurement. One preparation 'guaranteed to give the skin a pure white look' was made from white mercury, lemon juice, powdered white egg shells and white wine, a drastic method of beautifying the face which could result in severe 'burning' and often did; but which was frequently

used by the ladies who constantly sought to achieve the whiteness of face and hands which were the principal attraction of the
times.

Another preparation, used to cover up blemishes of the skin for
special occasions, was known as 'ceruse'. This was white lead
mixed with white of egg; it was applied to the face like a beauty
pack but was left on for the occasion. For contrast, the cheeks
were tinted with Spanish wool, which was a red dye, and black
beauty spots completed the decoration. During Queen Anne's
time, patching even took on a political significance, those stuck on
the right side of the face denoting a Tory supporter, those on the
left showing a partiality for the Whigs.

Older women, whose sunken cheeks gave away their age, used
'plumpers' for padding them. In *The Fop's Dictionary*, John
Evelyn describes them as 'very thin round and light balls . . . much
used by old court countesses' to improve their charms.

Perfumed baths now became the rage. They were introduced
shortly after the 'sweating houses' began to open in every London
street and to become as common as the gin shops. The devastations
of the Plague had at last made people think about personal cleanliness
and, later on, when the use of perfume became more fashionable,
fragrant herbs and essences gave the baths a greater piquancy.
During the Plague it also came to be appreciated that strongly
smelling leaves and resinous gums did possess valuable antibiotic
qualities and their greater use was advocated not only by the
medical profession but by those who were entrusted with the task of
re-building London after the Great Fire. Evelyn suggested to the
King that large areas of land should be filled with all manner of
scented plants 'such as yield the most fragrant and odoriferous
flowers and are apt to tinge the air upon every gentle emission at a
great distance . . . when the City would be sensible of the sweet and
ravishing varieties of the perfumes': a delightful idea but one which
Charles, because of his extravagance and costly wars, was unable to
put into practice.

Books containing suggestions on how to make all kinds of beauty
preparations began to appear, and Mary Doggett's *Book of Receipts*
(1682) was widely read at the time; it was the first 'best-seller' on
beauty treatment. One of her recipes was for making a lip salve. She
suggested using salad oil, bees-wax (sufficient in quantity to fill

two large nutmegs) and a sprig of rosemary and warming them over a fire. Then pour into a pot and, when it is required for use, add a spoonful of rose water before melting.

Snuff, in the form of powdered leaves of fragrant plants, had been taken by countrymen since earliest times to clear the head of a cold or of melancholia, but it was not until the reign of Charles II that 'stuff' taking became fashionable at Court, although during Shakespeare's day aromatic powders made of orris and the dried leaves of camomile and white pellitory were passed round after banquets. The principal ingredients of Elizabethan snuffs were camomile leaves and those of alehoof and pellitory, the latter being known as the Sneezewort, for according to Turner, 'the flowers make one sneeze exceedingly.' The leaves had a similar effect and from them a 'tea' was brewed. Peppermint, woodruff and thyme were also used in snuffs after they had been dried and ground to a powder, likewise the dried roots of the Sweet Flag.

Originally, the pouncet-box which came to be used for containing snuff, was for keeping pumice-stone. This was used in the preparation of parchment for writing, since its absorbent nature prevented the ink from spreading (blotting paper had in fact been invented and was in use at the beginning of the fifteenth century). Later, during Elizabethan times, a pouncet was the name given to any type of box which held scented toilet powder for placing between linen or for blowing about a room or on to a lady's hair with bellows. Shakespeare's 'pouncet-box' most likely contained leaves and roots to be taken as snuff.

It is possible, too, that tobacco snuff may have reached England during Shakespeare's lifetime, for the herb had been introduced into Europe in 1560 by Jean Nicot, French Ambassador to Portugal, who planted it in the garden of the Embassy in Lisbon; the first cigars were made about the same time, by Demetrio Pela, a Spaniard. It is believed that the word cigar was originally derived from the Spanish 'cigarral', little garden, for most gardens in the Iberian Peninsula had plants of Nicotiana tabacum. Certainly by the late Elizabethan era, the tobacconist was as firmly established in the city of London as the herbalist. Gerard, writing in 1597, said: 'The dry leaves are used to be taken in a pipe and set on fire and sucked into the stomach and sucked forth again from the nostrils.'

In France, tobacco snuff had been taken since the time of

Catherine de Medici who, after receiving a quantity from Jean Nicot, started the fashion at court. The habit quickly achieved such popularity that, in 1624, Pope Urban VIII issued an order banning its use from places of worship and excommunicating those who did not conform. But snuff-taking did not become really popular in England until the Great Plague, when men began puffing tobacco as they had never done before as it was thought to have valuable antiseptic properties. Snuff is essentially powdered tobacco, fermented in salt, then ground and scented. There are two forms: dry, which is made from tobacco stems; and moist, from the leaves. But the skill in its manufacture lies in the blending and in its flavouring with various attars for which cinnamon, cloves, lavender and bergamot were the most popular scents.

Snuff is made either plain or scented. There are two kinds of plain, Scottish and 'Rappee', the former being made from the stalks and consequently dry, though the best Scottish snuff also contains a portion of leaf. The dry snuffs are dried still further by baking in an oven and are afterwards ground to a fine powder. 'Rappee', which means 'little leaf', is made from tobacco leaf and is a moist snuff made by cutting the leaves into small pieces and placing them in a trough with common salt. The tobacco begins to heat, like compost, and gives off a strong smell of ammonia. After two months, it is taken from the trough to be dried and ground.

The odour of snuffs is distinguished by their relative strengths and, although the flavour reveals itself in the odour, the strength is in the after-effects shown by absorption in the mucous membrane of the nose. Some snuffs were prepared from orris root to impart its violet-like perfume; others from fennel, sage and rosemary. Tobaccos were also compounded with cascarilla bark or with the Tonka bean, which has the smell of newly mown hay and was often placed in snuff boxes for its flavour. Modern cigar connoisseurs are of the opinion that the aromas of cigars are as diversified as the bouquets of wines, but the Cuban manufacturers, who grow the finest cigar tobacco, place them in boxes made of Virginia juniper wood to improve their flavour before the cigars are exported.

In England, the two chief centres of the snuff-making industry are Kendal and Sheffield where snuff has been made since 1737 when Thomas Wilson, a shearsmith, rented the Sharrow Mill with its water-wheel and fine outbuildings from the Duke of Norfolk. He was followed by his son Joseph, a silversmith, who was associated in the manufacture of the first Sheffield plate and who carried on his business as a scythemaker until the firm began to make tobacco snuff in 1745. Though the original water-wheel is still in daily use, steam power was introduced in 1797, by which time the snuffs, usually sent out in bladders or barrels, had become famous throughout Britain.

Among the early snuffs were Sharrow Special and Gold Label; Tom Buck and Queen's. Later, other flavours were added to the range including Wallflower, Tonquin, Lavender, Jockey Club and High Toast, with Royal George, named after George IV, one of the most popular of all. Menthol and medicated snuffs are also manufactured. The recent decrease in cigarette smoking has resulted in doubled sales both at home and abroad. Figures released by the Society of Snuff Grinders, Blenders and Purveyors for 1970 show that total sales for the year amounted to more than one and a half million pounds, the biggest rise in export sales coming from the menthol and medicated blends which are becoming increasingly popular in the United States.

In *The Country Lady's Directory* (1732), there is a recipe which tells how perfumed snuff may be made by the housewife. First, a box must be obtained (a cigar box would be suitable), which is lined with dry white paper and the bottom is covered with a layer of snuff one inch deep. Over this is placed a layer of highly perfumed flowers, such as the tuberose, narcissus or Damask rose. Then more snuff and more flowers are added alternately, until the box is filled. Several days should elapse before the snuff is sieved from the flowers and placed in a canister to be used when required.

Dr. Johnson, who was particularly fond of snuff, carried it in his waistcoat pockets, which he had specially lined with leather to maintain its purity and to prevent it from falling through. By the early eighteenth century, the taking of snuff had achieved such importance among the fashionable that, on August 8, 1711, there appeared in *The Spectator* an advertisement to the effect that 'the exercise of the snuff-box according to the most fashionable airs and notions of the time, will be taught with the best plain or perfumed snuff at Charles Lillie's, perfumer, at the corner of Beaufort Buildings in the Strand, for two hours each day at noon, except Saturdays'. The advertisement went on to say that 'there will be likewise taught

The Ceremony of the Snuff Box, or rules for offering snuff to a stranger, friend or mistress'. But it was really at Bath that snuff-taking first became popular when Beau Nash set the fashion, and soon the snuff box had become as much a part of the dandy's dress as the gold-topped cane and buckled shoes.

The Parisian goldsmiths were the first to produce these delightful boxes made in all shapes, often of chased gold and enamel and, later, with exquisitely worked miniatures set into the lid. As pomanders were the most prized possession of the Renaissance courtier, so did snuff boxes come to hold a similar position from the beginning of the eighteenth century; and, if not actually classed as jewellery, they were a delightful manifestation of the goldsmith's art. A snuff box lid, which may be dated to about 1700, at one time in the Franks collection and now in the British Museum, clearly shows a lady's head-dress of the period, known as the 'commode', which was fashionable during the reign of James II. Here, the figures are in relief which stamps the box as being of English workmanship.

Messrs. Parker and Wakelin, whose premises were in the Haymarket and who were eventually to become Garrard and Co., produced some fine early snuff boxes in gold. One of their designers was Elias Russel who lived and worked in nearby Suffolk Street. Snuff boxes were also manufactured of Battersea enamel, made at York House, Battersea, between 1753 and 1756 when the factory was controlled by Stephen Janssen. It was a brilliant move when he obtained the services of Simon Ravenet, a French engraver, for he brought with him the technique of deepening the lines of his etchings with a graver, a considerable improvement on the method, originated by John Brooks, of decorating enamels by transfer printing.

One of the earliest masters was Daniel Gouers of Paris whose boxes of chaste gold are among the most prized possessions of collectors. A Dutchman, Gouers worked in Paris during the reign of Louis IX and raised the snuff box to artistic form comparable with the most elegantly conceived jewellery of the time. He was followed, in his close association with the Royal House, by Jean Ducrollay who perfected the art of fusing enamel and gold. To achieve this, it was necessary to fire the object in a temperature of about 1,700° F. and, as the melting point of gold is just below

2,000° F. it is obvious that great care was necessary in maintaining exactly the correct heat.

A superb example of the master's work is to be found in the collection of Mrs. Charles B. Wrightsman. It is a double snuff box made in gold, enamelled with flowers and leaves and set with miniatures of Louis XV and his Queen, together with members of their family. In the same collection there is a box in brilliant red lacquer inlaid with tortoise-shell, which was melted slightly before the gold could be inlaid. As the shell cooled, it contracted, holding the gold as tightly as if in a vice. Great care was needed to obtain the precise temperature for, if too high, the tortoise-shell caught fire.

During Georgian times, it was the custom to place the dried leaves of woodruff at the back of pocket watches so that when it was required to tell the time, the back could be opened also when the woodruff would release its pleasing scent. The leaves were also placed between the pages of books to keep them free from any mustiness.

Another of the famous French goldsmiths was Juste-Aurêle Meissonier, the royal goldsmith from 1724, whose picturesque designs in the rococo style have made his snuff boxes amongst the most prized possessions of collectors. One gold snuff box designed by the master made the world record price of £56,173 (or its equivalent value in francs) when auctioned in Paris in 1971. The box carried the arms of Maria Anna of Bavaria-Neuburg, wife of Charles II of Spain and was previously in the collection of the late M. David-Weill, one of the most distinguished French collectors of the twentieth century.

A writer in *The Connoisseur* for September 1754, when snuff-taking was at its height, had this to say of the habit: 'Church and playhouse continually echo with the music of the nose and in every corner you may hear them in concert snuffling, sneezing, hawking and grunting like a drove of hogs.' He suggests that snuff-taking became prevalent so that the men of fashion could display their white hands, or the brilliancy of a diamond ring, and he concludes by saying that these people would never have become addicted 'had they not been seduced by the charms of a fashionable snuff box, whilst there is always the fellow who upon opening the box, may have the opportunity to steal a glance at his own sweet person reflected through the mirror in the lid'.

In France, snuff-taking first became fashionable towards the end of the seventeenth century when François-Louis de Bourbon, Prince de Conti, one of the most popular men at the court of Louis XIV, had his snuff made with his favourite perfumes and would himself superintend its blending. Conti's close friend and cousin, the Grand Dauphin, was also a snuff addict.

During the reign of Louis XV, snuff boxes and scent bottles were made in the Sèvres porcelain factory which continues to flourish to this day. In 1759, Louis purchased the factory, which then became known as the Manufacture Royale de Porcelaine, and at about this time the services were engaged of E. M. Falconet, a sculptor of renown whose original ideas brought about a succession of designs of outstanding quality. The period usually considered to have produced the finest work at the Sèvres factory coincided with the development and fame of the Chelsea porcelain works which began production in 1750 and continued until 1784, when the workshops were demolished and the moulds removed to Derby. At the beginning, the factory was managed for Sir Edward Fawkener by a Flemish silversmith, Nicolas Sprimont, who then purchased the factory on Fawkener's death in 1759. But Sèvres was the dominant influence and all snuff boxes and scent bottles closely followed the French style. The bottles were made to represent animals and birds; others were in the form of harlequins and clowns while some followed the Chinese theme. Indeed, genuine Chinese scent bottles and snuff containers first appeared early in the eighteenth century, made of natural stone in jade and rock crystal and in the exciting smoky colours of amber and cornelian. They were in the form of bottles rather than boxes, being about four inches high with a narrow neck, and were

Chinese jade snuff bottle

carried by the Chinese in the folds of their sleeves. The finest examples date from the mid-eighteenth century, the Chien Lung period, when many bottles were painted on the inside. This was a most difficult operation and was performed with a fine brush inserted at the neck. After painting, the bottle was then 'fired'. The most exquisite interior-painted bottles are those of Yeh Chung-san, Ma Shao-hsuan and Kuan-Yu-tien, dating from the mid-eighteenth century. Snuff-taking had really begun in China during the reign of K'ang Hsi (1662-1722) when small bottles with spoons began to appear. The Chinese took their snuff as discreetly as possible, removing a few grains from the bottle and placing them on the nail of the forefinger before lifting them to the nose.

Towards the end of the eighteenth century, scent bottles were being produced in England in the blue jasper (white stoneware coloured by barium sulphate brought from the Derbyshire mines) for which the Staffordshire firm of Wedgwood was to become famous. One example, a double bottle made in the shape of a cigar with a screw top of silver at both ends, can be seen in the collection of the Houbigant Perfume Company of Paris, while several are in the Josiah Wedgwood collection at Barlaston. A number were made with a small ring at the top through which a cord or chain was threaded so that the bottle could be suspended from the neck or around the waist. By the end of the century, jasper was being used for various articles. In his book *Wedgwood*, Mr. Wolf Mankowitz describes an order for jasper being sent to the King of Naples by a merchant in Manchester which included snuff boxes, scent and smelling bottles, rings and door handles, bell-pulls and panels for the king's coach, all made in blues and greens and to the designs of Robert Adam and John Flaxman, who worked in Rome for the firm on reproductions of Etruscan design.

From the Staffordshire town of Bilston early in the eighteenth century, went scent bottles of the most exquisite design, enamelled by Dovey Hawksford who took to the road to sell his wares. The bottles were decorated in the Watteau style and many were probably the work of the finest of all transfer-painters, Robert Hancock, who at one time worked for the Wedgwood factory, who incorporated his designs on their pot-pourri jars and pomanders.

The early years of the nineteenth century saw the first examples of magnificent glassware produced at the Waterford factory in

Ireland. It was in 1783 that John Hill of Stourbridge left England
with fifty or more of the finest craftsmen, to set up as a glass maker
in Waterford, because of the imposition of a tax of a penny a pound
on all materials used by glass makers in England. After numerous
closures, the Waterford factory now flourishes as never before in its
chequered history. Several of the early Irish glass scent bottles
have survived and possess outstanding beauty, being in appearance
like miniature decanters with the familiar fluting which runs from the
base to about half-way up the side. This is an aspect of Waterford
glass which enables the collector to distinguish it from decanters
made by other firms.

To give as presents on special occasions, gold bottles of elaborate
design were now being made for wealthy patrons of the goldsmith's
art. These were usually fitted with a gold chain on each shoulder
of the bottle, the chains were attached to a golden ring to wear on the
finger, and the bottle was carried in the hand so that all could
admire its intricate beauty. Late eighteenth-century scent bottles,
designed by François Cheret the Parisian goldsmith, were even
decorated with a small clock let into the side, the face of which
opened to allow for its winding. The perfume may not have had the
same adverse effect on the working of the clock as it so often does
when a watch is worn on the wrist of someone who uses scent in
large amounts.

Back in the later years of Charles I's reign, perfumed finger rings
often adorned the hands of both sexes. These were first made with a
small hinged box attached to the ring and in which were placed a
few grains of civet or of scented powder which could be unobtrusively
inhaled by lifting the lid of the 'box' with the thumb. The rings
were also made with a lid pierced with tiny holes which allowed the
scent to escape unaided. These rings were usually worn for evening
occasions, for banquets and balls, when the scents would revive one
if fatigued by the oppressive atmosphere or by the exertions of
dancing.

During Regency times, the fountain ring came into fashion. With
the least pressure, a fine spray of perfume would arise to a height of
twelve inches or so and refreshed the air around; a lady would
also use it to release a jet of her favourite perfume on to her lover
as he took her hand to kiss it. The ring was filled by inserting it
into a cup containing the perfume and pressing a rubber 'ball' at

the back. The pressure was released when the perfume had been drawn into the ring, in exactly the same way as a fountain pen is filled.

The vinaigrette, of French origin, was also very popular at the time. This was a container for holding aromatic vinegar which was held to the nose 'to correct the bad quality of air' or to clear the head when conditions were oppressive. Vinaigrettes took the place of the pomander and were made by goldsmiths and silversmiths who lavished on them much of the craftsmanship they had put into their snuff boxes. Though usually constructed flat and rectangular with a hinged grille through which the perfume could escape, vinaigrettes were also made to the designs of flowers and birds or in the shape of horns and purses. The majority came from Birmingham workshops and were sometimes made to a rococo design and inlaid with precious stones: others may have carried on the lid a design of the owner's country seat.

Gold and silver vinaigrettes, stamped with hallmarks giving the initials of their maker, the town, year and the carat for gold, the lion for silver, have become collector's items, and the finest examples may make as much as £200 in the London salesrooms. This was in fact the figure paid recently for a rectangular vinaigrette in silver made by Nathaniel Mills in 1838, which shows on the lid Windsor Castle in relief. The craftsmanship of Mills was equalled by few others, but Gervase Wheeler, working contemporaneously, was almost as fine and so too was Samuel Pemberton at an earlier date. Joseph Taylor, whose 'watch-case' vinaigrettes had their own particular charm, was another craftsman in silverwork. Taylor's models were made to fit snugly into the waistcoat pocket and, if now no longer used for their original purpose, they can still be filled with stamps or peppermints.

Each vinaigrette held a fine sponge soaked in an aromatic vinegar which was made by distilling acetate of copper. This produced acetic acid which was aromatized with camphor and with otto of lavender or rosemary. The method was to dissolve the camphor in the acid, then to add the ottos. After a few days, the liquid was strained and was ready to pour on to the sponge. Another method was to take the leaves of rosemary, lavender, sage and mint, and to immerse them in rectified spirit for several days. The acetic acid was added and allowed to stand for several more days before straining. A 'rose vinegar' was made by mixing otto of roses with acetic acid which greatly accentuates the rose perfume.

The vinaigrette was a popular object to carry around until late Victorian times and, for almost a century, continued to be made to the original designs by the descendants of earlier craftsmen. Later, acetic acid was distilled from wood, while wine vinegar was even more highly rated since its odour of acetic ether was very much more refined than that obtained by the distillation of acetate of copper. During Victorian days, toilet vinegars were also prepared for use in the bath. One which was immensely popular was known as 'vinegar à la violette', made from otto of roses, extract of cassie, orris and white wine vinegar. Another was made by adding an ounce of acetic acid to a pint of Eau de Cologne. Only a very small amount was required to scent a bath.

Perfume or pastille burners came into use at about the same time as the vinaigrette during the reign of George III. They were first made of silver and, in an age of elegance, were carried into the dining-room with the dessert, to scent the room with aromatic perfumes and to banish the lingering smells of soup and meat which may be appetizing before a meal but not afterwards. The outstanding craftsman for silver perfumers was Matthew Boulton of Birmingham who, with John Fothergill as his salesman, was to achieve everlasting fame as one of the manufacturers of early Sheffield plate. As there was no assay office near him at the time, he applied for one to be set up at Sheffield. It opened in 1773 and from then on Boulton sent all his silver pieces to Sheffield for their marking.

One of the finest examples of his work is his Adam-style perfume burner of 1779, now in the U.S.A., where it was sold at the Parke-Bernet Galleries in 1969. It stands on three legs, the feet of which rest on velvet pads, and three griffins decorate the urn-shaped burner. There is no spirit burner beneath the urn as was more usual, and the fumes which escaped through the pierced lid were produced by the smouldering of scented pastilles of charcoal and resin.

From the Regency period onwards, pastille burners, made of bone china or earthenware, were to be found in many homes, to counteract the smells of inefficient sanitation. They were often made in cottage style, complete with chimney, through which the smoke poured forth, and walls covered with imitation hollyhocks and climbing roses.

These cottage burners were in fact only a slight modification of the gum resin burners of Richard I's time, the pastilles being made by mixing together ground sandalwood, gum benzoin and gum tolu, with otto of cassia and cloves. Potassium nitrate was then dissolved in mucilage of tragacanth (a gum exudation of Astralagus noted for its binding qualities and used in modern hand jellies and hair creams) was added to the mixture. This was beaten in a mortar and made into small cakes. When dry, these were placed in the cottage through a hole in the base and set alight, when they would smoulder for several hours.

Seraglio pastilles were made in a slightly different way. Gum benzoin, balsam of tolu, labdanum, sandalwood, potassium nitrate and poplar or willow tree charcoal were mixed together and to these ingredients was added a small quantity of mucilage of tragacanth. A well-made pastille should not develop an odour of its own, but simply volatilize the fragrant matter used in its manufacture.

The incense burners used at the French Court were of more elaborate design then the quaint models of English cottages and castles. From the Chantilly factory, which closed in 1800, came a series of porcelain burners of exquisite workmanship made in the shape of tree trunks. They were mounted on a base of gilded bronze with covers of similar material, and the porcelain was encrusted with flowers and leaves.

In the Victoria and Albert Museum there is a pair of white porcelain pastille burners with covers, mounted in silver-gilt and moulded with plum blossom in relief. They date from the early years of the eighteenth century and were made in Fukien province. They were later housed in the Japanese Palace at Dresden and had a considerable influence on the Meissen factory which commenced operations in 1710 and was the first in Europe to manufacture porcelain.

On a less elaborate scale was the perfume lamp, an object of Victorian times which was the invention of Mr. Isaac Deck of Cambridge. He introduced his lamp shortly after his discovery that spongy platinum would remain incandescent in the vapour of alcohol. Mr. Deck's lamp was made of glass, like a small decanter, and he filled it with Hungary water, 'trimmed' with a wick. Over the wick was placed a small ball of spongy platinum held in place by a thin glass rod inserted into the wick. The wick was then lit and allowed to burn until the platinum became red-hot, when the flame was extinguished. The platinum continued to burn, drawing the Hungary water up the wick and diffusing its fragrance about the room.

Chinese joss-sticks were burned in European homes just as they were in the temples of Buddha, and scented spills were also popular. These were made by steeping paper in a saltpetre solution, two ounces being dissolved in a pint of water. The paper is then dried and on to it is rubbed a solution made by dissolving myrrh in rectified spirit. This is applied to both sides of the paper which is hung up to dry. The paper is then cut into strips to be rolled into spills for lighting. They will burn slowly.

Perfumed wax candles were also burned in most upper-class houses during Georgian times. They were placed in cut-glass fixtures and were often the sole method of lighting an apartment. Today, scented candles can be obtained from the same people who made and sold them two centuries ago, though these candles' sole function is to perfume an apartment.

In almost every house, pot-pourris of fragrant flowers and leaves were to be found, shedding their delightful odours through every room. This was a method of scenting the home that had been popular from mediaeval times when herbs were gathered from the countryside to be dried and placed in muslin bags or open boxes, so that their fragrance would be brought to the full in the warmth of the room. Later, pot-pourris were made more lastingly scented with the introduction of Damask roses and white jasmine and by the addition of powdered cloves and allspice.

A favourite recipe of Charles II's wife was to take three parts of a basin of rose petals which had been dried in an airy room away from strong sunlight and to which were added a cupful of dried rosemary, thyme and lavender, together with the dried and powdered skin of an orange and some cloves. The whole should be well mixed together and placed in a pot-pourri bowl or jar made of decorated wood or china; the lids are pierced with a number of large holes through which the perfume escapes, yet the mixture is kept free from dust and from being carelessly scattered about the room. A well-made pot-pourri should retain its perfume for at least fifty years, which is the length of time guaranteed by Taylors of London for all their pot-pourris.

A moist pot-pourri will possess a more powerful perfume and is made by placing a six-inch layer of red rose petals in an earthenware jar. The petals are covered with a layer of salt and allowed to settle for several days before the addition of more rose petals and those of orange blossom, pinks and other highly scented flowers, together with rosemary and lavender. Then add another layer of salt, some powdered orange skin, a sprinkling of dried marjoram and a quarter of an ounce of powdered cloves. Keep the jar closed until the perfume is to be enjoyed.

During the eighteenth century, the pot-pourri bowl became the manifestation of the porcelain maker's art in England and in France. From the Chelsea factory in 1760 came a number of perfume vases of outstanding beauty, decorated with exotic birds and encrusted around the base with flowers and leaves representing those used in making pot-pourris. The lids were also ornamented with flowers and it was usual to remove them when entering the room and to replace them when leaving. In this way the strength of the pot-pourri would be maintained.

Even more elaborate in design and execution were the pot-pourri bowls of the Louis XV period, one of which was sold at Christie's in 1968 for the record price of fourteen thousand guineas. In the Louvre there is a pair of exquisite ormulu-mounted Japanese lacquer pot-pourri containers which were once in the collection of Madame de Pompadour in the Château de Bellevue. The perfume is released through apertures made in the ormulu mounting which surrounds the bowls beneath the snugly fitting lids.

By 1770, the use of perfumes had reached such amazing proportions that a Bill was introduced into Parliament laying it down that 'all women of whatever rank or degree, whether virgins, maids or widows, who shall from and after such Act, impose upon, seduce and betray into matrimony, any of his Majesty's subjects by scents, paints, cosmetic washes, artificial teeth, false hair, Spanish wool, iron stays, hoops, high-heeled shoes, and bolstered hips, shall incur the penalty of the law now in force against witchcraft and like misdemeanours and that the marriage upon conviction, shall be null and void'. The Bill, however, never reached the statute books and perfumes continued to be used on an ever-increasing scale.

Almost every house smelled with the fragrance of its writing paper which was impregnated with the scent of roses or violets by coming into contact with Spanish leather. Pin cushions and jewel cases were lined with quilted silk, which was filled with scented wadding, and the lids were covered with shells which had been steeped in a mixture of bergamot and sandalwood with a drachm of civet and one of musk added. Even precious stones were perfumed, being placed in a box containing a mixture of musk, civet and otto of rose, rubbed together with a little mucilage of tragacanth.

The year 1770, however, is one to be remembered by all who take a delight in perfumes and pleasant things, rather than as the year in which there was a genuine attempt to prevent their use by the law of the land. For this was when William Yardley set up business in partnership with Thomas Beedal as makers of buckles for shoes and decorative swords which were worn by dandies of the time. His ancestor, George Yardley, who was born in the year of the Armada, had been one of the early settlers in the New World, arriving in Virginia in the *Sea Adventurer* on May 15, 1609, eleven years before the Pilgrim Fathers left in the *Mayflower*. It was he who saved the colonists from starvation and disaster by persuading them to cultivate the land to its maximum potentiality so that, by 1620, they were able to send the English Government 120 pounds of tobacco in exchange for 'ninety respectable Englishwomen' who were to become their wives. George Yardley was not, however, able to take advantage of this unusual commercial exchange for, while on a short visit to England in 1618, he had married Temperance Flowerdew, besides being knighted by James I before returning with the rank of Governor. Both he and his wife died in their adopted country, and many Americans today can trace their ancestry to the Yardleys of Virginia.

By 1817, William Yardley was still trading as a maker of buckles and swords but, now that wigs were beginning to go out of fashion and men were using bear's grease and oils to set their own hair, he began macerating his Norfolk-grown lavender in bear's grease and distilling it in water, with the result that, by the time of his death in 1824, he had established another profitable business, selling lavender water and soap of similar fragrance. By the end of the century Yardleys had become the largest manufacturers of lavender products in the world.

Throughout our history, oils and pomades have been used on the hair, to keep it well groomed and perfumed. The ancient Britons wore their hair long but like all those he conquered, Julius Caesar compelled them to crop it. In France, too, men had long hair until Francis I was wounded in the head and had his own cut short. The custom spread to England, and was especially prevalent during Henry VIII's time when barbers were kept busy shaving and cropping. Afterwards, the head was washed in rosemary water which was good for the hair. In all barbers' shops, a censer was kept continually burning, to counteract the personal smells of the customers. Shakespeare refers to this in *The Taming of the Shrew*, when Petruchio compares the clippings of a tailor to the intricate design of 'a censer in a barber's shop'.

During early Stuart times, ringlets became fashionable. 'I know many gentlemen,' said Middleton in one of his plays, 'who wear longer hair than their mistresses.' This excess led to extremes in the opposite direction, when the Puritans had their hair cropped so short that they acquired the name of 'Round heads'; but at the Restoration, long hair once again returned to favour and both men and women powdered the hair with violet-scented orris and with other fragrant powders. Indeed, perfumery has never formed a separate branch of trade in England. It was either under the jurisdiction of the milliners or of the mercers who combined their trade with the sale of combs and toilet mirrors. The first people to deal in aromatics were the pepperers of London, a guild mentioned in the Pipe Rolls as early as 1179. They were a company of merchants who imported spices and aromatic gums from the East and, shortly after this date, they amalgamated with the spicers. They were originally known as the Pepperers of Soper's Lane while the Spicers were of the Ward of Chepe and each year they paid a toll of spices to the King. Many were of Italian origin and brought with them a considerable knowledge of their wares; their patron saint was St. Anthony and they dealt mainly in drugs for the medical profession. One of their members was Odin the Spicer, who was apothecary to Edward II's Queen, Isabella of France, and in the year before Bannockburn, it is recorded that he received the sum of sevenpence halfpenny for his services.

At the beginning of the fifteenth century, the spicers and milliners had settled in Bucklersbury where the first tobacconists began to

7

sell their wares a century or more later. The spicers held a position of importance in supplying aromatics to the wealthy for embalming purposes. Amongst the funeral expenses of Sir Edward Darrell, who died in 1549, there is the sum of thirty-seven shillings 'for spice for the embawminge of his corpse', and the spicers provided herbs and unguents for the embalming of Queen Eleanor's body before it left Lincoln on its long journey to London for interment in the Abbey of Westminster.

From the spicers, the trade in perfumes passed to the grocers and apothecaries; the milliners made up their own unguents and powders to perfume the gloves they sold along with other scented garments.

In 1617, the apothecaries deemed it necessary to break away from the Grocers' Company because, as their charter says, 'many unskilled and ignorant men ... do abide in our City of London which are not well instructed in the art or mystery of Apothecaries and do make a compound many unwholesome, hurtful, deceitful, corrupt and dangerous medicines and the same do sell ... to the great peril and daily hazard of the lives of our subjects ...'

They had a willing supporter in James I who met the Mayor and Corporation and told them that he had granted their charter 'from his own judgement for the health of the people'. The following year they took part in the Lord Mayor's procession under their own banner. The manufacture of perfumes for toilet purposes, however, remained with the surgeon-barbers and it was not until 1882 that they were granted their own charter when the Incorporated Guild of Hairdressers, Wigmakers and Perfumers came into being.

The first premises devoted entirely to making and selling perfumes was that of Charles Lillie who lived above the shop he opened in the Strand, at the corner of Beaufort Buildings, during the early years of the eighteenth century. This was something of an innovation and attracted much attention; the *Tatler* frequently praised his skills in devising new snuffs and perfumes. Shortly afterwards, a Mr. Perry opened a perfume shop, also in the Strand, at the corner of Burleigh Street where the London house of Elizabeth's Chancellor had once stood. In the Elizabethan era it was noted for its gardens, which were for a time in the care of John Gerard who also looked after the first botanic garden of the College of Physicians. Another London perfumer to achieve fame during the reign of Queen Anne, was

William Bayley who in 1711 opened his shop in Long Acre, then one of the more fashionable parts of town. Later he moved to Cockspur Street where he carried on business at the sign of 'Ye Olde Civet Cat', where he stayed for many years.

The early eighteenth century was a time of considerable activity in the manufacture and sale of perfumes and in 1730 Juan Floris set sail from his native Minorca to set up his sign in the fashionable quarter of London in Jermyn Street, directly opposite Sir Christopher Wren's newly built church of St. James. At the time, Jermyn Street was only slightly less exclusive than St. James's, for here was the location of 'Gentlemen's chambers' where men of substance kept up a separate bachelor existence. At the side of 89 Jermyn Street, a small door opened to a long narrow passage and a stairway, dimly lit by flickering candles, but on occasions bright with the presence of Admiral of the Fleet Lord Nelson who occupied 'chambers' above the Floris shop. Close by, at No. 11 Clarges Street, now demolished, lived Emma, Lady Hamilton, so that Nelson had not far to walk on his numerous visits to the house. Later, 'dearest Emma' moved to New Bond Street and purchased her perfumes and cosmetics at Savory & Moore's which stands today exactly as she knew it one hundred and fifty years ago. Other famous men who lived nearby included William Pitt whose lumbering coach must often have splashed the panels of many a lady's sedan chair on its way up the busy cobbled street to Floris's shop. Nearby, over a hosier's shop, Thomas Gray resided during the time he was writing his 'Elegy in a Country Churchyard'; and at No. 42, lived Thomas Lawrence, the fashionable portrait painter.

In 1800, the firm of Floris supplied the Prince of Wales with the fine tortoise-shell combs for which it was justly famed. His Royal Highness succeeded to the throne in 1821 as George IV and, in the same year, graciously bestowed on the firm the Royal Warrant, the first of many it has since received. The firm also dealt in sponges for the bath and in vinaigrettes, and made a speciality of its bone toothbrushes, two of which are mentioned in an invoice for March 25, 1810, for goods purchased by Admiral Wilson, who served with Nelson at Trafalgar. On the same invoice is an item for 'lavinder water' for which the firm was also celebrated, the total amount for goods supplied being £5. 3. 0. Nelson purchased his pomades and toilet requisites here, and in the firm's possession there is a letter personally written by Miss Florence Nightingale, dated July 25, 1863, thanking Mr. Floris for his 'sweet-smelling nosegay' and giving him a detailed account of the sickness record of the Army in India.

A catalogue of about the same date, which carries the royal cipher of Queen Victoria, describes the firm as being 'smooth-pointed comb makers and perfumers'; and, among a large number of articles for sale, mention is made of 'tooth picks in tortoise-shell'; 'smelling bottles with patent stoppers'; 'wicker-covered Eau de Cologne bottles'; 'Egyptian loofahs'; and 'Turkey sponges', which were of specially fine quality and suitable for vinaigrettes. Their scented pomades for the hair included Orange, Violet, Maréchale and Reseda perfumes, the last having the fragrance of mignonette. For fumigating apartments, a special mixture known as Eau à Brûler was recommended. This was made from one pint of Eau de Cologne, one ounce each of tincture of benzoin and vanilla, and half a drachm of otto of thyme, mint and nutmeg. It was burnt in a perfume lamp or in a small bowl held above the flame of a spirit lamp which was kept alight for several minutes before the room was occupied. Floris's Eau de Cologne was specially prepared for them by the Farina brothers, who had settled in Cologne in 1709 and soon became famous for their product.

The range of Floris perfumes for handkerchiefs numbered more than a hundred and included such famous odours as Rondeletia, Maréchale, Frangipani, Chypre and Esprit de Rose, while a number were concocted to cater for the tastes of the 'smart set' and were given more popular names like Jockey Club, Guard's Bouquet and Canterbury Violet.

Floris also made scented powders for sachets and to perfume drawers and writing desks, and smelling salts prepared with otto of roses, lily of the valley and lavender. From the mid-nineteenth century smelling bottles began to take the place of vinaigrettes and were prepared from concentrated liquid of ammonia. To each pint were added one drachm of otto of rosemary or lavender, one drachm of otto of roses and half a drachm of otto of cloves. Small bottles with their closely fitting glass stoppers were filled with an absorbent material, such as asbestos or the trimmings of Turkey sponges which were saturated in the scented ammonia. Transparent crystalline salts such as sulphate of potash were also used after being treated with alcoholic ammonia (this is alcohol which has been saturated with ammonia gas before being mixed with various ottos). Preston salt was another form of smelling salts but was neither so pleasant nor so lasting. It was prepared by ramming hard into a bottle a mixture of aesqui-carbonate of ammonia and freshly slaked lime and then pouring on a few drops of otto of lavender or bergamot.

The Red Rose perfume, for which the firm of Floris is justly famed, first came into prominence in the days when Rosa Lewis took over the lease of the Cavendish Hotel in Jermyn Street in 1902, a time when Edwardian elegance was at its height. Edward VII was a frequent visitor at the Cavendish and kept his own wine cellar there. He loved Rosa's quail puddings and her rose perfume which she obtained from the Floris shop only a few yards from the main entrance of her hotel. It was, so to speak, her trade mark, and, whenever she met the troop trains at Victoria during the First World War, the fragrance of her rose perfume was unmistakable, as familiar to all those returning from the trenches as was the Cavendish Hotel where they would congregate.

CHAPTER ELEVEN

SCENTS OF THE NEW WORLD

The primitive peoples and their love of scent – Aromatic barks – Russian leather – Bay rum – Perfumed waxes – Balsamic resins and their collection – Vanilla in commerce – Microfragrance.

SINCE that day in 1493, when Mercutio Frangipani, the botanist sailing with Columbus on his second expedition, first inhaled the delicious perfume of Plumeria alba as the ships approached the coast of Antigua, the New World has provided many scented plants for perfumery—which would have been considerably the poorer without them.

The Aztecs placed scented flowers on the graves of the departed and, when they withered, replaced them with others over a period of at least four years, during which time they believed that the soul was passing through various stages of purgatory on its long journey to heaven. Rich in scented flowers, Mexico and South America have given to commerce the 'linaloe' and the famed Balsam of Peru.

In his *Travels up the Amazon and Rio Negro*, A. R. Wallace tells of a perfume which the natives call 'umari'. This they use to rub over the body, and they also insert pieces of wool, steeped in the perfume, in their long plaited hair-locks. They obtain the perfume by lifting the bark of the tree Humirium floribundum and inserting pieces of cotton or wool, leaving them for a week or more until they have become saturated by the resinous secretion.

Around their necks they hang necklaces of rose-scented beads, made from the wood of Convolvulus scoparius. From this, the perfumer distills oil of rhodium, and from its dried and powdered wood the Victorians made sachet powders. One hundredweight of the wood will yield about three ounces of oil which has a pleasing rose-like perfume. It has come to be superseded by oil of geranium, which has the rose scent more faithfully reproduced and is obtained from plants which are more readily available.

In South America, a fragrant essential oil is obtained from the leaves and young wood of Boldoa fragrans, native of the Chilean Andes where it is found growing in isolated groups on mountainous slopes. It is a handsome small tree with highly scented flowers and aromatic leaves. Its cylindrical branches are clothed in a smooth grey bark though the twigs are rough and covered in stellate hairs. The bark and twigs are also aromatic, likewise the fruits which are greenish-yellow in colour, and little more than pea-size. They are dried and made into necklaces by the Chilians and, when warmed by the body or by the sun, they release the delicious scent of cinnamon which is also present in the leaves. These are reddish-brown in colour and covered with pellucid dots. When dried and powdered and scattered among clothes, they impart their aromatic perfume to them.

Another plant of the New World which has bark with a similar fragrance is Croton eleutheria, native of the Bahamas, its product being known commercially as 'cascarilla'. The branches are brittle and, when broken, exude a thick balsamic juice. The bark arrives on the market in short curled pieces or quills, each about three inches long. When quite dry it releases an agreeable aromatic smell and for this reason was once an important ingredient in fumigating pastilles. To the islanders, it is known as 'sweet-wood', and they use it to scent clothes and bedding.

The New World, in particular, abounds in trees and shrubs with fragrant wood and bark, one of the most important in perfumery being 'sassafras', the product of Laurus sassafras or Sassafras officinale of the natural order Lauraceae. A deciduous tree, it is common in woodlands from eastern Canada to Missouri where, in the south, it will attain a height of almost a hundred feet. The deeply furrowed bark is greyish-brown and possesses extreme fragrance.

The early French settlers in Martinique found that the natives decorated their heads with Talauma blossoms which appear at the ends of the branches, the large white flowers with their satin-like petals having a most powerful scent, especially at night. They were also used by the distillers of Martinique to flavour their wines and liqueurs. The Talauma has a scent comparable to that of the Rondeletia of Mexico and Havana, a shrub with handsome red flowers which grows on rocky promontories near the sea. Though not made from the flowers, the perfume is named after them and is an example of the perfumer's art in being able to reproduce their natural scent without the blossoms forming any part of it.

The French in Louisiana have recorded their enjoyment at gathering magnolia blossoms to make into garlands and to decorate their homes; the plants grow to a hundred feet in height with shining laurel-like leaves and large pale yellow cup-shaped flowers with a delicious fruity perfume. The southern United States is its natural home and here it begins to bloom early in May and continues until almost the end of summer. Its near neighbour is often Magnolia glauca, the Swamp Laurel, which grows in swampy ground close to the sea. It does not attain the stature of M. grandiflora nor is it as handsome, but in a gentle breeze, the scent of its blossom, resembling that of lily of the valley and being especially pronounced at eventide, may be detected at a distance of three miles or more.

The magnolia is found in old fields and on thinly wooded slopes where the trees are 'grubbed up' during winter when the sap is down. At this stage, the roots contain a large concentration of essential oil and from them and the external bark, which is light and spongy, crude oil of sassafras is distilled composed of about seventy per cent safrol with its pleasant aromatic odour. Safrol is present in the essential oil of the Camphor tree, Cinnamomum camphora, and is identical to shikomol, present in the fruit of the false Star Anise tree of Japan, Illicium regulosum, which for its many scented attractions is usually planted near Buddhist shrines throughout the land. From safrol, heliotropin is synthetically obtained, reproducing the scent of heliotrope in perfumery.

It is the bark of the sassafras roots which is the most fragrant part of the tree. When dug up, they are cleaned of soil and split into small pieces which are fed into a chopping machine capable of dealing with about 10,000 pounds of root an hour and which will cut them into slices less than half an inch thick. They are then placed in a steep tank to which steam under pressure is admitted and which will take two days and nights to extract the oil. The average yield is about one gallon of oil from every thousand pounds of root chippings. Baltimore was once the centre for the export of sassafras, both the bark and the root, as well as the crude oil which mostly went to European manufacturers of soaps and hair shampoos.

Further to the south grows the Sweet-scented Shrub of Carolina, the calycanthus, all parts of which have a different scent. The flowers, which are comprised of a large number of chocolate-coloured petals and sepals, have the aroma of ripe apples; the bark smells of cinnamon, and the roots of camphor. It is found on the banks of rivers and streams where it forms a bush about six feet high and remains in bloom throughout summer. The early settlers made use of the bark as a substitute for cinnamon and burnt the dried roots to fumigate their homes.

An aromatic, whose odour and flavour so much resembles a mixture of cinnamon, cloves and nutmeg, that it is known as 'Allspice', is the dried, unripened berry of a handsome evergreen tree, Eugenia pimenta or Pimento, native of Mexico and Costa Rica, of Trinidad and Jamaica and the Leeward Islands. Its grey bark and leaves are highly aromatic and the small white flowers are so powerfully scented that their perfume is carried quite a distance off-shore when a soft breeze is blowing. The flowers are followed by small berries which are gathered while green and dried on mats in the sun, to be removed under cover each evening to be protected from dew.

In Jamaica, large forests of Pimento trees are to be found near Kingston and St. Ann's, growing to a height of about 6,000 feet above sea level; and from Kingston the dried unripened fruit is despatched to the United States and to Britain. The berries yield an essential oil composed mainly of eugenol, the principle body of cloves, which when mixed in the proportion of three ounces to each gallon of rectified spirit, forms 'extract of allspice' which at one time was used in the manufacture of inexpensive carnation 'bouquets' and in scented soaps.

During the American Civil War, when allspice was difficult to obtain, the fruit and bark of Laurus benzoin acted as a substitute. Known as the 'spice-bush', it is found in damp, deciduous woodlands from Maine to Florida. The aromatic bark was used as a valuable tonic and stimulant and the essential oil of the bright red berries, the same size as olives, has a smell greatly resembling the clove, being 'warm' and aromatic.

The 'Sweet-fern' of North America, Comptonia asplenifolia, with its fern-like fronds sprinkled with resinous dots of golden-yellow, yields an essential oil with the spicy odour of cinnamon. It has a limited use in perfumery, in combination with other oils, including

7*

oil of wintergreen which is obtained from Gaultheria procumbens, the Ground Holly or Mountain Tea. It is a common plant of the pine forests of New Jersey and North Carolina, and all parts, including the small heath-like leaves and the crimson berries, yield the otto methyl salicylate. After treatment with a warm solution of caustic alkali, it yields salicylic acid and methyl alcohol used for perfuming soap.

Iceland Wintergreen was a popular handkerchief perfume in the United States a century ago and was prepared from esprit de rose; essence of lavender; extract of neroli, vanilla and cassie, using a half pint of each and five minims of otto of wintergreen. A similar oil, consisting mainly of methyl salicylate, is obtained from the inner bark and leaves of the Black Birch, Betula lenta, which is widely dispersed in North America; and from the White Birch, Betula alba, an aromatic oil known as 'Russian leather' is derived. It was given this name because the extraction was at one time used by book-binders to rub on to leather, to impart its characteristic perfume (caused by the principle Betulin) and also to preserve it. For many years, the extraction of the oil was a closely guarded secret of the Russian Government.

The libraries of all large houses in Britain and in the United States were once redolent with the smell of their leather-bound books, and in these rooms the scent has persisted to this day. A writer, referring to the Bodleian Library at Oxford, said that 'the aromatic scent of the Russian-bound books in the Mason Room, and the mellow odour emanating from the library of Francis Douce, distinguished those rooms from the rest of the Bodleian'. The same writer says that, when the Library was visited by James I, the floors of each room had been scrubbed clean with rosemary water as this was the monarch's favourite scent.

The islands of the West Indies are rich in plants with scented flowers and leaves and, in Antigua and Barbados, the air is filled with the fragrance of the West Indian Bay. From its leaves and branches is obtained, by distillation, oil of Bay which at one time was mixed with Jamaica rum to produce the best of all hair tonics, the celebrated 'Bay Rum'. Today, oil of Bay is adulterated with alcohol, to which are added oil of orange and pimento, eugenol with its clove-like perfume and pinene, both of which are among the principal ingredients.

The early settlers made ample use of the wax-myrtle, a shrub which abounds on the wastelands of Nova Scotia and as far south as Louisiana. It is also present on the islands of the Bahamas. Myrica cerifera was known to the Pilgrim Fathers as the Candleberry for they made night-lights from the white wax crust which encases the berries. Their method of collecting was to scald the berries with boiling rain water and to collect the wax as it floated to the surface. The yellow tallow was then re-heated and made into cakes which burn with a clear white flame, producing little smoke and emitting a most agreeable aromatic odour. At a later date, perfumed candles were made by incorporating Carnauba wax, obtained from the Wax Palm of Brazil, a tree which attains a height of almost a hundred feet in its natural habitat.

The wax forms on the scales which enclose the leaf buds and is secreted in such abundance that it falls to the ground to be collected. An alternative is to cut off the leaf-buds, to remove the wax by treating with boiling water and to collect it from the surface. It is then re-melted and made into cakes. It is harder than Myrtle wax and burns longer though its smell is not nearly so pleasing, resembling newly mown hay rather than the resinous scent of Candleberry wax. Each tree will yield about four pounds of wax during the season and, throughout the nineteenth century, England imported large quantities from Brazil to make scented candles; the natives of the Rio Grande also burned it to fumigate their primitive homes.

The Indians of North America obtained a similar wax from Myrica gale, the Sweet Gale, a native British plant which is also widely dispersed throughout North America. The leaves are odorous and yield an aromatic oil upon distillation, but it is from the small berries that the wax is obtained. This is yellowish-green in colour and, after collecting by the boiling water treatment, it yields a brittle wax which, when burnt, releases a delicious balsamic odour.

There is another species found on the islands of Jamaica and St. Domingo, the fruit of which yields Columbian wax; and, in the province of Para, Ocuba wax is obtained from yet a further species which grows only along the banks of the Amazon. Though each of these waxes is used for candle-making, the most suitable is Carnauba which has a melting point of 84° C., twice as high as that of other waxes, hence its commercial value.

The New World is rich in balsamic resins, and the three balsams of perfumery are indigenous to parts of Mexico and Central America. Balsam of Peru is the most important for it has an odour resembling that of vanilla. It is an interesting fact that almost all the importations from South America which are of use to the perfumer, have a similarity of odour. Vanilla, Tonquin, Heliotrope and the balsams of Peru and Tolu blend perfectly with each other to make 'bouquets' and sachet powders though, with the introduction of modern synthetics, they are not now so widely used as they were prior to the First World War when they were present in most of the better known perfumes such as Marcéhale and Stolen Kisses.

Balsam of Peru is obtained from the tree Myroxylon peruiferum, but it has no connection with the country of that name, being native only of El Salvador where it is found in dense forests near the coast. A century ago, the collection of its resin was on so large a scale that the strip of land where it abounds came to be known as the 'Balsam Coast'. It had a medicinal value for its 'healing' qualities, and the balsam was widely used in soap manufacturing to impart its pleasant smell and to make the soap wash with a creamy lather.

The Myroxylon is a handsome tree, growing about fifty feet tall in a pyramidal form, and all parts are fragrant with the balsamic exudations, even the calyx of the small white flowers. This yields the finest balsam but is rarely collected as the flowers are shortlived. Instead it is obtained from the trunk of the tree by natives who bring to their task an expertise which comes only after years of practice. About six feet up from the base of the trunk, incisions are made in the bark in such a way that four strips, each about 2 inches wide, are left intact as it is upon these that the future vitality of the tree depends. Between the strips, the bark is beaten with the back of an axe and several cuts are made with a sharp knife. Immediately, the balsam begins to flow and is set alight with a wax taper causing it to run more quickly; the flame is extinguished after an hour or so. Into the incision are stuffed cotton rags which, when saturated with the balsam, are placed in earthenware pots and have boiling water poured over them. The balsam is collected once a week and the average weight of resin will amount to about four pounds per tree. The work continues in this way from November until the end of April, after which no further resin is 'tapped' until the following

November. When treated with hot water, the balsamic resin rises to the surface where it is collected and placed in pans to be re-heated, and any impurities removed. It will then have the appearance of dark brown treacle.

With careful handling, a tree may be expected to yield for about thirty years. It is then rested for at least five years before 'tapping' is resumed, and will normally give another twenty years of production. During the height of the balsam-yielding season, the delicious fragrance is prevalent a mile or more off-shore, so thickly is the coastline covered with the trees. At one time 20,000 pounds of the resin were sold annually to merchants for export to European markets where it was in demand for making soaps and for incorporating into pastille burners.

From Mexico and El Salvador comes also Balsam of Tolu which is extracted in the same way but from a different species of the Myroxylan tree. The balsam, which is sold at ordinary temperatures, is however so mobile that, if pieces are placed in a jar in a warm room, they will quickly consolidate into a mass. Like pale treacle in appearance, it will dissolve in alcohol and at one time was used as a base for most perfumes, not only for its vanilla-like odour but to give a scent more permanence. Cinnamic acid and Benzyl cinnamate are the most important of its constituents.

Balsam of storax or 'gum storax' is the exudation of Liquidamber styraciflora, the Sweet Gum, a handsome North American tree whose resin has replaced that of the Near Eastern Storax officinalis (it also provides satinwood for cabinet-makers). The tree was first mentioned in a book by the Spanish botanist Hernandez, published in 1650; in it he describes how the sweetly scented gum exudes through the bark like 'liquid amber', hence the name which Linnaeus gave the genus. It was first planted in Britain, in Bishop Compton's famous garden adjoining Fulham Palace, in 1681.

Another species, Liquidamber orientale, native of Asia Minor, is a small shrubby tree yielding a liquid balsam much appreciated by people of the Near East to use in perfumery. The bark is often burnt in the home to counteract unpleasant smells and liquid storax will give greater permanence to the odours of flowers extracted by maceration. It was also used in the imitation of other scents as an alternative to vanilla, ambergris or benzoin or to complement them. When a perfume is applied, the alcohol is the first thing to evaporate, the attars being 'held' or 'fixed' by the resin or by one of the animal secretions. Without a fixative, as the perfume dies away, each substance used in its composition would become too noticeable, depending upon the strength of each as no two attars are exactly alike in their volatility. Thus, in a mixture of jasmine, rose and patchouli, the jasmine would be the first to evaporate and the perfume would then be completely changed in character. Then the rose scent would vanish, leaving only the patchouli to provide an odour which may be not at all to the liking of the wearer. Where a 'fixative' is employed, however, the perfume retains its original composition until it has evaporated entirely.

Perhaps no plant of the New World has been more widely used in perfumery and in confectionery than the vanilla, at least until the discovery of vanillin by Tiemann and Rieman in 1875 which was one of the most important advances in synthetic chemistry. Vanillin, the odoriferous principle of vanilla, is now obtained from coal tar; Dr. Wright obtained it from opium, and Tiemann from fir sap or resin.

The vanilla is an epiphytic plant of the tropical forests of Mexico and Brazil where it attaches itself to tall trees and pulls itself up into the sunlight, its greenish-yellow orchid-like flowers diffusing their sweet perfume in the warmth. During the last century, it was widely planted in Madagascar and Mauritius, in several islands of Indonesia, and in the West Indies where, grown commercially, the plant's climbing habit is restricted.

The pods or beans, as they are called, are about nine inches long and were first seen in England towards the end of the sixteenth century when John Morgan, an apothecary, showed one to Elizabeth I, saying that he knew not what it was except that 'it had been brought from abroad by Spanish merchants'. The pods, resembling runner beans, were imported in bundles of fifty or more, made secure at either end. To obtain the perfume, the pods are sliced before being placed in a gallon of alcohol and shaken up daily for about four weeks. By the end of that time, the delicious scent will have been extracted and all that needs to be done is to strain off the tincture which is now ready to include in 'bouquets' or for flavouring food. Extract of vanilla is combined with that of orange flowers to compose an imitation essence of sweet pea.

In its wild state, the plant will eventually become as thick as a man's thigh and as hard and woody as the tree against which it is growing. When grown commercially, the roots form numerous offsets which may be divided and re-planted. In its fourth year after propagation, it will bear pods of a suitable size for export and will continue to do so in ever-increasing quantities for about fifty years.

The pods are gathered in September, just before they are fully ripe, and are carefully dried so that they retain no excess moisture which would cause the pods to become mouldy during transit. When correctly harvested and cured, they are covered on the outside with needle-like crystals of vanillin, a condition known to the trade as 'frosted'.

It was Professor Johnson who stated that, physiologically, the scent of vanilla acts upon the system as an aromatic stimulant, exhilarating the mental functions, and increasing generally the energy of the animal system. In the perfumes of the last century, vanilla was almost always included as a complement to extract of Tonquin, which was obtained from the Tonquin bean, the fruit of Dipterix odorata. It is a tree of the laburnum family which grows in the tropical forests of Brazil and Guyana and on the island of Martinique where the creoles greatly appreciate the scent of new mown hay given off by the seeds. The natives place them in clothes-chests for the perfume is light and refreshing and it will keep away insects. When snuff-taking necessitated keeping bulk supplies in wooden boxes, a few Tonquin beans were usually included, especially when the snuff was not otherwise flavoured. The finely ground beans were also used in those sachet powders which at one time were sold in hosiers' shops for placing in drawers with clothes and linen. Like that of orris, the scent increases with age.

The bean is black in colour and, when dry, shines as if it has been polished. It is enclosed on the tree in a drupaceous single-seeded pod, in shape like an almond, and it releases its scent of newly mown meadow grass, like Sweet Vernal grass, only when it becomes dry. Its scent is due to the same principle, Coumarin, which was first made synthetically in 1868 by Sir William Perkin, discoverer of aniline mauve, since when the Tonquin bean has depreciated in value. Coumarin is pure white and is used in the manufacture of less expensive soaps and in perfumery. Extract of Tonquin is obtained by infusing the beans in rectified spirit, one pound of beans to a gallon of spirit; after a month, the extract is strained and is ready to use.

In Guyana and Venezuela, close to the coastline and along the banks of the Orapu and Coroni rivers, grow Galipea aromatica and G. officinalis, both renowned for the stimulating powers of their fragrant barks. That of G. aromatica is burnt by the natives to fumigate their homes whilst that of G. officinalis is better known as Angostura bark, from the name of the district near where it was first discovered. The tree grows to eighty feet or more in height and from a distance has the appearance of a palm tree. The lanceolate leaves are of brightest green and are filled with resinous dots, while the quilled bark is greyish-yellow with an under-surface of dark brown. Its bitter principle is known as Cusparine and to this it owes its peculiar odour. It acts as a tonic and stimulant and removes acidity arising from dyspepsia.

One of the earliest distillations in the United States was from Peppermint and when, in 1700, Charles Ray first saw the plant growing in England, in a Hertfordshire lane, and called it by its now familiar name, little did he realize how important it was to become in nineteenth-century commerce on both sides of the Atlantic. Fifty years later, there were at least five hundred acres under cultivation at Mitcham in Surrey and it continued to be a highly profitable crop until the middle of the nineteenth century when American competition and improved methods of distillation brought about a fall in its culture in England.

The distillation of oil of peppermint was begun in the United States in 1816 by John Burnett, who founded the industry in Wayne County, New York. Thirty years later, steam distillation was introduced when James Hall of St. Joseph County set up four large distilleries capable of producing 500 pounds of oil daily and which were fed by more than five hundred acres of peppermint. Before being taken to the stills, the plants were partially dried, for in this way they gave their essential oil within thirty minutes, and a larger amount could be distilled at one charge. The yield was about twenty pounds an acre.

The method of planting has been described by an American writer. 'It is an interesting sight,' he wrote, 'owing to the queer motions of the workmen' as they took, from a sack strung across their backs, a piece of root and dropped it into a furrow, covering it

Early scent containers by Yardley

Staffordshire porcelain pastille burners

(*Above*) Spode pastille burner

(*Below*) Staffordshire porcelain pastille burners

Sperm
Whale

Castor
beaver

Musk
deer

Civet
cat

Animals used in perfumery

with the feet before moving on. An experienced worker, in well-cultivated ground, would be able to plant about an acre each day.

The oil was packed in glass demijohns, capable of holding twenty pounds each, and from the samples, the refiners and exporters made their selections. Upon their judgment and skill in refining depended the quality of the oil. Peppermint oil owes its popularity to the solid compound menthol which achieved considerable publicity in 1879 when the *Lancet* drew attention to its value in relieving headaches and neuralgia. For this purpose, menthol cones were available in most homes merely to evaporate into the air, and wax menthol candles were burnt to relieve a cold in the head. Menthol came to be an important ingredient for flavouring snuff and has remained so until the present day. It was also used in the manufacture of inexpensive soaps.

In the United States, perfumes and cosmetics complemented each other, and beauty shops, as they are known today, began just a century ago when Marcel Grateau invented the waving iron. This was to revolutionize ladies' hair styling with its undulating waves which were held in place by setting lotions. Hairdressing salons and beauty parlours opened everywhere and unscrupulous operators brought the business into such disrepute that Congress considered it necessary to introduce the licensing of beauty parlours, a licence being granted only after extensive examinations and certification of the premises as being suitable for beauty treatment.

The rise of Hollywood as the centre of the film industry shortly after the First World War gave a much-needed impetus to American perfumery and cosmetology. It was at this time that several of the now famous beauty houses first began operations, catering not only for the American woman but for all who sought to capture the glamour of the celebrities of stage and screen.

One of the first to realize the potential of the huge American market for cosmetics and perfumes was François Coty who opened a branch in New York before the outbreak of the First World War and almost a decade before he established his business in England.

About the same time, Florence Nightingale Graham, the daughter of a Scotsman William Graham and Susan Todd, a Cornishwoman, opened her salon on Fifth Avenue, New York; and by 1922, her beauty parlours, under the Elizabeth Arden name, had become as famous in London and Paris as they were in America.

With her dynamic personality and amazing energy, Florence Graham began her working days as a nurse to a dental surgeon in her home town of Woodbridge, Toronto, but noticing how much more attractively groomed the women of the United States were, she determined to take up the dispensing of beauty as a career, extending her studies until she felt qualified to work out a complete method of skin care based on promoting natural processes. This was evolved on the principle of cleansing, toning and nourishing the skin as one bathes, exercises and feeds the body, and her original preparations are still the basis of treatment given by Elizabeth Arden salons everywhere.

Seeking a 'name' with which to launch her business, she hit upon the one by which she was to become so well known after reading the book, *Elizabeth and Her German Garden*. Arden was a corruption of 'garden', for, throughout her life, Florence Graham adored flowers and all things which grew, naming her lovely Blue Grass perfume after the distant panorama she could enjoy from her home in Virginia.

She realized that the ritual of beauty is steeped in perfume, beginning with the bath. Her fragrant milk softens and perfumes the water and the soaps hold their fragrance to the last thin wafer. Her bath oil clings to the skin, leaving a lingering scent, to be released again and again as the warmth of the body diffuses it.

The fame of her Fifth Avenue salon soon spread throughout America and further salons were opened in Boston, Washington and Chicago. Today there are beauty parlours in thirty-five cities in America, Europe and Australia, where women are offered a comprehensive beauty service, including lessons in exercises and posture; in massage and slimming; in hairdressing and facial treatment.

Because of their subtle powers of persuasion, perfumes have come to play an ever-increasing part in commercial advertising and have advanced considerably in this respect since the days when coffee houses sought to attract those who passed by with the appetizing aroma of ground coffee beans which reached the pavement through a discreetly placed ventilator. The same odour is now dispersed by synthetic means from stores and supermarkets who realize the part that perfume plays in attracting customers; while the beauty parlour, releasing a synthetic perfume of tropical subtlety, has been known to increase the number of its customers fourfold.

So important is it, when introducing a modern commercial product, to be quite certain that its fragrance has customer appeal, that firms have been set up specially to provide the necessary advisory service. In laboratories situated on the outskirts of London, experts at the Perfume Evaluation Board are continually sniffing to determine the right scent for new products and to evaluate new perfumes for wearing. It is their task to create suitable scents for almost every saleable item, from detergents to aerosols, from printer's inks to plastics, while in the United States there is at least one firm experimenting with perfumes to add to petrol, so that the appalling smell of exhaust fumes may be replaced by a more pleasing fragrance.

One of the most interesting introductions of modern perfumery is known as micro-encapsulation or micro-fragrance, an innovation of the Minnesota Mining and Manufacturing Co (3M) of America. Micro-fragrance has been evolved from early attempts to encapsulate oily liquids in spheres so minute that they have the appearance of talcum powder, and now makes it possible to incorporate smell with print so that perfumed products can be sampled and will add impact when the perfume is released. 3M micro-fragrance consists of millions of microscopic plastic capsules, each of which contains the exact smell it is wished to convey, and which are coated on to paper or self-adhesive tape. They can be incorporated in any form of printed material and will, in the future, come to be used to advertise cookery or gardening books, whose jackets will bear a strip which, when scratched with the finger-nail or with some other hard object, will release the smell of herbs or of a sweetly-scented flower. In the United States, the first children's book to contain these scented tapes, *The Sweet Smell of Christmas*, was published in 1970. All the characters there release their scent merely by the picture being scratched. Thus the Christmas tree exuded its familiar pine-resin scent and the gingerbread men, the smell of ginger, much to the enjoyment of young readers and scratchers.

Perfumes and toiletries are obvious subjects for micro-fragrance sampling. The firm of Coty was the first to use it, taking a full page in McCall's magazine to advertise their Imprévu perfume. The result was a considerable increase in counter sales after the interested reader had been invited to 'scratch the surface' of the yellow strip, which released exactly the fragrance of the perfume in the bottle illustrated alongside it.

The firm of Yardley tested the power of micro-fragrance on their 'Springflowers' toiletries, in a direct mail offer to two million American high school and college girls, half receiving the offer with a micro-fragrance sample, the other half without it. The result was a fifty per cent greater response from those who had received and tested the micro-fragrant sample.

In Britain, Avon's Brocade was one of the first perfumes to be launched using micro-fragrance and Elizabeth Arden followed with their Seaqua range of toiletries, a strip of micro-fragrant tape being afixed to a leaflet which was available for customers to scratch and smell in all stores and salons stocking the Arden range.

The life of an encapsulated oil is said to be equal to that of a bottled perfume, which will last almost indefinitely if kept sealed and in a dark place. The capsules are so small that one pound will be sufficient to coat almost 40,000 square inches of tape and, when coated, they are invisible to the naked eye.

'Scratch-and-smell' tapes are only a beginning, but already tourist boards in America are including micro-fragrance tapes in their brochures to advertise fresh sea breezes; and soon it may be possible to incorporate micro-capsules into tissue papers so that, when one applies a tissue to the nose, it will immediately release one's favourite perfume or an invigorating smell.

In the home, delicate scents may also be released simply by placing a few drops of essence on an asbestos disc and allowing a few seconds for it to absorb before placing it on an electric light bulb. As soon as the light is switched on and the bulb becomes warm, the essence will vaporize to create a fragrant and lasting perfume. the vaporization ceasing when the light is turned off so that one application of essence will last for several hours. It is an idea originating in America which quickly found favour in European homes.

CHAPTER TWELVE

THE COMPOSITION AND EXTRACTION OF PERFUME

The odour of flowers – Their composition – The antiseptic value of essential oils – The first synthetic scents – The perfume industry – Methods of extracting the essential oil.

THE strength of an odour when inhaled will play a large part in determining its unpleasantness. Most perfumes are pleasing only when inhaled in small amounts and are highly unpleasant when inhaled in bulk. Indeed, attar of roses in quantity is most disagreeable because it is so overpowering, and it does not represent the true rose perfume which is dependent upon a number of other substances for its delicacy.

These substances have a similar but not identical scent and whereas one substance may predominate, in company with it are closely related chemical compounds whose scents resemble that of the dominant scent. The effect is to shade or round off the predominant scent, like a note played on a violin which may have a certain sharpness on its own but which is mellowed by closely associated overtones.

In the rose scent, geraniol is the substance predominating but in association with it there are various other substances of different but similar scents, though they may not be chemically related. One is phenyl ethyl alcohol which has a scent similar to that associated with the rose. However, a mixture of the rose-scented substances to be found in attar of roses, though it gives a pleasantly sweet scent, in no way produces the rose perfume. At least eight other substances combine to produce the true rose perfume which may have undertones of a fruity or a spicy nature. The scent of the hybrid tea rose Fragrant Cloud has undertones of cinnamon or clove whilst that of Ena Harkness has the damask perfume combined with fruity undertones. The late Mr. Charles Curtis enumerated seventeen different rose scents including musk and myrrh, violet and clove. The petals of the most highly scented varieties have on their inner surface minute scent glands containing the volatile essence, which are clearly visible under a microscope, while on the petals of the Sweet Brier, the scent glands are clearly visible even to the naked eye.

Very few flower scents are built up around a single note, most contain two distinct scents, as with mimosa (the 'cassie' of the French perfumers) where the principal scents are violet and hawthorn. In hawthorn itself, there are the fishy smell of trimethylamine and the sweeter undertones of aniseed, caused by anisic aldehyde which is chemically related to anethol, the sweet substance of aniseed. Attar of jasmine is composed of benzyl acetate, with overtones of benzyl formate and shaded with methyl anthranilate and indol, also with some balsamic and various fruit-scented substances to give it a pleasing 'lightness'.

The wallflower contains most of the typical flower scents and among those which have been isolated from its attar are the main substances which make up the scent of violet, rose and orange blossom. The double yellow wallflower, Harpur Crewe, named after a Shropshire country parson of that name, emits a powerful violet-like scent which is also present in the mignonette and vine flower, two of the most difficult flowers from which to extract essential oil. Mignonette yields only o.oo2 per cent of essential oil, yet its scent is so powerful that it is used in perfumery at a strength of only 1 part in 500 parts of alcohol.

The composition of the essential oil of flowers is more complex than that of leaves, which accounts for the unique delicacy of flower scents compared with those of the latter. The essential oil of leaves usually consists of a single substance such as methyl salicylate which contains oil of wintergreen and coumarin. It is this which gives the sweet herby smell to new mown hay and to woodruff. A notable exception is the Rose-leaf Geranium in which are present geraniol and phenyl ethyl alcohol, these being the principal constituents of attar of roses and which account for the delicate rose perfume in the leaves of Pelargonium capitatum.

Many leaves contain substances which are not present in flowers and give the leaves their particular pungent quality. Eucalyptus is present in Yarrow and in Cotton Lavender and lends them its familiar herby smell; and borneol acetate occurs in conifer leaves and in Rosemary, and gives them their invigorating 'pine' scent. Lemon scent is due to citral which is present in Lemon-scented Verbena and in Lemon Grass. It also occurs in Lemon Thyme, in combination with eucalyptol. Geraniol is found in several species of Lemon Grass and in Australian pines whose essential oil may contain as much as ninety per cent geraniol.

The essential oil of lavender is made up of the bergamot-scented linalyl acetate, combined with eucalyptol and softened with a trace of rose. It is this slight perfume which gives the bay leaf such a pleasant smell, for it occurs together with the herby eucalyptol which would give the leaf a less attractive scent if not sweetened with rose.

The sweetly scented balsams were the first scents to be appreciated by man. Their principal substance is cinnamic alcohol which is present in the exudations of a number of trees and shrubs. It is in storax and in balsam of Peru, in balm of Gilead and in the exudation of the Balsam Poplar. These, together with the conifers which yield a resinous exudation when the bark is punctured, were used by primitive man for treating wounds for they have antiseptic qualities which also protect the plants from browsing animals. They were the earliest plants to inhabit the earth, being thornless and reproducing themselves by wind pollination as there were few insects to do the work. Man still uses their resinous exudations for medicinal purposes and in perfumery. Friar's Balsam is used for treating cuts and to heal a sore throat while tincture of myrrh is still the finest preparation to soothe a sore mouth.

Balsam is a resinous substance incapable of saponification, being insoluble in water but soluble in ether, alcohol and in oil. It contains cinnamic or benzoic acid, or both together. The principal source of benzoic acid is Styrax benzoin or benjamin which has the odour of the resin from which it is derived.

Oils extracted from fragrant leaves have a greater antiseptic value than those obtained by extraction from petals. Attar of roses is the exception, its antiseptic powers being more considerable than those of any other flower, with seven times the antiseptic strength of carbolic acid. The essential oil of the leaves of thyme is, however, even more potent, having twelve times the antiseptic value of carbolic acid. It was used to spray on the clothes of soldiers during the Crimean War to keep them free from lice, in the same way that rue was once strewn over the floor of the Old Bailey.

The scented substances, the essential oils, are the waste products of a plant's metabolism, occurring first amongst the by-products of the plant's chemistry to be thrown out as excreta. Some animal scents, too, have a similar origin, being secreted into the cavity formed around the lanoline glands. Indol, which is present in the essential oil of a number of heavily scented flowers, is also one of the products of the putrefaction of animal tissue, while methyl indol, the active principle of civet, is a well known excretary product. It is this animal quality which makes the jonquil, lily and narcissus seem oppressive and unpleasant when their scent is released in a badly ventilated room.

The recombination of the plant's metabolism plays an important part in the production of essential oils. In a series of interesting experiments conducted in Paris in 1908, Eugène Charabot traced the development of the essential oil of lavender and has shown how the slightly scented linalol of the unripe bud combines with acetic acid to give the richly bergamot-scented linalyl acetate of the matured inflorescence. This, by the evaporation of moisture in sunlight, becomes geraniol which, by polymerization, gives rise to nerol. By recombination with acetic acid, it becomes geranyl acetate.

In the production of artificial perfumes, acetic acid is believed to be the basic unit. Acetone and acetaldehyde can be produced from carbon and water and these chemicals can react to produce citral, from which a large number of chemicals present in essential oils are obtained.

The first authentic description of the essential oil of a plant (its attar) was given by Arnaldo de Vilanova, a Catalian physician living at the end of the thirteenth century, but another hundred years were to elapse before it became known that, although essential oils are insoluble in water, they may be dissolved in alcohol. The alcoholic solution then becomes an 'essence' from which is made the 'bouquet'. This is a mixture of extracts so compounded that no one odour predominates over another.

Those flowers with the thickest petals like the white jasmine, tuberose and lily, will produce the highest quality of essentail oil, for the cells contain a greater concentration of oil than those flowers which have thin, flimsy petals; also there will be less rapid evaporation. Jasmine and tuberose, however, produce little essential oil, although they continue to produce it as long as they remain alive so the amount supplied by the flower in its lifetime is considerable.

The essential oil of flowers is contained in epidermal cells in the petal, or in the bracts (as in lavender) which take the place of petals. It is not secreted by the nectaries nor by the anthers. As Mesnaud has shown in his experiments, it is the result of a transformation of the chlorophyll into tannoid compounds or pigments, and this process can be more readily understood if it is admitted that the floral organs of a plant are only leaves modified for the performance of a new function. This is why green petalled flowers have no perfume and white flowers are the most fragrant. Perfumes are made from white jasmine, orange blossom, the jonquil, tuberose, pinks and carnations, white violets and lily of the valley. The rose is one of the few exceptions. Not only are white flowers the most fragrant of all, but the majority of them have thick, velvet-like petals which ensure the greatest yields of essential oil. As pigment (colour) is bred into flowers, the perfume vanishes. This is the reason why so many modern roses of vermilion and scarlet colouring are entirely devoid of perfume and why the white form of Clematis montana is sweetly scented whilst the red-flowered variety, rubens, is scentless. The high degree of pigmentation to be found in autumnal flowers, mostly native of North America, accounts for their almost complete absence of perfume. These include the helenium, inula, helianthus, rudbeckia, all belonging to the Compositae family.

In leaves, the essential oil is stored in numerous ways. In the bay leaf and the leaf of St. John's Wort, as in the orange, the oil is stored in capsules, which are visible as pellucid dots when held up to the light. In the myrtle, the oil is embedded deep inside the leaf tissue and the scent is released only with considerable pressure. With lavender and rosemary, the oil is stored in goblet-shaped cells which are present immediately below the surface and are released by the sun or in a warm breeze. With certain plants, the exudation is secreted on to the unopened bud, as in the Balsam Poplar, where it is fixed with a sticky substance to prevent its evaporation. If held over a low flame, the resin melts and the balsamic fragrance is released. In the cistus, prevalent in Crete and other Mediterranean islands, the gum is secreted from glandular hairs usually found on the underside of the leaves.

The essential oil in leaves acts as a protection, not only from animals, but also from attack by ants and, as scented leaf plants are usually to be found in the most exposed places, and in the warmer parts of the world, the oxidized oil provides an invisible cloud which surrounds the plant, protecting it from scorching and preventing undue loss of moisture. It is a method by which the plant provides its own shelter and the warmer the weather, the more essential oil does it produce.

The essential oil or nectar is composed of numerous organic chemical compounds known as terpenes, which contain carbon and hydrogen (hydrocarbons of the formula $C_5 H8$) and give rise to a number of oxygenated derivatives, chief of which are the alcohols and their esters, aldehydes and ketones. Alcohols occur in several different forms, notably geraniol, the principal substance of attar of roses; and borneol, with its camphor-like smell, is present in a number of fragrant leaves. Another alcohol, menthol, is found in mints, and the principal substance of the clove is methyl eugenol which gives the pink and carnation their aromatic perfume. Eucalyptol is present in many scented-leaf plants, especially lavender, rosemary and sage.

By the combination of an acid and an alcohol, an ester is produced; for instance, when acetic acid combines with alcohol (ethyl alcohol) to give the ester ethyl acetate, a volatile liquid with a lemon-like scent as in magnolia blossom. This lends a light fruity scent to perfumes. Another ester, linalyl acetate, is the most important constituent of Bergamot oil and is the real vehicle of the bergamot smell. It is also one of the chief constituents of lavender oil. Linalyl acetate, by evaporation, becomes geraniol, which in turn by polymerization becomes nerol; with the addition of acetic acid, this changes to geranyl acetate which adds softness to the scent.

Aldehydes, of which citral is the most common, are mostly present in leaves like those of Lemon Grass. Their names end in 'al' and by oxidation they become alcohols.

The violet scent is caused by a ketone, 'ionone' in the violet flower and 'irone' in orris root. The same compound is present in animal musk. Shakespeare's reference in *Hamlet* to the fleeting perfume of the violet flower is interesting and shows his keen observation of nature. In a room in Polonius's house, Laertes says:

> A violet in the youth of primy nature,
> Forward, not permanent; sweet, not lasting.
> The perfume and suppliance of a minute. No more.

This strange quality is due to a substance known as ionine, derived from the Greek ion, from which the violet took its name. Ionine possesses the ability to dull the sense of smell within a very short time and so it is not the flower which, as some believe, loses its fragrance when cut, but it is our own powers of smell which are lost. If, after several minutes to allow the sense of smell to recover, the flower is smelled again, the perfume will return, only to disappear once more, as it begins to tire the senses. It is this elusive quality that has endeared the flower to all for it is never possible to enjoy an excess of its perfume. The scent of the violet gives the impression of consisting of but a single sweet substance shading off to the fragrance of cedarwood and then to the mossy perfume of damp woodlands.

The chemical principle which causes the odour of orris root flower was isolated in 1893 by Tiemann and Kruger who, in a memoir presented to the French Academy of Sciences, stated that it was due to a ketone which they named irone. This they obtained by exhausting the orris root with ether. The extract was distilled in a strong current of steam and dilute sulphuric acid was added to the oily substance remaining in the retort. The pure irone then passes over on distillation. The substance is freely soluble in alcohol, ether and chloroform.

Experimenting further with a view to obtaining irone synthetically, Tiemann and Kruger discovered that an isomeric ketone, ionone, which has the odour of violets, may be obtained from the aldehyde citral. By the action of alkalines with acetone, citral is converted into the ketone pseudo-ionone, which, by the action of dilute acids, is then converted into the isomeric ketone, ionone. The structure of irone was finally established in 1947 following Ruzicka's years of experimentation.

Irone, which has a delightful violet odour, costs almost £12 an ounce and, though a synthetic, it is more expensive than most natural oils. Indeed, it should not be thought that synthetic odours are less valuable in perfumery than those odours made with natural oils. Long before Ruzicka's work with irone, Sir William Perkin, inventor of the analine dye, discovered in 1868 the synthetic manufacture of Coumarin, with its scent of newly mown hay. Synthetic perfumery now took a considerable step forward and the use of chemical compounds in the creation of new perfumes ran complementary to the use of natural oils, though synthetics lack the 'warmth' of natural substances.

Yet, one of the great perfumes of the world, Chanel No. 5, created by Ernst Beaux in 1923, was one of the first to contain synthetic odours. Coty's L'Aimant and Lanvin's Arpège followed in their use of synthetics and, with Chanel No. 5, became three of the most popular of all the world's great perfumes, a position they have retained ever since.

L'Aimant, which means 'magnet', clearly underlining its hidden appeal, was introduced in 1927 by François Coty, after he had spent five years perfecting it. It was time well spent for it soon became a favourite with women throughout the world. It may be described as being a subtly balanced floral 'bouquet' based on jasmine but with the top-note a vibrant and lasting synthetic, blended with natural citrus and floral oils including Bulgarian rose, Italian bergamot, Algerian geranium and, of course, jasmine. The middle or body-note includes vanilla from tropical South America and vetivert from the Orient whilst the base note has the animal warmth of Himalayan musk and of civet from Ethiopia. One of the all-time classic perfumes, it is blended from materials obtained from all parts of the world.

It is remarkable that at exactly the time François Coty was perfecting and introducing his L'Aimant perfume, Mme Jeanne Lanvin was crowning her creative ability as a couturier with the introduction of Arpège which was also to become a star creation in the world of fragrance. Like Coty's L'Aimant, it was an immediate success and has retained its popularity through the years. A perfume of surpassing beauty for the woman of good taste, Arpège is an 'arpeggio' of the most delicately scented of all flowers, there being included in its make up, the attars of jasmine, Bulgarian rose, camellia and lily-of-the-valley. It is said that the volume of flowers used each year to make Lanvin perfumes would be equal in bulk to those needed for a building of the size of the Arc de Triomphe.

As an alternative to the famed attar of rose from Bulgaria which costs more than £20 an ounce, a new synthetic rose oil recently intruduced as Attarose ABR 5000 is now being used. But Bulgarian attar, though the most expensive and desirable of all rose attars is by no means the dearest of attars. That of jasmine costs twice as much whilst the essential oil of the tuberose is priced at £2,500 a pound and is used only in the most expensive perfumes.

The use of synthetic perfumery in the future must be on an ever-increasing scale for the chemist now has a number of new devices to help him to discover nature's secrets. Ultra-violet spectroscopy, gas-liquid chromatography and NMR spectrometry enable him to identify essential oils and even trace elements which may be present in the most minute quantities.

New synthetic preparations continue to appear each year and more recent discoveries have been terpineol, a product of turpentine which reproduces the odour of purple lilac, and styrolyl acetate which has an odour resembling gardenia flowers. Further developments of synthetic perfumery included the synthesis of phenylethyl alcohol by Radziszewski, and the manufacture of hydroxycitronellal in 1905. This enabled the lily-of-the-valley fragrance to be added to the list of synthetic perfumes. Shortly afterwards, Blanc discovered how to manufacture cyclamen aldehyde.

A synthetic heliotrope perfume was first obtained in the U.S.A. by Messrs. Schimmel and Co. of New York, following the distillation of oil of sassafras, obtained from the bark of the Laurus sassafras. Crude oil of sassafras contains about ninety per cent safrol which has a pleasant aromatic odour. By treating it with permanganate of potash, safrol yields piperonylic acid known in perfumery as heliotropin, which has a scent resembling the sweet cherry pie smell of wild heliotrope.

The synthetic perfume of citrus is provided by linalyl acetate, a product of linalool present in oil of lavender. It was the Frenchman Bouchardat who found that acetic anhydride reacted with linalool at ordinary temperatures to form linalyl acetate, which has a sharp lemon-like smell; and he took his experiment a stage further when he saponified linalyl acetate with alcoholic potash which, when heated to 230° F. and combined with four equivalents of bromine, forms an alcohol which has the identical rose scent of geraniol.

From earliest times, man has sought to imitate nature by

reproducing the scents of flowers and leaves, and when it is realized that the chief soap-flake and detergent manufacturers each use as much as a hundred tons of perfume each year, it is understandable that only a small proportion of their requirements can be provided by natural oils. Today, more than two-thirds of the materials used in perfumery and in manufacturing processes are man-made, but, try as he may, man cannot reproduce in the laboratory exactly the scent of many flowers, though he can create aromatic chemicals which give off an odour greatly resembling those flowers.

The terpenes are present in all essential oils, particularly in the oil of orange blossom and in ylang ylang, while benzine compounds are prominent in the attars of most heavily scented flowers. Many of the scent substances of essential oils contain in their molecules a closed ring of six carbon atoms, known as 'the benzine ring'. Nitrogen compounds are also present in orange blossom and in all the more heavily scented flowers. The ester methyl anthranilate, which has the scent of orange, becomes methyl-methyl anthranilate when a compound of the methyl group is added to the acid. This is to be found in the skin of tangerine oranges and gives a delicious scent to the essential oil. Anthranilic acid and indol always occur together in the essential oil of heavily scented flowers like the jonquil and lily so that, when inhaled in large numbers or close to, there are always present the disagreeable undertones of excreta.

The natural perfume industry is now concentrated in the south of France, and in the valleys of northern Bulgaria, where the world's finest attar of roses is produced. Italy and Spain produce much of the essences of the citrus, and lavender water is still manufactured in England, but the flower perfumes are produced almost entirely in Bulgaria and around the small town of Grasse, situated at the foot of the Maritime Alps, in the valley of the Var, about ten miles inland from the Mediterranean. Here, the principal flowers grown are violets, jasmine, cassie (acacia), orange and rose. The land is densely planted, as many as a hundred thousand jasmine plants occupying a single acre of ground from which, over an entire season, they may be expected to yield about 7,000 pounds of flowers, the perfume being obtained by enfleurage or maceration.

The orange tree requires a deep well-prepared soil for it to be long-living, and it may be expected to attain at least a hundred years of age. It will begin to bear bloom and fruit when six years old and will reach maturity at about eighteen years when each tree will yield in a single season, which lasts for about a month, twenty-five pounds of blossom. A hundred orange trees occupying an acre of ground will produce, during the season, about 2,500 pounds of blossom which will yield by distillation about two pounds of neriol worth more than £500.

The mimosa or cassie tree requires rather less room for its development and an acre will accommodate about 300 trees which, upon maturity, will attain a height of about twelve feet and will spread out their branches to about half that distance. Like all flower perfumes, with the possible exception of the rose and orange, the cassie flower has its scent extracted by enfleurage and, as the fluffy yellow ball-shaped flowers open in succession, this enables the manufacturer to make repeated changes of blossom. In this way the fat used for extraction may be fully charged with the perfume, and consequently those flowers which open over several weeks, rather than all at the same time, are the most valuable for the extraction of their scent. This enables the plants to be picked over daily without loss of quality and the fat to be recharged over a long period so that the extract will be of high concentration. About ten pounds of cassie flowers will make one to two ounces of attar.

Around Grasse, harvesting the flowers continues throughout the year, beginning with the mimosa in January. In February the jonquil is in bloom and remains so until the end of April when the orange blossom will be ready for harvesting; its picking continues until the end of June. From early July until October, the jasmine and tuberose are harvested, with the violet remaining in bloom almost the whole year.

The rose is one of the few flowers to have its essential oil unharmed by the process of distillation, which is mostly used for the extraction of the odorous principle from leaves, barks and woods. Though in the south of France large areas are down to rose growing to supply the manufacturers with blossom, it is in the Rose Valley of northern Bulgaria that the finest attar is produced. Here, at Kazanluk and for miles around, the fields are carpeted with the pink Damask rose and its perfume is overwhelming at the height of the season. It takes about 250 pounds of rose petals to produce an ounce of the attar and June is the busiest month for collecting the flowers, when girls in their national costumes gather the roses and pile them high into wicker baskets. As many as ten thousand pickers are employed at the height of the season, when they make their way to the fields shortly after daybreak, before the rising sun causes evaporation of the essential oil from the petals. There is an old Bulgarian saying that 'when the skirts are wet, the harvest is good', and in a vintage year, which is as important to the rose grower as it is to the wine makers of France, the crop will yield as much as two tons of attar of such outstanding quality that imitators cannot hope to match it by a chemical process.

Almost a thousand varieties of the Damask rose are cultivated in Bulgaria and, at the research stations, scientists are continually working out new methods to improve the culture of the plants and the extraction of the perfume. Already it has been possible to reduce by always twenty-five per cent the number of flowers required to make an ounce of attar. In his *Sylva Florifera*, Henry Phillips, John Constable's friend, tells of a perfumer in Paris making attar of roses for the Court of Louis XVI who said that it required two tons of flowers or a hundred million petals to yield a pound of oil. At today's prices this would be worth more than £300.

A large proportion of the attar is exported to France where the world's finest rose perfumes are made. The United States and Japan are also important customers, and each year more attar is made for the demand always exceeds supply.

Several of the new African states have begun to take an interest in the production of odorous substances. In the valley of the Limpopo and in the Shire valley of southern Malawi, scented leaf plants such as marjoram, lavender and thyme are being grown commercially, and in Tanzania, eucalyptus, rosemary and dill are now distilled and the distillations sent to European manufacturers.

The extraction of essential oil is carried out by several methods, including distillation; extraction; enfleurage; and expression. The method of obtaining the essential oil by distillation is suitable only for those flowers whose attar will withstand considerable heat without suffering change. In addition, the flowers must contain a large amount of attar for the method to be profitable.

Only stainless steel and glass vessels are used in the manufacture and mixing of scents, copper and iron containers now being obsolete as they do not give the same purity of odour.

During the height of the season, the flowers are gathered without interruption and distillation continues throughout the night. The blooms are taken to the still, which is a large tank fitted with a perforated tray. When it is almost filled, a steam jet is started at the base and this makes its way through the perforations and through the mass of blossom. The steam which is driven off is laden with essential oil which is then cooled, and the oil, being insoluble in water, rises to the top. The water is run off and the oil collected.

The method of extraction whereby the attar is washed from the flowers by a volatile solvent such as petroleum ether is more gentle than steam distillation and results in the most concentrated of all essences. The flowers are placed on perforated trays in a vat which is hermetically sealed. At one end is a solvent tank, at the other end a vacuum still. The solvent is allowed to run through the percolators until it arrives at the still highly charged with the scent. Here it is distilled off at low pressure and returns to the solvent tank, the scent remaining in the retort. The process is repeated again and again so that every particle of attar is extracted, the final product being solid and wax-like and known to the trade as a 'floral concrete'. Before being used, however, it is washed with alcohol which dissolves the essential oil from the solid. The alcohol is then removed by distillation to leave behind the pure essential oil which is then known as a 'floral absolute'. This is the most concentrated form of floral scent and when diluted will give the identical perfume of the flower. The jasmine will yield about 0.25 per cent of 'floral concrete' and sometimes the petals are put under pressure to release more of their essential oil. Besides alcohol, other volatile solvents used for extraction are benzene, butone, and lythene which is a low boiling, purified fraction of petroleum.

Mignonette, jasmine, tuberose, white lilac, lily-of-the-valley and the violet will give up a greater percentage of their perfume by enfleurage or absorption than by any other method though, being carried out entirely by hand, this is one of the most expensive forms of extraction and only those flowers which continue to give off their essential oil after they have been gathered are suitable for the treatment. No heat is used in the process, which ensures that the most delicate perfumes are in no way damaged.

The flowers are collected and conveyed to the rooms with all possible speed. There they are spread out on large sheets of glass enclosed by a frame and reinforced by a wire base. The frames are

8

three to four inches deep and are known as 'châssis', some of the more important manufacturers employing as many as four or five thousand trays each season.

First, a layer of fat about half an inch thick is spread over the glass, and into the fat the flowers are sprinkled so that they entirely cover the surface. On top of the frame, others are stacked as they are greased on both sides and filled with flowers. Maybe as many as twenty frames are piled one upon the other and here they remain for three days and nights while the fragrance of the flowers is absorbed by the fat on both sides of the glass. The trays are then taken down and the flowers replaced with fresh ones, though the same fat is retained. It may take fully a month before the fat is saturated with the scent and, during that time, the flowers are changed every two or three days. Because of this, it is necessary for the flowers to continue to bloom over a long season, at least two months being the required time for successful enfleurage to take place. At the end of a month, the fat is scraped from the glass and the scent is then extracted by an alcoholic solution. About one ton of jasmine blossom will be required to extract one pound of 'floral absolute'.

Extract of jasmine is prepared by pouring alcohol on to the pomade and allowing them to remain together for two weeks. Two pounds of pomade should be used to every quart of spirit, the pomade being cut up before the alcohol is added. With mignonette, a pint of alcohol is used to extract the scent from every pound of pomade. After the essence has been filtered, it is usual to add an ounce of extract of tolu to give it greater permanence.

The oils of the same flowers may be made to yield their perfume by first saturating muslin cloths in olive oil and placing them over the frames which have had the glass removed. The cloths rest on the wire supports and over them the flowers are spread out, to be removed and replaced by others as previously described. Again, after about a month, the oil will have become saturated with their scent and it is then removed from the cloths under considerable pressure and the scent extracted by an alcoholic solvent.

One of the greatest difficulties when using fat, is to ensure that it is entirely free from any odorous principle, and when it is to be used for pomade, it must be prevented from becoming rancid. A century ago, Dr. Charles Redwood, writing in the *Pharmaceutical Journal* (Vol. XIV, No. V), suggested that if a small quantity of gum benzoin was added to the fat, this would prevent its rancification. The finest fat oil is known as oil of Ben which is colourless, tasteless and inodorous and never becomes rancid. The Behen tree is the Hyperanthera moringa, an Eastern tree now naturalized in the West Indies, the seeds of which yield twenty-five per cent of oil. Benzoic acid, prepared from the resinous gum of Styrax benzoin by the humid process, is also odourless.

By a simple method of enfleurage, a perfume can be made at home which, though not in any way to be compared with that of the professional perfumer, will be pleasing enough when used for sprinkling on clothes and linen.

To three-quarters of a pound of animal fat and a quarter of a pound of lard, add a quart of water into which has been dissolved a teaspoonful of alum. Then bring to the boil and, when the fat has dissolved, strain through muslin and allow to cool. The fat, which collects on the surface, is separated from the liquid and re-heated. It is then poured into two shallow dishes and is allowed to cool again.

The flowers are then spread over the fat of one dish to a depth of several inches and over them is placed the inverted second dish with the rims in contact with each other. The dishes remain undisturbed for two days when the flowers are removed, to be replaced by others. Each alternate day they are changed until the flowers have finished blooming or for about a month, by which time the fat will have fully absorbed the perfume. It is then scraped into a wide-necked jar with a screw top and the same amount (by bulk) of spirits of wine is added. The top is screwed down and the jar placed in a dark cupboard for two or three months, being shaken up each day to extract the scent. The liquid is then strained through muslin and will carry a perfume similar to that of the flowers. If given a fixative such as a drop of oil of sandalwood, it will intensify the scent and be more lasting.

By maceration, yet another form of extraction, purified fat is put in a porcelain pan and is melted by steam heating; cassie and orange are flowers which have their perfume extracted in this way. The flowers are thrown into the warm fat and allowed to digest for several hours before being removed with a strainer. Fresh flowers are then added and the process is repeated nine or ten times until the fat has become saturated with the scent of the flowers. After straining, the pomade is re-heated but is now kept only sufficiently warm to allow any impurities to settle; this will take about forty-eight hours. When finally cool, this becomes the cassie pomade of commerce and, to extract the attar, six pounds should be mixed with each gallon of rectified spirit. After a month it is ready to draw from the pomatum, by which time it will have become olive green in colour with the violet-like scent of mimosa. Only by enfleurage and maceration may the delicate scents of so many flowers be obtained. The 'washed' pomatum or residue can be re-heated and used for hair dressings, for it will still retain much of the delicate odour of cassie, one of the most 'flowery' of all perfumes and, with jasmine, present in almost all the great floral 'bouquets'.

Expression is only used when a plant—for instance the orange and its peel—is particularly strong in essential oil. It is usual to place the peel in large muslin bags which are then put in a vessel of stainless steel for crushing; this is done by a plate which fits inside the vessel or by rollers. During the pressing, a powerful water jet is played on to the peel to separate the juice from the solids; the liquid leaves by a number of small holes at the bottom of the tank where the essential oil is collected with the water, from which it is then separated by extraction.

CHAPTER THIRTEEN

THE ART OF THE MODERN PERFUMER

Definition of 'perfume' – The velocity of odours – Scents and their musical
allusion – Concocting a perfume – Animal fixatives – Perfumes for grooming and
personal hygiene.

THE *Encyclopaedia Britannica* defines 'perfume' as being 'a
composition of scented substances whose fragrance gratifies the sense
of smell and which is commonly associated with personal adornment'. Perfume is not merely a pleasant smell, it is a sensation
brought about by a blend of materials each with its own particular
odour and resulting in one paramount and pleasant impression. A
perfume which satisfies the senses may consist of at least a hundred
different substances, each with its separate identity, but which
blend to produce an agreeable composition, like the chords of a
piece of music built around a main theme to produce the complete
score.

Because of their intangible nature, music and perfumes have a
close affinity and, in a famous essay, Francis Bacon likens the scent of
flowers to musical notes, describing the breath of flowers in the air
'as it comes and goes' as like the warbling of music. In *Sylva
Sylvarum*, he takes the allegory a step further, judging scent and
other pleasing odours to be sweeter in the air at some distance,
'for we see that in sounds likewise, they are sweetest when we
cannot hear every part by itself.'

Eleanor Sinclair Rohde has described the fragrance of flowers as
their music, none the less beautiful because it is silent. 'In every
scented flower and leaf,' she said, 'their perfume is exhaled by substances so perfectly blended as to give the impression of a single
scent.' Shakespeare alludes to the allegory between the sound of
music and scent when, in the famous opening speech of *Twelfth
Night* made before a company of musicians, Orsino, Duke of
Illyria declares:

> If music be the food of love, play on,
> Give me excess of it; that, surfeiting,
> The appetite may sicken, and so die.
> That strain again; it had a dying fall:
> O, it came o'er my ear like the sweet sound
> That breathes upon a bank of violets,
> Stealing and giving odour.

Again, the poet draws attention to the unique character of the violet's perfume which, after a few seconds, so soon tires the olfactory nerves that its fragrance vanishes, lost in the warm south wind of early summertime. Later, the Duke dismisses his musicians, coolly unconcerned;

> Away before me to sweet beds of flowers;
> Love-thoughts lie rich, when canopied with bowers.

Here, Shakespeare is alluding to the seductive quality of fragrant flowers which the perfumer tries to imitate in composing his 'bouquets'.

Just as there is an analogy between colour and sound, the ancients identifying the musical gamut as the 'chromatic' scale to give proof of the existence of a universal law of harmony, so there is an accepted criterion for measuring the intensity of an odour in the same way that sound (notes) is measured. When alcoholic solutions of various essences are allowed to evaporate in the open air, they undergo natural analysis, the most volatile being the first to evaporate, the less volatile disappearing later. Dr. Septimus Piesse called this 'the velocity of odour' and it was his opinion, since accepted in perfumery, that odours affect the olfactory nerves in direct proportion to their force of volatility. In other words, he believed that the force of volatility of essence, or the rapidity at which they evaporate, would always be in proportion to the rapidity with which the odorous waves might be propagated. Thus, bodies possessing a low degree of volatility are known as strong odours; those with a high volatility are the delicate odours. To give an analogy between odours and sounds, the loudest notes are produced by sonorous waves which are the most slowly propagated; and the most powerful odours are produced by the most slowly propagated odorous waves.

Scents, like sounds to the ear, affect the olfactory nerve in a similar way. Just as there is an octave in music, so there is an octave of odours in which, for example, heliotrope, vanilla and almond blend together; and on a higher scale, citron, lemon and verbena, for in each, similar chemical substances are to be found. To the undisciplined nose, many odours are alike, but to the perfumer, as to the tea blender and tobacco manufacturer, almost all scents are different and the slightest variation in scale is readily detected. An experienced perfumer may have at least two hundred odours in his laboratory and can readily distinguish each by smelling.

The art of the perfumer is both skilful and complex. If a perfumer wishes to make a 'bouquet', he must use such odours as to form a 'chord' so that each is in harmony, in the same way that an artist blends his colours. To make a 'bouquet', every odour must first be brought to a certain standard of strength, otherwise one odour may 'kill' all others used with it. The odour of camphor, for example, is three times as intense as that of the rose, so that it is necessary to bring the strength of one down to that of the other. Again, attar of orange blossom by distillation has very little of the true orange smell because water vapour acts chemically upon an essence, reducing its strength. Essences obtained by enfleurage, however, have the odour of the flower faithfully reproduced. It is only by enfleurage that the essences of jasmine, acacia, tuberose and violet are reproduced without loss of character for they are the most difficult of all flower scents to imitate.

The perfumer works at an 'organ', to use yet another metaphor of music, where the ingredients are arranged around him in scales of scent. There may be as many as ten tiers, each accommodating a hundred bottles, carefully marked and arranged on three sides so that each one of the thousand or so may be reached with ease and notes made of the ingredients used. The perfumer relies on his trained sense of smell to create a symphony of fragrance which may take a year to compose, adding a touch of one, then another, using maybe a hundred different odours until he is satisfied that the right blend has been achieved. This is known as the 'chord'. The 'base notes' are those which have the heaviest and most lasting fragrance while the 'top notes' have the most immediate effect upon the sense of smell, though they are quickest to evaporate. He has to adjust the balance every so often, replacing those lost in the process of extraction or toning down if the odour is too fierce, too pronounced; and all the time he must guard against creating an artificial perfume, remembering that one false 'note' will completely ruin the harmony. He must never lose sight of the maxim that a perfume is a blend of materials, resulting in an overall and pleasant impression.

From the whole floral kingdom there are more than four thousand scented substances available to the perfumer with which to compose his works, the most famous perfumes being likened to the world's great symphonies; and each is built up around three basic parts, the 'top notes', 'middle notes' and the back or 'bass notes'. The harmony of the three basic notes is known in perfumery as 'layer blending'. In music, the concerto places the emphasis on a single instrument in the orchestral accompaniment and, in the same way, a perfume is built round an odorous chemical substance or otto. To arrive at the final score there may be as many as a hundred variations or amendments before the finished product satisfies its creator and those whose business it is to launch it on the market. So intricate is the composition of modern perfumes that the slightest deviation in the use of one odour or another will entirely change the character of the perfume. In perfumes, odour ingredients may occur to the extent of ten to twenty per cent; in toilet waters five to ten per cent.

The 'green and woody' perfumes will form a 'bouquet' of chord C and may be composed of sandalwood, geraniol, acacia, orange blossom and camphor as the main ingredients around which the perfume is built up. Lancôme's Magie, with its soft flowery bouquet in which jasmine strikes the dominant 'note' and with its muffled overtones of cedar and sandalwood, fixed with ambergris, civet and musk, is representative of the 'green' perfumes. Hermès exquisite Calèche, with its subtle composition of rose, gardenia, lilac and musk and with its 'green' top note, may also be classed with the most sophisticated of the 'green and woody' perfumes. Sandalwood and vetivert often strike the dominant note in perfumes of this group.

Several of the top selling American perfumes are based on the 'heavier' scents which are less popular in Britain than they were at one time. The perfumer modifies his 'heavy notes' with amyl salicylate, a product of oil of wintergreen, and with methylnonylacetaldehyde which gives a perfume a lighter, more flowery odour.

The spicy perfumes, with their blend of musk and carnation, built up around the alcohol eugenol, have a warm, 'heady' fragrance, which is the dominant 'note' of Caron's Bellodgia and Lancôme's

Fidji which is manufactured under the name of Guy Laroche. They begin with a green aldehyde note, complementing tuberose, jasmine, lilac, ylang-ylang, carnation and orange blossom, followed by the 'woody' notes of cedar and sandalwood and with undertones of several Arabian balms and of myrrh, musk and ambergris which hold together the many delicate perfumes until its complete evaporation.

The 'bouquets' exist only as an alcoholic solution, obtained from a fatty body by way of enfleurage, and these are the most delicate of perfumes, built up around the white jasmine, acacia and lily-of-the-valley. They possess a flowery lightness which has retained for them a unique popularity since the beginning of the century. They are obtained from essences or, to use the French word, esprits, the name given to those simple odours which exist in alcoholic solution extracted from oils or fats in which the flowers have been repeatedly infused. Lanvin's Arpège may be likened to an arpeggio of jasmine, rose, and lily of the valley, the most difficult of all flower perfumes to reproduce. Caron's Fleurs de Rocaille is also a blend of jasmine and rose and in addition has overtones of ylang-ylang, with its honeysuckle scent, and petit grain which is obtained from the distillation of the leaves, twigs and unripened fruit of different species of citrus. The name 'petit grain', small holes, is derived from the small globular ducts to be seen in orange leaves when held up to the sunlight. Petit grain bigarade is obtained from the leaf of the Seville orange and petit grain limon is the distillate of lemon leaves. The orange scents, in one form or another, are present in almost all perfumes.

To prevent the too-rapid evaporation of the odour of a perfume, there must be a fixative to replace the wax or resin of a flower or leaf and to act in a similar way. The best of all fixatives are animal secretions, which have been employed in perfumery since earliest times. Musk, with its long-lasting strength, was used in India and China at a remote period in history and was included among the presents sent by Saladin to the Greek Emperor of Constantinople in 1189.

In a manuscript of 1398, in the British Museum, there is mention of 'boxes made to kepe muske in', possibly the first reference to musk in England. By Elizabethan times it was an important article of perfumery. In a room in the Garter Inn at Windsor, Mistress

8*

Quickly tells Falstaff of the many exciting gifts given to Mistress
Ford to win her affections: '. . . there has been knights and lords and
gentlemen with their coaches . . . with gift after gift . . . smelling
so sweetly, all musk . . .' And, true to her Creole heritage, the
Empress Josephine loved the scent of musk more than any other.
She had her rooms filled with it daily, and a hundred and fifty years
after her death, her dressing-room at Malmaison still carries the
unmistakable smell, even though, during that lapse of time, the
walls must have been frequently washed and the woodwork painted.
A contemporary authority says she always carried a laced handkerchief smelling strongly of musk which she constantly pressed to
her nose.

When adulterated, musk has a sweet smell but, according to
Chardin, so powerful is it, that when it is removed from the animal,
hunters are required to have their mouth and nose covered with
linen as fresh musk is capable of bringing about haemorrhage and
even death if inhaled too near. It is the most powerful of all perfumes
and, though this is something of an exaggeration, it is said that a grain
of musk will perfume a room for a year without losing weight. Its
penetrating smell will affect everything near it, and the East India
Company during Victorian times refused to include musk in any
shipment of tea. In perfumery, musk seems to act as an aphrodisiac,
giving a perfume a 'lift' and stimulating the senses of those who
use it and inhale it.

Musk is obtained from the musk-ox and musk-rat, but it is from
the musk-deer (Moschus moschiferus) that the finest product comes.
This interesting animal inhabits the Himalayas, extending from
Afghanistan across northern India and to western China, always
roaming in dense forests just below the snow-line. It is only from the
male animal that the musk is obtained and this is most abundant at
the time of rutting when it is thought that the scent may play a part
in courtship. The pod or small bag, which is really a gland, is near
the navel, between the flesh and the skin, and is about two inches
long, being about the size of a walnut. There is a small orifice
through the skin, into which a man's little finger can be inserted, but
it has no other connection with the animal's body. It would seem
that the musk is a secretion of waste products. Indeed, the dung of
the male musk-deer (and only the male) smells strongly of musk at
most times of the year.

The musk-deer is a delightful nocturnal ruminant, about the size of a roebuck, with grey fur and two projecting teeth from the upper jaw which it uses to root up the herbs from which the musk-like odour is said to be derived, though the undergrowth in its habitat consists chiefly of juniper. Tonquin musk is of the finest quality. It comes from the Chinese province of Szechuen, and Tavernier, the French traveller, writing early in the seventeenth century, recalls bringing back with him almost eight thousand pods, which he sold to European perfumers.

To the Chinese, the animals are known as shay-leang, meaning 'scented animals', and it is during the first months of the year that their capture usually takes place, when hunger drives them from their snowy haunts into the valleys. They were at one time killed with bows and arrows after which the pods were cut away, though the natives were also proficient at removing the musk from the pod and allowing the animals to go free again.

The pod forms with the animal; it is present at birth and for about two years the musk remains as a milky substance with a most disagreeable smell. As the animal grows it increases in quantity and becomes hard, like grain. When the contents have been removed from the pod, it is known as 'grain-musk' and is reddish-brown, but it turns black with age. It is usual for a pod to contain about two drachms, as most are taken when the deer are quite young; but an old animal may yield almost an ounce of musk, though of an inferior quality. Its scent is similar to that of honey, and as a consequence flowers which have a musky smell are often classified with those of honey perfume.

The pods are wrapped singly in silk and are placed in a small box known as a 'caddy' which contains, by weight, about twenty ounces. 'Grain-musk' which has been extracted from the pods is more expensive. In each 'caddy' was included a Chinese 'chop-paper', a circular praising the quality of the musk and the integrity of the firm who supplied it. 'We beg honourable merchant who favour us with custom, to remember firm's seal; certain shameless scoundrels having falsely assumed our designation. Our wares are genuine, our prices true,' ran the citation, and it usually ended by sending good wishes to the customer.

The buyer of musk today may consider this to be little more than a pleasing salutation from the vendor, but once there was more to it than that for, when musk first came to be used by the perfume industry, the integrity of many suppliers remained in doubt. In his *Journal of Sporting Adventures in Chinese Tartary*, Colonel Markham says that he had often seen pods offered for sale which were merely a piece of the skin of the animal, tied up to resemble a musk-pod before being filled with some musk-like substance and rubbed over with musk to make it smell. Sometimes, the musk was taken from the pod which was then filled with dried blood, while on other occasions small pieces of lead were inserted into the pod to increase its weight before it was sewn up. The Chinese musk exporters damaged their reputation by such practices and it became necessary for the more reliable merchants to give notice that they supplied only musk of the finest quality.

Civet, a sex gland secretion of the civet cat (Viverra civetta) of Ethiopia, Burma and Thailand, has been used as a fixative for a long time. The secretion is formed in a double glandular receptacle and is yellow in appearance, of an oily or slimy nature and with a disagreeable smell; yet, on dilution, it is most pleasing. Bulleyn, writing in 1564, mentions 'muske and zenet' and Pomet tells of having received a civet cat as a present from a friend who was in the retinue of the King of Siam. The animal was placed in a cage, for the civet cat is a ferocious beast, untameable, and the irritation of being caged brought about a greater secretion of the substance, which Pomet found on the bars of the cage. 'The bars,' he wrote, 'became covered with an unctuous moisture, thick and brown, with a very strong and disagreeable smell; so that all the time I kept this animal, I took care to gather the civet from the pouch every other day, not without trouble and hazard, because it put the creature to some apprehension.'

The Dutch were the acknowledged experts in keeping and breeding the civet cat, a member of the feline tribe which will attain a length of about three feet, its black fur being striped or ringed with white. At Amsterdam, once or twice each week, the cats were placed in a narrow cage so that they could not turn and attack those who sought to extract the civet through the orifice of the pouch (similar to that of the musk-deer). This was done with a small wooden spatula which was scraped into a vessel, about a drachm being obtained during each operation. Cats in captivity secreted more civet than those in the wild, since the quantity depends upon the

amount of food and nourishment the animal takes. The Dutch fed
their cats on fish, boiled meat and eggs, as the price they obtained
for the product was highly remunerative and they could well afford
to give the animals a substantial diet.

The lighter the colour of the civet, the better the quality. Lemery,
a French chemist of the seventeenth century, said that it was to
be preferred to musk because the scent was finer; and added, 'it
comforts the spirits and is good against all diseases of the head and
brain.'

During Shakespeare's time, civet must have been used undiluted
for, like others at a later date, he always referred to its scent as
being oppressive. In its pure state it was used to rub on to the body
to attract the opposite sex—as Don Pedro tells in *Much Ado About
Nothing*: '. . . he rubs himself with civet: Can you smell him out
by that?' To which Claud replies: 'That's as much as to say, the
sweet youth's in love.' To the poet Cowper, its smell was so unpleasant that he could not bear to remain in a room with anyone
using it:

> I cannot talk with civet in the room,
> A fine puss gentleman that's all perfume.

Yet, when diluted, it has more of a floral fragrance than musk, and
the perfumer would find it impossible to imitate some floral scents
without it. Civet needs only to be diluted to an infinitesimal amount
for its smell to be highly agreeable, in the same way that attar of rose
or patchouli have an unpleasant sickly odour before being diluted.
With a thousand times their volume of spirit added, their fragrance
becomes most pleasing. In Victorian times it was usual to place some
civet in a small box in the drawer of a desk so that it would impart
its perfume to writing paper kept with it. Valentines and birthday
cards were scented in the same way.

Extract of civet was prepared by rubbing in a mortar an ounce of
civet with an ounce of orris root which would 'break up' the civet. It
was then placed in a gallon of rectified spirits and, after maceration
for a month, was strained off and was then ready to use as a 'fixing'
ingredient for essences of delicate odour.

But probably of more value to the perfumer than either musk or
civet is ambergris, an excretory product found in the intestines of
the spermaceti whale (Physeter catodon). Soluble in alcohol, its

essence is able to 'bring out' the scent of the attars with which it is mixed, imparting to them an ethereal fragrance which is long-lasting and unattainable by any other means. In the solid, it is as permanent as musk and will retain its perfume for three centuries or more, while on fabric, used in an unadulterated form, it will prove almost indestructible, retaining its powerful smell for many years, even after repeated washings.

The ancients believed ambergris to be vegetable matter—hence its name amber-gris (grey)—as it floats on the sea in large grey lumps. It was found mostly off the coast of China and Japan and around Greenland, from where it floated to the Faroe Islands and down the western shores of Ireland. *The Philisophical Transactions* gives an account of a lump of ambergris being found off the coast of Sligo in 1691 which weighed fifty-two ounces and was sold in London for £100. Usually, it is found in lumps weighing about a pound which at present day prices would be worth a little under £100. Pomet described it as being 'the most expensive commodity in France' and he believed it to be honeycomb taken from the sea! It is a wax-like inflammable substance, ash-grey in colour, and may be formed by the hard bird-like beak of the cuttle fish which the sperm whale consumes in large amounts and which it is unable to digest. It is thus frequently spewed up and floats away on the water where it is collected by fishermen. It has a smell resembling that of labdanum and the resin of the Balsam Poplar.

Powdered ambergris was used to make into a paste of sweet-smelling substances to place in cassolettes, small perforated boxes of ivory which were carried in the pocket or handbag, to be produced and inhaled when an oppressive atmosphere caused fatigue or when unpleasant smells brought about nausea. The odour of ambergris is obtained by alcoholic extraction, when it becomes a tincture. It is used only in the manufacture of the more expensive perfumes and is added at an advanced stage in their composition. Constantin Wériguine of the Society of French Perfumers has said that tincture of ambergris has about it a feminine, carnal smell, caressing and warm . . .' It adds warmth and softness to a perfume, giving it a more seductive quality.

Castor, a glandular secretion of the beaver (Castor fiber), has characteristics similar to that of civet, though with nothing like the same odour. It is now rarely used though it was, at one time, included in the less expensive perfumes when its exportation from Canada was the sole prerogative of the Hudson's Bay Company. Castor is formed in pear-shaped membranous pods or bags which are present near the back groins. They would appear to be lymphatic glands and, when removed from a mature animal, the bags are about four inches long. Two kinds of castor are known, different in their chemical composition and in their scent; but, in the natural state, they are almost scentless.

A standard extraction is made by dissolving two ounces in a gallon of spirit, no more than a quarter of a pint of which should be mixed with a gallon of other scented substances otherwise, as with civet and musk, its smell will be dominant.

Sweet gums and resins which harmonize with the attars are also used by the perfumer as fixatives, and the oils of cedarwood and sandalwood, being less expensive than animal fixatives, contribute 'warmth' and staying power to perfumes.

In England, perfume is usually known as 'scent', when describing the manufactured product; the Americans follow the French in their use of the older word 'perfume', as used in the Bible and by Shakespeare, which would seem to be more appropriate for the sophisticated product, while scent is better suited to describe the smell of a flower or leaf, or sweet smells in general.

To find out if a perfume suits one's personality, it is necessary to 'wear' it. Sniffing from a bottle is only the preliminary step. It must then be applied to the skin, to the bosom or the throat or to the inside of the wrist where, in a few seconds, the warmth of the body will release the most subtle qualities of the perfume and provide instant excitement. If it does so, it is right for your personality but, if there is no reaction, take a walk in the fresh air, then on the other wrist try some other perfume. If this does not satisfy the emotions, it is not advisable to try any others until twenty-four hours have elapsed, otherwise one will be too confused to make the right choice.

Perfumes should be kept in a cool, dark place. Under warm conditions and exposure to strong light, their quality will deteriorate. Always 'wear' perfume on the body rather than on the clothes and, as most perfumes will evaporate within three to four hours, should one be away from home for a longer period, carry in the purse or handbag an atomizer or flacon to renew the application whenever desired. Modern cream perfumes do not evaporate so readily nor do they deteriorate so quickly in heat and light. They also spread more easily, being absorbed into the skin with the minimum of application.

The first of the great modern perfumers was François Coty. He was born at Ajaccio, Corsica, Napoleon's birthplace, in 1873, and his ideas and skills were to revolutionize the perfume and cosmetic industries of the world by the time he was forty.

He arrived in Paris at an early age, at a time when ostrich feathers littered the floor of every fashion house. This fact attracted his attention, and at first he set himself up as a salesman of ostrich feathers, but being friendly with a young chemist who had his premises near Coty's apartments, he frequently watched his friend compounding toilet waters and hit upon the idea of making his own, and presenting them in containers of artistic design. Realizing that he would have to accumulate a storehouse of knowledge before he began in business, Coty moved to Grasse and there spent two years growing and harvesting flowers and learning how to extract their scent.

Then, after borrowing a small sum of money from his grandfather, he set up in business on his own in Paris, in the Rue de la Boétie. The shop had only two rooms, one of which he used to prepare his scents, the other to display them, and it was not long before he had attracted several important customers for his rose perfume. His first five hundred bottles, taken by a well-known store, were sold within days after a bottle had broken and the perfume spilled on the floor; so life-like was the rose bouquet that Coty became, almost overnight, the 'rage' of Paris. The broken bottle had brought him instant success. It was one of many exquisite bottles, made for Coty by the famous artist in French crystal, Jacques Lalique, which were to become almost as famous as the perfumes inside them. Coty's Rose perfume was followed by his L'Origan, Chypre and then L'Aimant, each one of which came to enjoy a world-wide reputation.

François Coty died in 1934 after having founded one of the world's most important perfume houses and had lived to see the manufacture of perfumes and cosmetics become big business, with millions of pounds changing hands each year in all parts of the world in the promotion of allurement and hygiene. Three years after opening his premises in the Rue de la Boétie, Coty had made enough money to acquire a villa at Suresnes, near the Bois de Bologne, where the present factory and offices are still to be found, a monument to his courage and skills. His success rested upon his acute sense of smell and his instinctive good taste. 'Give a woman the best product you can compound,' was his philosophy. 'Present it in a container of simple, but impeccable taste, charge a reasonable price for it, and a great business will arise such as the world has never seen.' This has been the formula for success since the Queen of Sheba marketed her perfumes throughout the Near East some three thousand years ago.

SELECT BIBLIOGRAPHY

ART OF PERFUMERY, THE. Charles H. Piesse.
AROMATICS AND THE SOUL. Dr. D. McKenzie.
BOOK OF PERFUMES, THE. Eugene Rimmel.
BOOK OF RECEIPTS. Mary Doggett.
BUTTERFLY HUNTING IN MANY LANDS. Edward Longstaffe.
FLORA ODORATA. F. T. Mott.
FLOWERS, THEIR ORIGIN. J. E. Taylor.
GARDEN OF HEALTH. William Langham.
HERBALL OR GENERAL HISTORIE OF PLANTES, THE. John Gerard.
HISTORY OF GARDENING IN ENGLAND. Alicia Amherst.
MYSTERY AND LURE OF PERFUME. C. J. S. Thompson.
ODOROGRAPHIA. J. C. Sawer.
PLANT LORE OF SHAKESPEARE. Henry Ellacombe.
PLANTS OF THE BIBLE. Harold and Alma Moldenke.
SCENT OF FLOWERS AND LEAVES, THE. F. A. Hampton.
TRAVELS UP THE AMAZON. A. R. Wallace.

INDEX